THE RISE OF HISTORICAL WRITING AMONG THE ARABS

Modern Classics in Near Eastern Studies

Series Editors: Charles Issawi and Bernard Lewis

A. A. DURI

The Rise of Historical Writing Among the Arabs

Edited and Translated by Lawrence I. Conrad

Introduction by Fred M. Donner

PRINCETON UNIVERSITY PRESS

Published by Princeton University Press, 41 William Street, Princeton, New Jersey 08540
In the United Kingdom: Princeton University Press, Guildford, Surrey

Library of Congress Cataloging in Publication Data will be found on the last printed page of this book

ISBN 0-691-05388-X

This book has been composed in Linotron Galliard

Clothbound editions of Princeton University Press books are printed on acid-free paper, and binding materials are chosen for strength and durability. Paperbacks, although satisfactory for personal collections, are not usually suitable for library rebinding.

Printed in the United States of America by Princeton University Press, Princeton, New Jersey

Translated from the Arabic, *Baḥth fī nash'at 'ilm al-ta'rīkh 'inda l-'Arab*, Beirut, 1960

The translation and preparation of this volume were made possible through a grant from the translation program of the National Endowment for the Humanities, to which we would like to express our deep appreciation.

Publication of this book has been aided by a grant from the Paul Mellon Fund of Princeton University Press.

Contents

Introduction by Fred M. Donner vii

Note on the English Translation
by Lawrence I. Conrad xix

Preface 3

1. The Rise of History Among the Arabs and Its Development During the First Three Centuries A.H. 12

2. Origins of the Historical School of Medina: ʿUrwa—al-Zuhrī 76

3. The Beginnings of Historical Folklore: Wahb ibn Munabbih 122

4. Origins of the Historical School of Iraq: Its Rise and Development Until the Third Century A.H. 136

5. Motives for the Writing of History and the Historical Views Embodied in the Works of the First Historians 152

Bibliography of Works Cited 161

Index 177

Introduction

The study of early Islamic history, more perhaps than most historical fields, has been plagued by uncertainties about the reliability of its written sources. No branch of history is, of course, entirely free of such historiographical controversy; but the disagreement and debate over sources for early Islamic history and their reliability have hung like an ominous cloud over the field almost from the moment scholars began scientifically to work it in the mid-nineteenth century, and show little sign of dispersing even today. The persistence of this problem is doubtless in part due to the fact that the scientific study of early Islam is still a very young subject, scarcely a century old; it is also partly attributable to the relatively small number of scholars who, in any given generation, choose to dedicate themselves to this study. As a result of these factors, it is fair to say, the field as a whole remains poorly developed; vast areas have never been worked at all, or have only been touched on superficially, and much fundamental spadework remains to be done before the full outlines of early Islamic history will begin to emerge clearly. Under such circumstances it is hardly surprising that drastic reinterpretations both of early Islamic history itself, and of the role of various sources for it, should periodically arise.

In this case, however, the historiographical debate is more than just a reflection of the efforts of a fairly young historical field to define itself; rather, it also derives in large measure from the nature of the sources themselves. For the great majority of the information about early Islamic history on which modern historians rely is derived not from contemporary documents, but from literary compilations that only attained their present form a century or even two centuries or more after the events they purport to describe. The relatively late date of the sources does not necessarily make them fraudulent, of course, and it became generally accepted by modern historians that some of the information in these sources—perhaps most of it—is considerably older material that was preserved and transmitted until it found its way into the literary compilations now available to us. But the lateness of the sources does, at least, mean that the existence of anachronistic and tendentious accounts of a spurious character that might be woven in with more authentic older material cannot be dismissed out of hand. As a result, sharp disagreement has persisted among historians of Islam on what and how much material in the extant sources is older, as it has on the question of how old this "older" material actually is and what interests and attitudes it reflects. Finally, it has been asked how—and even whether—scholars can discriminate between "authentic" older material and tendentious, fabricated, or anachronistic accounts of more recent provenance.

As already noted, this debate in modern scholarly circles goes back virtually to the beginnings of Western historiographical studies. M. J. de Goeje, in his *Mémoire sur la conquête de la Syrie* (first edition, Leiden, 1864), decided that many of the contradictory historical accounts about the conquest of Syria were unreliable, and concluded that only a certain fraction of them—he favored those purveyed by the historian al-Wāqidī—could be accepted as trustworthy. Similarly, Julius Wellhausen, in his *Prolegomena zur ältesten Geschichte des Islams* (Berlin, 1899), tried to demonstrate that the accounts about the conquests of Iraq transmitted by Sayf ibn ʿUmar were romanticized, filled with evidence of tribal chauvinism, chronologically absurd, and in other ways gave an appearance of unreliability. For a time such studies seemed to provide the desired critical basis on which the historian could rely when evaluating the historical traditions with which he had to work in studying the early Islamic period; and for many years (and, to a certain extent, even today) "critical method" in working with these sources came to mean, for many, simply rejecting accounts derived from Sayf ibn ʿUmar's collections and relying on other early authorities, such as al-Wāqidī, instead.

In the meantime, however, there appeared Ignaz Goldziher's classic *Muhammedanische Studien* (Halle, 1888-90), which first demonstrated that among the collections of *ḥadīth*s (sayings) attributed to the prophet Muḥammad—even in those collections that had been most carefully screened by Muslim scholars to sift out forgeries—there were many *ḥadīth*s that careful analysis of content revealed certainly to be products of a later period and not authentic utterances of the prophet at all. Because the methods used by medieval Arab scholars to transmit and verify *ḥadīth*s were in many respects similar to those they used to deal with historical accounts, Goldziher's conclusions cast a shadow of doubt on the reliability of all historical accounts. Far more than the studies of de Goeje and Wellhausen, therefore, Goldziher's critique was disturbing in its implications for historians of early Islam—or, at least, should have been; and ever since his day, scholarship in the field of early Islamic history has suffered from what might be called a collective schizophrenia, a profound division over the assumptions that should properly underlie efforts at historical reconstruction. Some scholars have treated the Arabic sources as fully reliable, adopting only those criticisms that they could not in good conscience ignore (e.g., Wellhausen's rejection of Sayf's traditions) and picking their way through the remaining material according to their own (often not explicit) criteria for determining what was and what was not "authentic." Typical examples of this approach are W. Montgomery Watt's studies of the life of the prophet, *Muhammad at Mecca* and

Muhammad at Medina (Oxford, 1953 and 1956). Other scholars have adopted a much more skeptical attitude toward the sources in the light of Goldziher's conclusions, and have come to denounce more and more of the received corpus of historical traditions as spurious or otherwise unreliable, sometimes eschewing the study of early Islamic history altogether for studies of Islamic law or other phenomena that took definitive form only in later centuries. We might see in the works of Joseph Schacht, Goldziher's main successor in the study of Islamic law, the first culmination of this trend.

It proved much more difficult, however, to find a middle ground between these two extremes—a position that neither embraced the sources too credulously, nor adopted a sweeping and (because unexamined) unwarranted skepticism toward them. Leone Caetani, in his compendious *Annali dell'Islam* (10 vols., Milan, 1905-1926), tried to examine early Islamic history with a critical eye to the sources. But many practicing historians who dealt with the early Islamic period in the years after World War I either saw no need to defend the sources, or seemed for one reason or another at a loss to do so, and hence chose to pass in silence over the issues at stake. One reason for such attitudes was probably the fact that it was simply easier to proceed on the assumption that the "standard" interpretation of early Islamic history was essentially sound than it was to undertake the arduous, and perhaps threatening, task of reconsidering the sources; for to do the latter might well require a radical revision of one's view of early Islamic history as well.

There was, however, a reason why historians of early Islam could not mount a serious or coherent defense of their sources during the first half of the twentieth century, even had they wanted to do so. That reason was the generally poor grasp of the historiographical tradition itself and of how it had evolved; for in order to judge or to comment on the historicity of these sources, one had first to understand clearly how, and why, they had come into existence in the first place. Yet at the beginning of the century few detailed studies of important Arab historians or of the growth of the historiographical tradition had yet been undertaken. True, the latter nineteenth century had seen the appearance of Ferdinand Wüstenfeld's *Die Geschichtschreiber der Araber und ihre Werke* (Göttingen, 1882), and at the turn of the century had appeared the first edition of Carl Brockelmann's monumental *Geschichte der arabischen Litteratur* (Weimar, 1898-1902), but both of these essentially provided merely a list of the main early Arab historians and their works, with no attempt to examine the interrelationship of various writers, the historicity of their work, or the growth of the historiographical tradition as a whole. More penetrating syntheses of Arabic historiography were simply not yet feasible in the absence of a full supply of detailed studies. Thus we find that even those general works from the early twentieth century that were explicitly devoted to Arabic historiography, such as David Margoliouth's *Lectures on Arabic Historians* (Calcutta, 1930), have only very vague and general things to say about how the historiographical tradition evolved, and represent very little progress over Wüstenfeld's essay of fifty years earlier, which had been published before the appearance of most of the early critiques of the Arabic sources that had generated the historiographical debate in the first place.

The first wave of historiographical critiques had not fallen entirely on deaf ears, however; there was a flurry of interest in historiographical research during the first quarter of the twentieth century, when such scholars as Josef Horovitz, C. H. Becker, and Johann Fück attempted to unravel in a painstaking and systematic way how particular aspects of the historiographical tradition had developed, or tried to present a fuller picture of some of the early Arab historians and their relation to other writers before and after them. Into this category can be placed such researches as Horovitz's essay on the use of *isnāds* or chains of authorities, Becker's examination of the Sīra (the standard biography of the prophet Muḥammad) and its relation to the *ḥadīth* and other material, and Fück's monograph on Ibn Isḥāq (Frankfurt, 1925). The motivating assumption underlying this work was the idea that the general reliability of the Arabic historiographical tradition, in the face of the criticisms raised against it, could only be demonstrated by showing that the tradition itself was something that had evolved naturally, and was not merely a composite of spurious and tendentious fragments pasted together at a much later date. In order to show this, however, one had to understand the historiographical tradition much more fully, and the object of these researches was to help meet this need.

For reasons that are far from clear, the pace of such detailed historiographical research slowed in the period following World War I—perhaps because the war itself had left in a shambles the European academic establishment, particularly that of Germany, which had led the van in these historiographical studies. There were a few noteworthy exceptions, of course, notably some of the studies by Brockelmann, Horovitz, and Robert Brunschvig—but by and large the detailed study of historiographical issues seems to have fallen into neglect after about 1925, and few new names were to take up the challenge for some decades. Evidence of this attitude of neglect can even be found in the first edition of the *Encyclopaedia of Islam*, which appeared in Leiden between 1913 and 1934. This massive reference work did feature biographies of a number of important early Arab historians (e.g., Ibn Isḥāq, al-Wāqidī, Sayf ibn ʿUmar, al-Zuhrī, al-Madāʾinī, Abū Mikhnaf, ʿUrwa ibn al-Zubayr, etc.), but some of these were rather spare first attempts; and of the articles on fundamental historiographical topics, such as *isnād, ḥadīth*, or *taʾrīkh* (dating, history), many were very brief and displayed the general lack of sophistication of this branch of Islamic studies. Readers had to await the appearance of the Supplement to the first edition, which appeared in 1938, to read the pioneering article on "Ta'rīkh" (History) by H.A.R. Gibb, one of the relatively few scholars to take up the question of historiography in earnest during the inter-war period. Among practicing historians dealing with the early Islamic period, the general attitude seems to have remained, for the most part, one of benign neglect of historiography. Few took up Caetani's lead, and even as late as the 1970s some authors still found it possible to construct novel interpretive histories of early Islam without any reference to historiographical issues or methods. M. A. Shaban's *Islamic History, 600-750 A.D./132 A.H.—A New Interpretation* (Cambridge, 1971), can be cited as a case in point.

It was only after World War II that the pace of research on early Arabic historiography again quickened and concern for the subject spread. Shortly after the war appeared two articles that focused attention anew on the relation between Arabic legal and historical texts: Brunschvig's "Ibn ʿAbdalḥakam et la conquête de l'Afrique du Nord par les Arabes" (Faculté des Lettres de l'Université d'Alger, *Annales de l'Institut d'Études Orientales* 6 [1942-1947], pp. 108-155), and J. Schacht's "A Revaluation of Islamic Traditions" (*JRAS*, 1949, pp. 143-154). But the main impetus to the accelerated pace of historiographical study was provided by the appearance of three books. The first was Franz Rosenthal's *A History of Muslim Historiography* (first edition, Leiden, 1952). Its purpose was not to address the debate over the historicity of the sources that most concerned historians, an issue that Rosenthal deliberately and explicitly sidestepped: ". . . we are not concerned here with the value of historical works as source material for the writing of the history of a particular period" (p. 6). The author intended, rather, to examine the conception of history held by Muslim scholars and to trace the development of history as a branch of Arabic literature and science. Nevertheless, Rosenthal's contribution provided a fuller treatment of the origins of Arabic historiography than had Gibb's brief survey of the subject in the *Encyclopaedia of Islam*, and began the process of synthesizing the rather large number of isolated studies of detailed aspects of Arabic historiography that had accumulated over the preceding decades. A further step, and one of greater importance for practicing historians, was taken with the appearance of the second book, Nabia Abbott's splendid *Studies in Arabic Literary Papyri, I. Historical Texts* (Chicago, 1957). This work provided an even more detailed survey of the crucial earliest phases of Arabic historiography, and did so in a manner that emphasized, on the basis of papyrological evidence, the generally reliable character of the process by which historical accounts were transmitted. The book thus provided strong, if still somewhat general, support for the view that the Arabic accounts were as a whole reliable as historical sources, even if some distortions and spurious material may have crept in.

The third work, however, really represented the culmination of the long series of diverse efforts to trace the evolution of early Arabic historiography in such a way as to be useful to the historian. It was ʿAbd al-ʿAzīz al-Dūrī's *The Rise of Historical Writing Among the Arabs (Baḥth fī nash'at ʿilm al-ta'rīkh ʿinda l-ʿArab)*, which appeared in Beirut in 1960. Dūrī's book was, and remains, noteworthy for several reasons. First, it provided the most comprehensive overview of the growth of early Arabic historiography that had yet appeared. Drawing in part on the results of many scattered critical studies and monographs devoted to individual traditionists and historiographical issues, the author was able to sketch out a much clearer and more highly nuanced picture than had previously existed of the rise of various schools of Arabic historical writing and of their methods. But Dūrī did not merely synthesize the work of others; he also relied heavily on his own independent researches into early Arabic historiography, efforts that became manifest not only in this book, but also in a number of studies of more restricted aspects of the subject that appeared over the years. Among them were his articles on "The Iraq School of History to the Ninth Century—A Sketch" (1962), and "Al-Zuhrī: A Study of the Beginnings of History Writing in Islam" (1957), as well as his monograph *Dirāsa fī sīrat al-nabī wa-mu'allifihā Ibn Isḥāq* (Baghdad, 1965) on Ibn Isḥāq and his biography of the prophet.

The Rise of Historical Writing Among the Arabs is especially noteworthy because Dūrī is himself a practicing historian, with many fine publications on early Islamic history to his credit (see Bibliography). It was therefore natural that in approaching the problem of historiography he should do so with the question that historians always want most to have answered uppermost in his mind—namely, how reliable are the sources under scrutiny as evidence for reconstructing "what actually happened"? This concern Dūrī wove together with his analysis of the earliest historical accounts according to the genre to which they belonged (popular story, genealogical tradition, tribal "battle-day" narrative, etc.) and according to the methods used by the various local schools of historical writing that emerged in Medina, Iraq, and elsewhere. The result was not only a more detailed and sophisticated analysis of the rise of early Arabic historiography in general, but also the elaboration for the first time of a set of general guidelines for assessing the reliability of a given account on the basis of its origin and its formal characteristics. This made the book particularly useful to historians, and also provided more support for those who viewed the Arabic sources as essentially reliable for reconstructing history, since the lack of consistent criteria for weeding spurious and tendentious material out of the Arabic historiographical tradition had all along been one of the main factors leading skeptics to reject the whole tradition as essentially useless for historians.

The importance of Dūrī's book was quickly recognized by most serious students of early Islamic history, and its utility has endured and doubtless will endure for some time to come. Since its appearance in 1960, a great number of additional historiographical studies have been undertaken, and the subject has in some respects changed so greatly that it can hardly be considered the same field that Dūrī worked in the 1950s. Some scholars, such as Fuat Sezgin, Ursula Sezgin, Raif Khoury, and others, have provided us with highly detailed studies of individual transmitters or—in the case of Fuat Sezgin and his massive *Geschichte des arabischen Schrifttums* (Leiden, 1967—)—with an extensive catalog and summary of the whole historiographical tradition for the first four Islamic centuries. The thrust of their work clearly follows that of Abbott and Dūrī, in that they take the historiographical tradition as a whole to be an organic development that can be used by historians if it is sufficiently well understood. On the other hand, scholars imbued with a more skeptical attitude have also been active, producing new studies asserting that the historiographical tradition is at best highly suspect, and at worst, useless. Albrecht Noth's *Quellenkritische Studien zu Themen, Formen, und Tendenzen frühislamischen Geschichtsüberlieferung* (Bonn, 1973) rejects the notion that the different historiographical "schools" of which Dūrī (and his predecessors) spoke used fundamentally different methods of handling material, thereby calling into question the notion that one school's view of the past might be, in general, more "accurate" than that of another. He also develops a much more detailed form-critical analysis of the content of early Arabic historical accounts than had Dūrī, emphasizing as he does so the view that the historicity of material displaying highly formalized characteristics is questionable. More recently still, a radical source criticism has been put forward by several English scholars. In *Hagarism* (Cambridge, 1977), Michael Cook and Patricia Crone present the view that the Arabic sources for early Islamic history are late, full of contradictions, and essentially useless for reconstructing the religious concepts of early Islam; while John Wansbrough's *The Sectarian Milieu* (Oxford, 1978) goes even further, arguing that the sources represent later religious polemic and can tell us nothing about the history of the early Islamic era. That is, the authors assert explicitly and uncompromisingly the skeptical thesis that had been implicit since the late nineteenth century, but had only been rather timidly embraced by practicing Islamic historians.

The debate over the historicity of the Arabic sources thus continues to rage, and it is yet too early to tell what the issue of the debate will be. Pending its outcome, however, ʿAbd al-ʿAzīz al-Dūrī's *The Rise of Historical Writing Among the Arabs* will certainly continue to hold an important place in the literature as the clearest and most historically useful exposition of the general development of Arabic historiography, even if certain details in the picture he has drawn must be modified by more recent research. And, if it turns out that those who argue for the general historicity of the Arabic sources are ultimately vindicated in their debate with the skeptics, it will be in no small part because of the convincing picture Dūrī has drawn. It is therefore a pleasure to welcome the appearance of this book, so useful as an introduction to the Arabic historiographical tradition and so important as a contribution to the long-standing debate, in English translation.

Fred M. Donner

Note on the English Translation

In his introduction Professor Donner has discussed ʿAbd al-ʿAzīz al-Dūrī's work and its place in the modern scholarship on Arab historical writing. Here I will limit my remarks to considerations which have dictated the course I have followed in editing and translating the book.

As published in 1960, *The Rise of Historical Writing Among the Arabs* consisted of two parts: a study of the genesis and early growth of Arab historical writing, and a copious collection of extracts from medieval historical texts. This latter section not only documented points raised in Duri's study, but also exposed the reader, in a direct way, to the style, method, and content of the historical writings of various scholars of early Islamic times. In the present volume, however, only the study of early Arab historical writing has been included, since the historical texts in English form would serve poorly the purposes for which these selections were intended. At the same time, I have tried to make the English edition more useful to students and non-Arabic-speaking historians by supplementing the notes to the original Arabic text. References to scholarly works, in both Arabic and western languages, on early Arab historical writing have been added: some earlier studies are cited with the absence of the section of historical texts in mind, but most are intended to guide the reader to more recent literature pertaining to points raised by Professor Duri, and to subsequent research published by the author himself on these subjects. I have also added further references to primary sources where this has seemed appropriate, and have tried to elucidate points and allusions in the text with which a foreign reader may not be familiar. To differentiate this material from the original, all additions have been set within square brackets. Notes not in the original Arabic text are lettered rather than numbered.

A special problem arose with the technical terms of medieval Islamic scholarship which frequently appear in the text. I have preferred, for the most part, to leave these in their Arabic forms, since they convey particular nuances, ideas, and conceptions which cannot but be obscured by rendering them into the terminology of another culture which approaches neither history nor historical writing in the same way. Also, I felt that as an introduction to the subject the translation should serve to familiarize the reader with the historiographical vocabulary of medieval Islam. To facilitate this, the index indicates in italic characters the pages where the reader can find definitions or explanations for the technical terminology used in the text.

The Arabic text itself presented a further problem. Circumstances at the time made it impossible for the author personally to supervise the book through every stage of the printer's work, or always to refer to the same edition of a given source. In editing the work, I have corrected typographical errors in the text and notes wherever I have found them,[1] and have tried to standardize the notes and to refer the reader to better editions of texts published since 1960. Simple corrections have been made without comment, but wherever a change has involved an actual addition, such material, as above, has been set within square brackets. In a few places, bracketed material represents departures from the text based on better editions

[1] Some of these I should point out to readers who may notice what seem to be discrepancies in comparing this translation with the Arabic original: e.g., read *ʿidda* for *ʿadam* on p. 24, l. 11 of the Arabic text, *maʿa asfārihi* for *maʿa asfalūhu* on p. 45, l. 11, *al-Ḥijr* for *al-hujja* on p. 65, l. 9, *al-qātima* for *al-qāʾima* on p. 98, l. 14, *ahl al-Yaman* for *ahl al-nabī* on p. 111, l. 6, *fī l-taʾrīkh* for *wa-l-taʾrīkh* on p. 136, l. 18.

for quotations from certain primary sources published since 1960 (pp. 77, 84), or on Professor Duri's suggestions for limited clarification or revision (pp. 67, 91).

In the preparation of this translation I have benefited greatly from the co-operation of Professor Duri himself, who read a draft of the entire translation and made suggestions for a number of improvements to the text and additions to the notes. I am also grateful to Professors Fred M. Donner and R. Stephen Humphreys for their own careful reading of the translation and suggestions for changes and improvements. For errors and shortcomings which remain, however, I alone bear responsibility.

Beirut Lawrence I. Conrad
1 February 1983

THE RISE OF HISTORICAL WRITING
AMONG THE ARABS

Preface

Historical writing and the theories concerning it have been the subject of particular interest among historians in recent years, due to the important ways they affect both historical research itself and the direction in which such research is oriented. Discussion of this subject is no longer limited to asking whether history is a science or an art; or, more properly speaking, to efforts to relate history to one of the two fundamental fields of knowledge. Instead, informed opinion has focused its attention on the importance of history as a vital concern in its own right, with its own fundamental principles, research methods, and goals, and its own particular importance among the various fields of knowledge. Indeed, some have even called the modern age the "Age of History."

Historical writing has been affected by the economic, social, and intellectual revolutions of modern times, as is manifest in the growth of the various fields of historical inquiry, and in speculation on the philosophy of history and on the ways the subject can be approached. The general crisis through which the West has passed since the dawn of this century has had an obvious impact on historical studies. Before this crisis it was customary to view Western civilization as the climax in the development of the civilization of all mankind. It was also customary to regard all the history of mankind from a Western perspective, as if the pivot of world history was the West and all other history was merely prefatory or marginal to that of the West. But the two World Wars and the great changes that accompanied them made it clear that Western civilization was only one stage of many in the course of human civilization, and that the ascendancy of the West, which became manifest especially in the nineteenth century, was itself but a historical phase which was rapidly drawing to a close. Realization of this was reinforced by the appearance of new forces in the world, with their own cultural outlooks and achievements, and a vital role of their own to play in shaping the future of mankind. This is true of the United States, and also applies to the rise of the Soviet Union and the important roles both nations have played in world affairs, both cultural and otherwise.

This was also an era characterized by nationalist movements and revivals, especially in Asia, and by the emergence onto the stage of world events—in particular after the Second World War—of ancient peoples who adopted cultural perspectives imbued with their own distinctive character and historical roots. This shook the Western theory maintaining that Western civilization would come to dominate the world and efface older stagnant civilizations, and that, culturally speaking, the world was destined sooner or later to become Westernized.

These and other developments led to a reconsideration of the various historical theories and of the very concept of historical writing. If history is essential to the understanding of the present, then these monumental changes in the world could not be understood from the study of Western history. Moreover, general developments in the first half of this century made it clear that Western civilization is not the ultimate goal of cultural development and has not been the only influential civilization in the world. These developments also demonstrated that the Western view of history could not retain its parochial character, viewing matters only from a Western angle, if it wished to achieve a comprehensive understanding of the present.

There is another view that was overturned as a result of these developments. It is now clear that an understanding of the present cannot be achieved through an understanding of the immediately preceding period by itself, and that the gradual advance of history cannot in itself explain these great revolutions, cultural or otherwise. Rather, preceding eras have sometimes had far-reaching effects on present developments. In other words, since the overall historical evolution of mankind may have had a great influence on these developments, the study of the great revivalist movements demands a return to the consideration of the fundamental roots of cultures and peoples.

All of these factors have engendered a new view of the discipline of history. This is a view which is worldwide in outlook to the extent that it places importance on other civilizations in addition to that of the West, and calls attention to the inter-relationship of civilizations and the reciprocal exchange of influence in the course of their interactions. This new view is also regional to the extent that it emphasizes the importance of studying the history of a given people on its own terms while keeping in mind overall historical developments. In this way it has become evident that it is necessary to rewrite the histories of certain countries afresh, and to do so in a way that will reflect the orientation of the new historical awareness in these countries and contribute to the understanding of their reawakening. This, in turn, places the primary responsibility for the writing of the history of any people on its own historians if a sound view of its history is to be achieved.

As Arabs, we may here ask ourselves where Arab history stands with regard to these new intellectual perspectives. We can state unequivocally that we have only just begun to resolve the task at hand, for many recent works are from the pens of outsiders, whether Western or Eastern, authors who grew up in other cultures and foreign environments, and it is only to be expected that their writings should be affected by the intellectual perspectives prevailing in these cultures and environments. Some of these writings have served historical studies, but others have set forth foreign views or perspectives which we initially accepted, but which now must be radically revised. We have a pressing need to understand modern theories and perspectives on historical writing, so that we may benefit from the insights they offer and make use of them in our own historical research. This does not mean, of course, that we can simply follow in their footsteps, or superimpose the Western method of historical research letter for letter onto our own studies. But we can make use of many of the schools of thought and research methods we find, as a preliminary step towards the establishment of historical methods derived from the essential character of Islamic historical studies.

It is particularly important that we pay attention to the "history of history"; that is, to the evolution of historical writing and to the historical methods and ideas which have accompanied this evolution. And here one of our most pressing needs is to study and research the history of history among the Arabs, for without this, critical historical writing is impossible. We would not be able to scrutinize our sources, to criticize the different accounts, and to distinguish what is reliable from what is doubtful, what is primary from what is secondary, and what is genuine from what is fabricated. Without a critical study of historians and the evolution of historical writing among the Arabs, we would not even be able to distinguish historical accounts from mere stories. We need to understand the reasons for the evolution of historical writing among the Arabs, to perceive the factors which motivated it, as well as the perspectives of those who wrote it, their historical ideas, their method of examining various accounts and setting down a text, and their view of the importance of history and its role in cultural activities and in public life. It is important that we be cognizant of the various factors which led to fabrication and confusion in the writing of history, from the effects of political and partisan currents in society, to the role of storytellers, the impact of the Shuʿūbīya movement, and religious influences. It is also important that we consider the effect of general developments on the development of historical writing. Without the study of these aspects of the subject it would hardly be possible to understand the worth of the historical sources available to us, or for us to criticize the research done by others, or for us to free our history from the defects which have marred it in the past and still do so at present.

In this domain it will not help us to utilize the technical methodology of *ḥadīth* for the study of history, or to place our faith on the high reputations which some historians enjoy. Al-Ṭabarī, for example, is one of our outstanding sources; but a perusal of what he wrote about early Islam shows us that in fact we have before us a melange of the historians and other authors on whom al-Ṭabarī relied, like Abū Mikhnaf, Sayf ibn ʿUmar, Ibn al-Kalbī, ʿAwāna ibn al-Ḥakam, Naṣr ibn Muzāḥim, al-Madā'inī, ʿUrwa ibn al-Zubayr, al-Zuhrī, Ibn Isḥāq, al-Wāqidī, Wahb ibn Munabbih, Kaʿb al-Aḥbār, and so forth. They differ in accuracy, outlook, style, and method of presentation; and each of them requires a special historical study.

Let us take a specific subject, the biography of the Prophet Muhammad, as an example. The earliest sources available to us are the *Sīra* of Ibn Isḥāq and the *Maghāzī* of al-Wāqidī, followed by Ibn Saʿd and al-Ṭabarī, after which we might turn to late sources like Ibn Sayyid al-Nās (*ʿUyūn al-athar*) and Ibn Kathīr (*Al-Bidāya wa-l-nihāya*). But although this may at first appear to be a reasonable way to proceed, it in fact places us on perilous ground fraught with danger. The *Sīra* of Ibn Isḥāq (which was revised by Ibn Hishām) is the oldest biography of Muḥammad to come down to us, followed by the *Maghāzī* of al-Wāqidī. On a close examination of Ibn Isḥāq we see that the accounts and reports which he transmits differ in importance. The solid historical material in his book is derived primarily from al-Zuhrī and certain scholars of *ḥadīth*, while another component portion of his reports is taken from popular stories dominated by elements of entertainment, piety, or boasting, and accompanied by a large amount of fabricated poetry. A third portion is derived from the *Isrā'īliyāt* and the legends and reports of Wahb ibn Munabbih, especially in matters related to the pre-Islamic period. At this point the differing value and importance of these three component parts which provided biographical material for Ibn Isḥāq become apparent; in a serious study one cannot be content with citing the reports of Ibn Isḥāq without distinguishing between the three elements mentioned above.

From another point of view, we might say that Ibn Sayyid al-Nās or Ibn Kathīr are late, that their information is taken from earlier well-known historians, and that, consequently, they are of secondary importance. This may be true for many of the reports these two authorities relate, but on close examination we find that each of them contains primary materials derived from historians earlier than Ibn Isḥāq—such as the generation of al-Zuhrī—that are not found in the biography of Ibn Hishām, and in this way we can acquire important additional historical material. After all this we can, by studying the early and subsequent sources, perceive the evolving conception among Arab historians of the Prophet's biography. When we compare the *Sīra* of Ibn Hishām with *'Uyūn al-athar*, for example, we witness a shift from simple historical reports in the early sources (e.g., 'Urwa ibn al-Zubayr and al-Zuhrī) to accounts in which the elements of piety and religious sanctity are predominant, and in which religious sentiment and a tendency to exaggerate are strongly intertwined with the historical view of the narrator. In such manner we can undertake a truly historical study of the Prophet's life founded on a sound evaluation of the sources and on a critical historical approach to the accounts in which this material has been preserved.

However, the study of this subject is difficult and troublesome since the primary historical writings have not come down to us in their complete form; rather, what we have from them are only selections scattered in later historical works. This means that we must collect and organize these selections so as to obtain an approximate idea of the structure of these earliest sources. Such an endeavor implies the reclassification of the historical materials which have survived to modern times, especially those for the first three centuries after the Hijra, and tracing them back to their original sources–all in all, a difficult, slow, and perilous task.

There is a second difficulty: namely, that these selections are usually (with rare exceptions) attributed to their original authors without reference to the works from which later writers took them. This compels us to resort to a great deal of supposition and conjecture as we attempt to gain knowledge about the original sources from which these selections are taken. Moreover, even after all this effort we are likely to obtain only broad outlines, which may or may not form a coherent whole, of these earlier historical compositions.

In spite of these difficulties, it is my feeling that one cannot study Arab history without undertaking such an endeavor, or without reorganizing the historical materials according to their sources. Otherwise, history will be mixed with legend and belles-lettres, and early accounts and later reports will be regarded as being of equal value. Neither the logic of history nor historical method will permit this.

The following pages represent a first attempt to study the evolution of historical writing among the Arabs, a collection of sketches linked both by chronological period—the first three centuries after the Hijra—and by their unity of subject. In the first introductory essay I have dealt with the rise of historical writing and its development to the end of the third century A.H.; the general and summary manner in which I have done so makes this section virtually a collection of biographies elucidating the general lines along which the discipline developed. The second essay deals with the evolution of the historical school of Medina as embodied in the works of its forerunner, ʿUrwa ibn al-Zubayr, and its true founder, al-Zuhrī. This section helps us to understand the origins of the biography of the Prophet. The third essay deals with Wahb ibn Munabbih as a storyteller and narrator primarily interested in legendary tales. His influence appears both in the *Isrāʾīlīyāt* and in stories about the pre-Islamic period, and likewise he represents the outlook of the tradition of Yemenite legend. I have discussed this in order to make it clear that he did not have a serious influence on the writing of the Prophet's biography, as some Orientalists have believed. The study of the Prophet's biography was developed by historians from among the scholars of *ḥadīth*, not by storytellers. The legendary element seeped into the Prophet's biography at a later time, and was subject to criticism by the historians.

The fourth essay deals with the evolution of the historical school of Iraq (Kufa and Basra), the other school of history among the Arabs. This school arose independently, from roots which differed from those of the Medinan school, and revealed the effect of particular circumstances, conditions, and motives associated with the tribal perspectives which existed within the newly established Islamic framework. It is my view that the evolution of historical writing among the Arabs can be traced to these two schools in Medina and Iraq.

In the fifth essay I turn to the motives which led to the rise of historical writing among the Arabs, and to the historical views and ideas which they wished to express and embodied in their writings.

We are passing through a period of comprehensive revival, and I hope that historical studies will have their own role and influence in this auspicious period.

ʿAbd al-ʿAzīz al-Dūrī

CHAPTER ONE

The Rise of History Among the Arabs and Its Development During the First Three Centuries A.H.

I.

Among the Arabs, historical writing has been an integral part of general cultural development.[1] Its links with the dis-

[1] For some general works on historical writing among the Arabs, see Ferdinand Wüstenfeld, *Die Geschichtschreiber der Araber und ihre Werke* (Göttingen, 1882); Carl Brockelmann, *Geschichte der arabischen Literatur* (Weimar and Berlin, 1898-1902); Supplement (Leiden, 1937-1942); 2nd ed. (Leiden, 1943-49); Johann Fück, *Muḥammad ibn Isḥāq: literarhistorische Untersuchungen* (Frankfurt am Main, 1925); Josef Horovitz ["The Earliest Biographies of the Prophet and Their Authors," *Islamic Culture*, I (1927), pp. 535ff.; II (1928), pp. 22ff., 164ff., 495ff.;] translated by Ḥusayn Naṣṣār as *Al-Maghāzī al-ūlā wa-mu'allifūhā* (Cairo, 1949); D. S. Margoliouth, *Lectures on Arabic Historians* (Calcutta, 1930); H.A.R. Gibb, "Ta'rīkh," in *EI*[1], Supplement (Leiden, 1938), pp. 233ff. [reprinted in his *Studies on the Civilization of Islam*, edited by Stanford J. Shaw and William R. Polk (Boston, 1962), pp. 108ff.]; Régis Blachère, *Histoire de la littérature arabe* (Paris, 1952-66); Franz Rosenthal, *A History of Muslim Historiography* (Leiden, 1952); [2nd ed. (Leiden, 1968). See also Ignazio Guidi, "L'Historiographie chez les sémites," *Revue biblique*, VI (1906), pp. 509ff.; Israel Friedländer, "Muhammedanische Geschichtskonstruktionen," *Beiträge zur Kenntnis des Orients*, IX (1910), pp. 17ff.; Émile Amar, "Prolégomènes à l'étude des historiens arabes par Khalīl ibn Aibak aṣ-Ṣafadī," *Journal asiatique*, 10th Series, XVII (1911), pp. 251ff.; XVIII (1911), pp. 5ff.; XIX (1912), pp. 243ff.; Rudi Paret, *Die legendäre Maghāzi-Literatur: arabische Dichtungen über die muslimischen Kriegszüge zu Mohammeds Zeit* (Tübingen, 1930); G. Richter, *Die Geschichtsbild der arabischen Historiker des Mittelalters* (Tübingen, 1933); translated by M. Saber Khan as "Medieval Arabic Historiography," *Islamic Culture*, XXXIII (1959), pp. 240ff.; XXXIV (1960) pp. 139ff.; Ilse Lichtenstädter, "Arabic and Islamic Historiography," *Muslim World*, XXXV (1945), pp. 126ff.; Zeki Velidi Togan, "Kritische Geschichtsauffassung in der islamischen Welt des Mittelalters," *Proceedings of the Twenty-Second Congress of Orientalists*, edited by Zeki Velidi Togan (Istanbul, 1953-57), I, 76ff.; translated by M. S. Khan as "The Concept of Critical Historiography in the Islamic World of the Middle Ages," *Islamic Studies*, XIV (1975), pp. 175ff.; Julian Obermann, "Early Islam," in

cipline of *ḥadīth* and with belles-lettres are particularly strong and deserve special attention. Moreover, the rise of Islam, the subsequent creation of an empire, the clash of various views and cultural currents, and the development and experiences of the new Islamic community, or *umma*, are all of vital concern to us if we are to understand the earliest stages in the development of historical writing in this milieu.

The Idea of History in the Ancient Near East, edited by Julian Obermann (New Haven, 1955), pp. 237ff.; B. Spuler, "Islamische und abendländische Geschichtschreibung: Ein Grundsatz-Betrachtung," *Saeculum*, VI (1955), pp. 125ff.; Nabia Abbott, *Studies in Arabic Literary Papyri* (Chicago, 1957-72), I, 5ff.; Joseph de Somogyi, "The Development of Arabic Historiography," *JSS*, III (1958), pp. 373ff.; Fuat Sezgin, *Geschichte des arabischen Schrifttums* (Leiden, 1967—), I, 235ff.; Ignaz Goldziher, "Historiography in Arabic Literature," in his *Gesammelte Schriften*, edited by Joseph de Somogyi (Hildesheim, 1967-73), III, 359ff.; Hamida Murtaza, "The Origin of the Muslim Historiography," *Journal of the Pakistan Historical Society*, XVI (1968), pp. 198ff.; Albrecht Noth, "Iṣfahān-Nihāwand: eine quellenkritische Studie zur frühislamischen Historiographie," *ZDMG*, CXVIII (1968), pp. 274ff.; K. Jahn, "Universalgeschichte im islamischen Raum," in *Mensch und Weltgeschichte: Zur Geschichte der Universalgeschichtsschreibung*, edited by A. Randa (Salzburg and Munich, 1969), pp. 145ff.; Walther Braune, "Historical Consciousness in Islam," in *Theology and Law in Islam*, edited by Gustave E. von Grunebaum (Wiesbaden, 1971), pp. 37ff.; D. M. Dunlop, *Arab Civilization to A.D. 1500* (London, 1971), pp. 70ff.; Gernot Rotter, "Abū Zurʿa ad-Dimašqī (st. 281/894) und das Problem der frühen arabischen Geschichtsschreibung in Syrien," *Die Welt des Orients*, VI (1971), pp. 80ff.; Albrecht Noth, "Der Charakter der ersten grossen Sammlungen von Nachrichten zur frühen Kalifenzeit," *Der Islam*, XLVII (1971), pp. 168ff.; *idem*, *Quellenkritische Studien zu Themen, Formen und Tendenzen frühislamischer Geschichtsüberlieferung*, I: *Themen und Formen* (Bonn, 1973); *idem*, "Die literarisch überlieferten Verträge der Eroberungszeit als historische Quellen für die Behandlung der Unterworfenen Nicht-Muslims durch ihre neuen muslimischen Oberherren," *Studien zum Minderheitenproblem im Islam* (Bonn, 1973), I, 282ff.; Gernot Rotter, "Formen der frühen arabischen Geschichtsschreibung," in *Deutsche Orientalistik am Beispiel Tübingens*, edited by Gernot Rotter (Tübingen and Basel, 1974), pp. 63ff.; Nisar Ahmed Faruqi, "Some Methodological Aspects of the Early Muslim Historiography," *Islam and the Modern Age*, VI (1975), pp. 88ff.; Tarif Khalidi, *Islamic Historiography: the Histories of Masʿūdī* (Albany, 1975); Claude Cahen, "Notes sur l'historiographie dans la communauté musulmane médiévale," *REI*, XLIV (1976), pp. 81ff.; John Wansbrough, *The Sectarian Milieu: Content and Composition of Islamic Salvation History* (Oxford, 1978). On related literary developments in early Islamic times, see William Marçais, "Les Origines de la prose littéraire arabe," *Revue africaine*, LXVIII (1927), pp. 12ff.; Ruth Stellhorn Mackensen, "Arabic Books and Libraries in

Although it was in early Islamic times that historical writing appeared among the Arabs, elements of cultural continuity oblige us to turn our attention back to the pre-Islamic heritage. Both nomadic and other more settled societies existed in the Arabian peninsula in the period of the Jāhilīya; and although the satisfactory information available to us is meager and generally the product of later times, we will consider it briefly here by way of introduction to the present study.

Inscriptions and carvings in southern Arabia attest to the emergence of four kingdoms during the period extending from 1200 B.C. to 527 A.D. These kingdoms all followed similar paths of development. They began as theocracies ruled by a priest-king, or *mukarrib*, exercising both religious and temporal power, and then gradually evolved into secular kingdoms ruled by families of warriors and landowners.[2] These kingdoms left inscriptions which, based on what we have learned so far, are datable to the period extending from the eighth century B.C. to the seventh century A.D. These inscriptions record a variety of actions, such as acts of charity and

the Umaiyad Period," *AJSL*, LII (1935-36), pp. 245ff.; LIII (1936-37), pp. 239ff.; LIV (1937-38), pp. 41ff.; Franz Rosenthal, *The Technique and Approach of Muslim Scholarship* (Rome, 1947); C. A. Nallino, *La Littérature arabe des origines à l'époque de la dynastie umayyade*, translated by Charles Pellat (Paris, 1950); Régis Blachère, "Regards sur la littérature narrative en arabe au Ier siècle de l'hégire (= VIIe s.J.-C.)," *Semitica*, VI (1956), pp. 75ff.; Franz Rosenthal, *Knowledge Triumphant* (Leiden, 1970). For some of the events which will frequently reappear in this book, the following works offer important historiographical discussions: Julius Wellhausen, *Prolegomena zur ältesten Geschichte des Islams*, published in his *Skizzen und Vorarbeiten*, VI (Berlin, 1899), pp. 3ff.; M. J. de Goeje, *Mémoire sur la conquête de la Syrie*, 2nd ed. (Leiden, 1900); W. Sarasin, *Das Bild Alis bei der Historikern der Sunna* (Basel, 1907); W. Montgomery Watt, *Muhammad at Mecca* (Oxford, 1953); *idem, Muhammad at Medina* (Oxford, 1956); Erling Ladewig Petersen, *'Alī and Mu'āwiya in Early Arabic Tradition* (Copenhagen, 1964); Elias S. Shoufani, *Al-Riddah and the Muslim Conquest of Arabia* (Toronto, 1972); Fred M. Donner, "The Bakr b. Wā'il Tribes and Politics in Northeastern Arabia on the Eve of Islam," *Studia Islamica*, LI (1980), pp. 5ff.; *idem, The Early Islamic Conquests* (Princeton, 1981).]

[2] Jacques Ryckmans, *L'Institution monarchique à l'Arabie méridionale* (Louvain, 1951), pp. 25ff.

piety, submission of tax payments, irrigation projects, the building of walls and fortifications, and military campaigns.[3] Although some of these inscriptions are religious in nature, others are essentially efforts to record human actions and perpetuate the memory of important deeds.[4] In these inscriptions we at first find a confused method of dating events; but later on a fixed calendar beginning with the year 115 B.C. was introduced, leading to a fixed system of dating.[5] This development, along with the interest in recording human actions, may have inspired the emergence of some measure of historically minded thinking. Al-Hamdānī lends credence to this possibility when he refers to royal documents and Ḥimyarite records that were preserved and consulted again later,[6] and to the *zubur*, the documents and genealogical records which some families and clans preserved.[7]

[3] *Répertoire d'épigraphie sémitique*, vols. V-VII, edited by J. Ryckmans (Paris, 1929-50), nos. 2695, 2706, 2789, 2975, 2999, 3021, 3391, 3943.

[4] Ryckmans, *L'Institution monarchique*, pp. 71ff., 77; *RES*, nos. 3858, 3943; *Corpus inscriptionum semiticarum*, Part IV (Paris, 1889-1931), no. 6215; G. Ryckmans, "Inscriptions Sub-Arabes," *Le Muséon*, XLV (1932), pp. 294f.; Sidney Smith, "Events in Arabia in the 6th Century A.D.," *BSOAS*, XVI (1954), p. 431.

[5] Ryckmans, *L'Institution monarchique*, p. 282.

[6] In his account of a Yemenite scholar, al-Hamdānī says that the man was "the heir to whatever written accounts of their learning that the kings of Ḥimyar had stored away in their treasuries," and that "he read the old *zubur* of the Ḥimyarites and their ancient inscriptions in their *musnad* alphabet." See his *Al-Iklīl*, vol. I, edited by Oscar Löfgren (Uppsala, 1954), p. 5. He also mentions that genealogies of the descendants of al-Hamyasaʿ "were recorded in the treasuries of the Ḥimyarites, as were the genealogies of the kings descended from ʿAmr ibn Hamdān"; *Iklīl*, X, edited by Muḥibb al-Dīn al-Khaṭīb (Cairo, 1368/1949), p. 30.

[7] Al-Hamdānī says, concerning the genealogies of the Laʿwīs, "The genealogies of the Laʿwīs are based on solid documentation (*muqayyadat al-uṣūl*) . . . I have taken them on their authority related from an ancient record (*zabūr*) in the handwriting of Aḥmad ibn Mūsā"; *Iklīl*, X, 111. Elsewhere he says that he has taken the genealogy of Banū Laʿwa "that was related on their authority in their own time in the town (Rayda) and based on the records (*zabūr*) they possessed. This genealogy has been compared with what Hishām ibn Muḥammad ibn al-Sā'ib al-Kalbī and other genealogists have related"; *Iklīl*, X, 119f. He also says, "The Marwānids of the Yemen . . . act according

Yemenite accounts found in the primary literary sources, however, are generally of a legendary character, to such an extent that even the events of the sixth century A.D., which was then the relatively recent past, are muddled.[8] In these sources we find, in place of any reliable accounts, narrators like Wahb ibn Munabbih (d. 114/732) and ʿUbayd ibn Sharya,[a] who furnish us with a fanciful romantic story of the history of the Yemen which is an amalgamation of popular fables and *Isrāʾīlīyāt*, or tales of the ancient Israelites.[b] In this way they attempted to glorify the Yemenite Arabs, ascribing to them glorious achievements in war, craftsmanship, language, literature, and even religion—all in order to prove that they had surpassed the Arabs of the north in such achievements, or that they were in no way inferior to them in these respects.[9] They set forth these accounts of their own past in a style which resembles the style of the stories in the *ayyām al-ʿarab*, the "Battle-Days" of the Arab tribes, including a very ample measure of forged verse to strengthen the impression made by the story. This is a phenomenon which calls for further attention. Its causes appear to be associated with the circumstances in

---

to the genealogies that their ancestors set down and preserved by transmission from one illustrious ancestor to the next"; *Iklīl*, X, 30f. [On the *zubur*, see *EI*¹, IV, 1184f. (J. Horovitz).]

[8] In the opening section of his *Iklīl* (I, 4), al-Hamdānī criticizes the historical accounts about the Yemen and says, "I found most people stumbling about in lost confusion, as the blackest darkness surrounded them in the dead of the night." He considers the lack of precision in chronicling events to be an element contributing to this confusion.

[a] [On Wahb ibn Munabbih, see Chapter Three below. ʿUbayd ibn Sharya was an oft-quoted transmitter of reports who supposedly died in the mid-first century A.H. Abbott (*Studies*, I, 9ff.) discusses him in detail and considers him to be a historical figure, but other scholars have raised serious doubts as to whether he was any more than a fictitious character to whom many folkloric tales were attributed. See F. Krenkow, "The Two Oldest Books on Arabic Folklore," *Islamic Culture*, II (1928), pp. 234ff.; *EI*², III, 937 (Franz Rosenthal).]

[b] [On this literature, see *EI*², IV, 211f. (G. Vajda).]

[9] Ibn Hishām, *Kitāb al-tījān fī mulūk Ḥimyar wa-l-Yaman*, edited by F. Krenkow (Haydarabad, A.H. 1347), pp. 35, 47f., 52f., 74, 86f., 110, 162.

which the Arabs found themselves in the early Islamic period. Political circumstances and geographical factors certainly exerted an influence in this, since partisan feeling and rivalry between the northern Arabs (Muḍar) and southern Arabs (Yemen) were most particularly responsible for such reports of the past as these. These Yemenite narratives may in turn have been partly responsible for the partisan spirit which arose among the genealogists of the north.[10] The remoteness of southern Arabia may have deterred the learned men of the north from traveling to Yemen and gathering information directly from the area.[11] Moreover, these early narrators, or ***ruwāt***, were more nearly storytellers than they were historians. Thus, the accounts of Yemen that have come down to us are of little value and devoid of historical conception. Yet, from another point of view, it is likely that the idea of fixed dating (the calendar) among the Yemenites had an influence in the establishment of a fixed calendar (the Hijra dating system) among the Muslims.[12]

In the north of the peninsula, the Lakhmid kings had "books," preserved in the churches of al-Ḥīra, which contained accounts of the Arabs of the city, their genealogies, and biographies of their rulers. Similarly, they were familiar with many Persian accounts of the Iranian past.[13] But although

[10] Al-Hamdānī (*Iklīl*, I, 4) considers the partisan feelings, or *ʿaṣabīya*, of the genealogists of Iraq and Syria to be one of the factors that contributed to the confusion over the genealogy of the Yemenites, and says that "the method of the genealogists of Iraq and Syria is similar, in that they abbreviate the genealogies of Kahlān and Mālik ibn Ḥimyar in order to make the number of their ancestors correspond to the number ascribed to the sons of Ismāʿīl." [I.e., they compress Yemenite lines of descent to avoid conceding that the great families of the south are of greater antiquity than those of the north.]

[11] Al-Hamdānī, *Iklīl*, X, 30. About the northern chroniclers, he says that "they have made very few journeys to see their counterparts living in Yemen; and in the path followed by their learned men they encountered naught but some leavings from departed caravans"; *Iklīl*, I, 4.

[12] Al-Suyūṭī, *Al-Shamārīkh fī ʿilm al-taʾrīkh*, edited by C. F. Seybold (Leiden, 1894), p. 9.

[13] Al-Ṭabarī, *Taʾrīkh al-rusul wa-l-mulūk* (Cairo: Ḥusaynīya Press, A.H. 1336),

some historians in later periods made use of these books and accounts in their own works, we find nothing which indicates that the Arabs of al-Ḥīra themselves had any clear conception of history.

The Arabs of the north had oral accounts of stories about their gods, and also accounts of their social affairs and their great exploits. The principal part of these accounts are concerned with their raiding expeditions and battles (*ayyām*) and their genealogies. These accounts are intimately related to the organization, views, and customs of society, as is reflected most prominently by the ideas of *muruwwa*, the totality of the bedouin virtues, of *nasab*, noble family origin, and of *ḥasab*, the distinction of great deeds and exploits, since individuals were expected to know their ancestors and the noble deeds which they had performed. As the *ayyām* were thus the subject of special concern in tribal society, the tribes had tales and narratives of their past deeds. These tribal accounts circulated both orally and in the form of prose. In the oral accounts, however, poetry plays a fundamental role, since it either appears throughout the story or comes at the end, depending on whether or not the poet has taken part in the events described. This poetry does not carry the story forward, but rather gives it vitality and authority. And, with the passage of time, it came to be considered the solid evidence which confirmed the validity of the story. As Ibn Fāris puts it, "Poetry is the register (*dīwān*) of the Arabs, through which genealogies are preserved and great deeds are displayed, and from which language is learned. . . ."[14]

II, 127 [edited by M. J. de Goeje *et al.* (Leiden, 1879-1901), I, 770]; Ibn Hishām, *Sīrat Rasūl Allāh*, edited by Muṣṭafā al-Saqqā *et al.* (Cairo, 1355/1936), I, 321 [edited by Ferdinand Wüstenfeld (Göttingen, 1858-60), I, i, 191]; Ḥājjī Khalīfa, *Kashf al-ẓunūn ʿan asāmī l-kutub wa-l-funūn*, edited by Şerefettin Yaltkaya and Kilisli Rifat Bilge (Istanbul, 1941-43), I, 35.

[14] Al-Tibrīzī, *Sharḥ al-ḥamāsa* (Cairo, 1335/1916), I, 3; al-Suyūṭī, *Al-Muzhir fī ʿulūm al-lugha*, edited by Aḥmad Jād al-Mawlā *et al.* (Cairo, n.d.), II, 470.

The *ayyām* stories had originated in evening tribal gatherings (*majālis*), and were an orally transmitted assemblage of collective tribal accounts. They were the common property of the tribe, and remained so until the second/eighth century, when these accounts were gathered and compiled in written form. At the same time, however, we must bear in mind that the political and social currents of the early Islamic period exerted a distinct influence on the *ayyām* literature. Accounts of the "Battle-Days" are chronologically confused, and generally reflect partisan tendencies and represent the views of only one side. Moreover, they lack coherence and order, and embody no concept of history. Nevertheless, they do contain certain historical facts. Their fundamental importance is that they persisted through the early Islamic period, and their style affected the early stages of historical writing, especially in Iraq.

The presence of poetry in the *ayyām* made them a subject of keen interest to philologists, genealogists, and historians (e.g., Abū ʿUbayda, al-Madāʾinī, Ibn Qutayba, Abū l-Faraj al-Iṣfahānī, and Ibn ʿAbd Rabbih), and likewise, the *ayyām* eventually became an element in historical accounts. Ibn al-Athīr tried to present accounts of the *ayyām* in historical sequence.[15] Ḥājjī Khalīfa considers the *ayyām* to be a branch of history, saying, "The study of the *ayyām al-ʿarab* is a branch of learning in which one studies the momentous events and great ordeals which occurred among the Arab tribes . . . and it is appropriate that the above-mentioned field of learning be placed among the branches of history."[16]

For modern historians the importance of the *ayyām* ac-

[15] Ibn al-Athīr, *Al-Kāmil fī l-taʾrīkh* (Cairo, A.H. 1290), I, 209, 219, 220, 225ff. [edited by C. J. Tornberg (Leiden, 1851-71), I, 502ff.].

[16] Ḥājjī Khalīfa, *Kashf al-ẓunūn*, I, 204. On the *ayyām*, see Werner Caskel, "Aijām al-ʿarab: Studien zur altarabischen Epik," *Islamica*, III (1930), pp. 1ff.; Aḥmad al-Shāʾib, *Taʾrīkh al-naqāʾiḍ*, 2nd ed. (Cairo, 1954), pp. 53ff.; *EI*[1], I, 218f. (E. Mittwoch); [*EI*[2], I, 793f. (E. Mittwoch); E. Meyer, *Der historische Gehalt der Aiyām al-ʿArab* (Wiesbaden, 1970); ʿAbd al-Jabbār al-Bayātī, *Kitāb ayyām al-ʿarab qabla l-Islām* (Baghdad, 1976)].

counts lies in their persistence into early Islamic times, and in their style. The style of the *ayyām* stories is direct and full of vitality, a realistic approach in which prose is blended together with poetry. This style had its effect on the beginnings of historical writing among the Arabs, and its influence was particularly strong in the tribal milieu.

Tribal life is characterized by its adherence to tradition, and has only a confused and limited notion of time. This is because time, from the tribal point of view, is punctuated by great events which tribesmen customarily take as starting points for dating events or fixing matters of chronology; when an important event occurs, whatever preceded it is disregarded and subsequent events are dated according to it. In some times and places, like al-Ḥīra and Mecca, the tribes were in contact with other cultures. But their interest in these cultures was limited to their own immediate and particular affairs, and we have no evidence indicating the presence of other outside influences.

The era of the Jāhilīya left no written literature, and was rather a period of oral culture. Although its legacy in general contributed to the persistent interest in *ayyām* and in genealogies, and to the survival of a certain style in relating accounts, i.e., the pseudo-historical storytelling style, it is nevertheless devoid of any genuinely historical view of its subject matter.

II.

New views arose with the emergence of Islam. The Qur'ān expounded a serious conception of the past, called attention to the limitations of the Arabs' earlier recollections, and traced history back to the beginning of Creation. The Qur'ān stressed the lessons and warnings provided by the history of bygone times, and recalled the experiences of past nations and peoples in order to emphasize the spiritual and ethical precepts they involved. It set forth a universal view which conceived of history as a succession of prophetic missions—all essentially a single message preached by various prophets, the last of whom, Muḥammad, was the *khātam*, or "seal," of the prophets and messengers. This view made its influence felt by directing attention to the history of the prophets and to the *Isrā'īlīyāt*. Yet this universal conception of history was limited to the periods which preceded the rise of Islam; for later times, attention was focused on the history of Islam. The Muslims were the successors of the previous nations among whom past prophets had carried out their missions, and their own deeds and affairs were thus deserving of special interest. This point of view was buttressed by the famous *ḥadīth*, "My community will never agree on an error," a *ḥadīth* important in establishing the concept of communal consensus, or *ijmā'*. Finally, the Qur'ān stated that the Prophet's words were of divine inspiration, and that his life was an example for Muslims to emulate. Here we find an immediate motive for the study of the Prophet's words and deeds.

The Arabs of Islamic times felt that they were possessors of a message of great significance, and that they were passing through an important stage in history. The great conquests, for example, made them aware that they had an important role to play in history, and this recognition had a powerful impact on historical studies. It was in this era that 'Umar ibn al-Khaṭṭāb established a fixed calendar, the Hijra dating system. This became a vital element in the rise of historical thought; and the temporal fixing of events, or rather their classification in chronological order, has been the backbone of historical studies ever since. 'Umar also initiated the *dīwān* system, or the recording of the names of warriors and their families according to tribe. This gave genealogies new importance and provided further incentive for studying them.

Considering these views and factors, and surveying the rise of historical studies, we notice that the first manifestations of such writing originated from two fundamental perspectives: the Islamic perspective, which arose among the scholars of *ḥadīth*, and the tribal perspective, or that of the *ayyām*. These two outlooks reflect the two great currents in early Islamic society: the tribal current represented by the enduring persistence of the tribal heritage, and the Islamic current embodied in spiritual principles and activities. Each of these two perspectives had a cultural center in which it was predominant: the Islamic perspective thrived in Medina, the abode of prophetic *sunna*, and the tribal perspective in Kufa and Basra, the two new garrison towns which were centers of tribal activity. All three cities were centers of vigorous cultural activity in early Islamic times. Each perspective developed its own school of historical writing, and each school exerted its own influence upon the other. In the end, however, the Islamic perspective prevailed as the viewpoint of the scholars of *ḥadīth* rose to a dominant position in historical writing, as we shall see later below.

III.

Men of learning considered it their natural role and essential task to devote their attention to the words and deeds of the Prophet, whether as sources of spiritual guidance, or as sanctions providing precedents applicable to jurisprudence, administrative organization, and the affairs of everyday life. Similarly, Muḥammad's military campaigns and the expeditions of his Companions were a matter of special interest and pride among Muslims in general, and were favored topics of conversation at evening gatherings. Interest in these events was further reinforced by the fact that participation in the campaigns and other activities of the Prophet was a factor in improving one's social status, and also a point considered in the determination of stipends in the *dīwān* registers. Before long, the Companions themselves came to be regarded as paragons for later generations to emulate in word and deed, and thus their sayings and activities also came to be included in the *ḥadīth*.[17] Eventually, through the course of the first century A.H., interest broadened to include the activities of the entire Islamic community. These various considerations all manifested themselves in historical studies.

The study of the *maghāzī*, or military expeditions of the Prophet, began in Medina in conjunction with the study of *ḥadīth*. The scholars of *ḥadīth* continued to show interest in the *maghāzī*, but some of them, in studying the life of the Prophet, began to do so in a manner which moved beyond the limitations of the juridical aspects of the subject. The pioneers of *maghāzī* studies were scholars of *ḥadīth*, as is confirmed by the way in which the learned regarded the *maghāzī* authors. This also explains the importance of the *isnād*,[c] the chain of authorities transmitting a report, in assessing the value of the *maghāzī*; this meant that the value of a *ḥadīth* or other account depended upon the reputation of the *ḥadīth* scholars or transmitters who figured in the chain of authorities. This point of view very early on gave rise to a critical attitude towards the *ruwāt*, the sources who transmitted the information. It introduced the element of investigation and inquiry into the gathering of the various accounts, and laid a firm foundation for historical studies. On the other hand, narratives and popular tales about the *maghāzī* were also passed along by word of mouth. Storytellers, the *quṣṣāṣ*, went to great

[17] See Joseph Schacht, *The Origins of Muhammedan Jurisprudence* (Oxford, 1950), pp. 3ff.

[c] [The development of the *isnād* and its evolution as a critical tool are still topics of considerable controversy. For some of the more important views, see Ignaz Goldziher, *Muslim Studies*, edited and translated by S. M. Stern and C. R. Barber (London, 1967-71), II, index; Leone Caetani, *Annali dell'Islam* (Milan, 1905-26), I, 29ff.; Josef Horovitz, "Alter und Ursprung des Isnād," *Der Islam*, VIII (1918), pp. 39ff.; Schacht, *Origins*, pp. 38ff.; J. Robson, "The Isnād in Muslim Tradition," *Transactions of the Glasgow University Oriental Society*, XV (1955), pp. 15ff.; Abbott, *Studies*, I, 8f.; II, 5ff., and frequently thereafter; M. M. Azmi, *Studies in Early Hadith Literature* (Indianapolis, 1978), pp. 212ff.; Michael Cook, *Early Muslim Dogma* (Cambridge, 1981), pp. 107ff.]

lengths in relating these accounts and turned them into a kind of folklore,[d] but although some of this did in later times find its way into certain biographies of the Prophet, the attitude towards transmitted accounts, and the methods employed in their criticism, essentially continued to follow the methodology of the scholars of *ḥadīth*.

The earliest studies of the Prophet's life were also referred to as the *maghāzī*, a word which from a linguistic point of view means the raids and military campaigns of the Prophet, but which actually extended to the entire period of his prophetic mission.[e] Such studies were taken up by some of the most prominent descendants of Muḥammad's Companions.[18] Let us now consider these writers.

We begin with Abān ibn ʿUthmān ibn ʿAffān (d. between 95/713 and 105/733), a scholar of *ḥadīth* inclined towards the study of the *maghāzī*. One of his students set his *maghāzī* materials down in writing, but this is described as a work of *ḥadīth*.[19] Excluding a solitary reference to him in al-Yaʿqūbī,[20]

[d] [On the *quṣṣāṣ* and the tales (*qiṣaṣ*) they related, see Goldziher, *Muslim Studies*, II, 145ff.; *idem*, *Die Richtungen der islamischen Koranauslegung* (Leiden, 1920), pp. 58ff.; J. Pedersen, "The Islamic Preacher," in *Ignace Goldziher Memorial Volume*, edited by Joseph de Somogyi (Budapest, 1948), I, 226ff.; *idem*, "The Criticism of the Islamic Preacher," *Die Welt des Islams*, New Series, II (1953), pp. 215ff.; Charles Pellat, *Le Milieu baṣrien et la formation de Ǧāḥiẓ* (Paris, 1953), pp. 108ff.; *EI*², IV, 733ff. (C. Pellat); V, 185ff. (C. Pellat). Cf. also p. 28, note f below.]

[e] [For some detailed remarks on the *sīra-maghāzī* connection, see Theodor Nöldeke, *Geschichte des Qorāns*, 2nd edition, revised by Friedrich Schwally *et al.* (Leipzig, 1909-38), II, 220f.]

[18] See Horovitz, "Biographies"; [also Fück, *Muḥammad ibn Isḥāq*, pp. 1ff.; *GAS*, I, 235ff.].

[19] Ibn Saʿd, *Kitāb al-ṭabaqāt al-kabīr*, edited by Eduard Sachau *et al.* (Leiden, 1904-40), V, 156. [Further light is shed on this matter in al-Zubayr ibn Bakkār, *Al-Akhbār al-muwaffaqīyāt*, edited by Sāmī Makkī al-ʿĀnī (Baghdad, 1392/1972), pp. 332ff. According to this report, the *amīr* Sulaymān ibn ʿAbd al-Malik asked Abān in A.H. 82 to write for him "*siyar al-Nabī* and his *maghāzī*," and Abān replied, "I have them with me, checked and documented from sources I trust." A copy was made for Sulaymān, but he destroyed the sheets later for political reasons.]

[20] *Taʾrīkh*, edited by M. T. Houtsma (Leiden, 1883), I, 3.

we find no one among the historians who transmits or reports information on his authority, whereas in the books of *ḥadīth* we do find accounts handed down through him. Abān ibn ʿUthmān thus seems to represent an intermediate stage between the study of *ḥadīth* and the study of *maghāzī*.

The founder of *maghāzī* studies appears to have been the famous jurisconsult and *ḥadīth* scholar ʿUrwa ibn al-Zubayr (d. 94/712), since he was the first to compose a book on the *maghāzī*.[21] Part of his work on the subject survives as quotations cited in the works of such historians as al-Ṭabarī, Ibn Isḥāq, al-Wāqidī, Ibn Sayyid al-Nās, and Ibn Kathīr. These borrowings are the earliest surviving writings on the history of the *maghāzī*. They cover various aspects of the Prophet's life, such as the beginning of the Qur'ānic revelations, some of the raids, and some of the personal affairs of the Prophet, although in his accounts ʿUrwa does not go into detail on the fighting during the campaigns. He set down some of his lectures in writing, while part of his historical writings comprised written replies to questions addressed to him by the Umayyad court.[22] He used the *isnād* in a form which reflects the attitude of his day. He apparently relied on *ḥadīth* materials in his written replies, but set forth a continuous narrative (or story) without mentioning the chain of authorities who had transmitted it. In his accounts of such important events as the beginning of Qur'ānic revelation and the Hijra, however, he does give his *isnād*. The attitude towards the *isnād* in his day was still flexible, and on its use there were as yet no detailed rules, which appeared later.

ʿUrwa's style of writing is direct and far removed from literary affectation, and at the same time his attitude is realistic, unequivocal, and free from exaggeration. His social position

[21] Ḥājjī Khalīfa, *Kashf al-ẓunūn*, II, 1747; al-Sakhāwī, *Al-Iʿlān bi-l-tawbīkh li-man dhamma l-ta'rīkh* (Damascus, 1349/1930), p. 99.

[22] See Ibn Saʿd, V, 132ff.; al-Ṭabarī, *Ta'rīkh*, I, 1180, 1284, 1634.

enabled him to gather historical information from its earliest sources, especially from ʿĀʾisha and the family of al-Zubayr, who were his kinsmen. He also had access to some written documents, and made reference to verses of the Qurʾān pertaining to the events he describes.[23] Although he does cite poetry from time to time,[24] this is not indicative of any influence by the style of the *ayyām*, but rather reflects ʿUrwa's own fondness for verse and the role of poetry in the culture of his time.

ʿUrwa's interest in history also extended to the period of the Rāshidūn caliphs, and included such topics as the Ridda wars and the battles of al-Qādisīya and al-Yarmūk.[25] It is thus at an early date that we find an interest in events affecting the *umma*. Unfortunately, the accounts which have come down to us from ʿUrwa are few and far between. They are insufficient for us to gain any clear conception of his *maghāzī* work, or even of the structure (assuming any such structure existed) according to which he arranged his accounts.

Let us note here that if we seek to understand the development of historical writing, we must bear in mind that academic studies, even in the early *maghāzī* tradition, were collective endeavors, and that the activities of individuals were part of the work of a particular school. Everyone who took up a career of learning added his own studies and research to those of his masters, and in this way both preserved the learning of the school to which he belonged and added to it other material which had come to his attention.

The role of one of ʿUrwa's contemporaries, Shuraḥbīl ibn Saʿd (d. 123/740), reflects the social attitude developing at that time. Participation in the various aspects of the Prophet's

[23] See Ibn Hishām, I, ii, 754; al-Balādhurī, *Futūḥ al-buldān*, edited by M. J. de Goeje (Leiden, 1866), p. 79; al-Ṭabarī, *Taʾrīkh*, I, 1180f., 1288.
[24] Al-Ṭabarī, *Taʾrīkh*, I, 2348.
[25] Al-Ṭabarī, *Taʾrīkh*, I, 1185, 1199, 1242.

mission was becoming a standard of steadily increasing importance in determining one's social status, thus Shuraḥbīl gave lists of the names of the Companions who had participated in great events, such as the warriors who fought at the battles of Badr and Uḥud and the groups of Muslims who emigrated to Abyssinia and to Medina.

In the following era there were three scholars primarily responsible for the advancement and extension of *maghāzī* studies: ʿAbd Allāh ibn Abī Bakr ibn Ḥazm (d. 130-35/747-52), ʿĀṣim ibn ʿUmar ibn Qatāda (d. 120/737), and Muḥammad ibn Muslim ibn Shihāb al-Zuhrī (d. 124/741). Their works firmly established the framework for *maghāzī* writings, and laid out the greater part of the materials used by Ibn Isḥāq and later by al-Wāqidī. Of these early works, however, only selections have survived to modern times.

Al-Zuhrī was the first true historian of these three authors;[26] for rather than confining himself to supplementing the *maghāzī* account of ʿUrwa ibn al-Zubayr,[27] he undertook a broad-ranging search to collect the accounts and *ḥadīth* in general circulation in Medina and wrote down whatever he found in order to aid his memory. He subjected these accounts to careful examination and arranged them within a clear and solid framework. A study of those of his accounts as have survived suggests that he was the first to endow the *sīra*—and this is the term he uses—with a definite structure, and to set down its outlines in unequivocal form. His format for the *sīra* begins by providing some information on the pre-Islamic era relevant to the life of the Prophet Muḥammad. He then takes up the important aspects of the Meccan period of the Prophet's life, the Hijra to Medina, and discusses Muḥammad's mil-

[26] I have already written a separate study devoted to this historian ["Al-Zuhrī: a Study of the Beginnings of History Writing in Islam," *BSOAS*, XIX (1957), pp. 1ff.]; I will therefore omit references to the sources here, but will return to al-Zuhrī in Chapter Two below.

[27] Al-Sakhāwī, *Al-Iʿlān bi-l-tawbīkh*, p. 89.

itary campaigns and the conquest of Mecca, some of the embassies he dispatched, and the delegations which came for audiences with him. Al-Zuhrī also speaks about other activities of the Prophet, and then his final illness and departure from this life. He strictly follows the chronological sequence in describing events of the *sīra*, and gives the dates for the most important ones.

Al-Zuhrī took most of his materials for the *sīra* from *ḥadīth*. We find only a slight trace of the *qiṣaṣ* tales in his writing, and similarly, we detect a faint echo in his materials from the *qiṣaṣ al-anbiyā'* ("tales of the prophets") literature,[f] in which he appears to have been interested. Al-Zuhrī was fond of poetry, as were the other men of his age, and in fact was quite knowledgeable on the subject. But his use of poetry in his *Maghāzī* was limited, and in his writing he was far removed from the style of the *ayyām*.

The studies of al-Zuhrī also covered the era of the Rāshidūn caliphs, since his scrutiny extended to the important events and major problems in the early history of the *umma*. These included the election of Abū Bakr as caliph, the establishment of the *dīwān* system, the collection of the Qur'ān, the *shūrā*, the *fitna*, the murder of ʿUthmān, the election of ʿAlī, the First Civil War, and the passage of political authority to the Umayyads. In this way he demonstrates the importance of the experiences through which the community had passed. From another standpoint, we should also note that al-Zuhrī was a learned genealogist. He wrote a book on Quraysh genealogy, and Muṣʿab al-Zubayrī mentions him as a source in his book *Nasab Quraysh*.

Al-Zuhrī provided his accounts with *isnāds*, and he was re-

[f] [On the *qiṣaṣ al-anbiyā'*, see Tilman Nagel, *Die Qiṣaṣ al-anbiyā': ein Beitrag zur arabischen Literaturgeschichte* (Bonn, 1967); J. Pauliny, "Einige Bemerkungen zu den Werken *Qiṣaṣ al-anbiyā'* in der arabischen Literatur," (*Graecolatina et Orientalia*, I (1969), pp. 111ff.; Raif Georges Khoury, *Les Légendes prophétiques dans l'Islam depuis le Ier jusqu'au IIIe siècle de l'Hégire* (Wiesbaden, 1978).]

nowned for the strength of the *isnāds* in which his name appeared. In this respect his attitude is representative of that of his age, inasmuch as he sometimes shows preference for accounts passed down through the descendants of the Companions, the *tābiʿūn*, to satisfy the conditions of *isnād* criticism. He did, however, introduce a new element, the collective *isnād* under which he combined a number of accounts into a single continuous narrative. In doing so he took an important step towards continuous historical writing. Al-Zuhrī also rendered another important service to historical studies in that he committed his accounts to writing. He is considered the first to have done so in any systematic fashion, and a considerable quantity of his writings was kept in the imperial library at the Umayyad court.[g] As for the accounts stating that he was coerced into writing down his works, these are echoes of disputations which arose after al-Zuhrī's time.[28]

The studies of ʿUrwa ibn al-Zubayr and al-Zuhrī cast light on the origins and scope of historical writing. From these works it appears that, in addition to the *sīra*, interest in the great tribulations and events which the Islamic community had experienced was a factor of fundamental significance in the rise of historical writing. Qur'ānic exegesis, considering the many references in the Qur'ān to Muslim affairs, was another factor. Administrative exigencies, such as organization of the taxation and *dīwān* systems, were also motives for writing.[29] Finally, the social status and the respect which scholars enjoyed in society were both elements promoting the quest

[g] [The evolution and role of library collections have been discussed in several useful works. See Mackensen, "Arabic Books and Libraries"; Abbott, *Studies*, I, 20ff.; Youssef Eche, *Les Bibliothèques arabes* (Damascus, 1967), pp. 9ff.]

[28] Ibn al-Jawzī, *Ṣafwat al-ṣafwa* (Haydarabad, A.H. 1355-56), II, 78; al-Dhahabī, *Tarājim rijāl rawā Muḥammad ibn Isḥāq ra'īs ahl al-maghāzī ʿanhum*, edited by August Fischer (Leiden, 1890), pp. 67, 69, 72; Ibn Kathīr, *Al-Bidāya wa-l-nihāya* (Cairo, 1351-58/1932-39), IX, 344.

[29] Al-Bukhārī, *Al-Ta'rīkh al-kabīr* (Haydarabad, 1360-79/1941-59), IV, 32; al-Dhahabī, *Tarājim*, p. 45.

for knowledge, as ʿUrwa ibn al-Zubayr and al-Zuhrī confirm.[30]

We should note that the accounts of these authors are distinguished by their candor and their essentially humane character, and that the exaggeration we find among the historians of later times is of only rare occurrence in these earlier works. The inclination, for example, towards fatalism in explaining events, a tendency promoted by the Umayyads, has no obvious manifestations in the work of either ʿUrwa or al-Zuhrī. We rather find that the deeds of the Prophet are sometimes presented as actions of divine inspiration, and yet in other situations are deemed nothing more than practical human initiative, as, for example, in the story of the Battle of the Ditch.

The studies of ʿUrwa and al-Zuhrī thus demonstrate that the outlines of the Prophet's biography were laid out in the first century A.H. The writers responsible for this were not storytellers like Wahb ibn Munabbih, but rather were scholars of *ḥadīth* with an admirable capacity for criticizing and scrutinizing the various accounts available to them. Storytellers who promoted popular tales, and in them adopted tales from the *Isrāʾīlīyāt*, only made their influence felt after the epoch of al-Zuhrī.

Due to his own influence in the spheres of folklore and the *Isrāʾīlīyāt*, this is an appropriate place to turn our attention to Wahb ibn Munabbih (d.110/728).[h] By both birth and culture Wahb was a Yemenite, and he elaborated a point of view which was alien to the Medinan school.

Wahb wrote a book about the *maghāzī*,[31] and a fragment from the work has been discovered by Professor Becker.[i] But

[30] See al-Balādhurī, *Futūḥ al-buldān*, pp. 19f., 61, 384.

[h] [Also see now Raif Georges Khoury, *Wahb b. Munabbih* (Wiesbaden, 1972); also his *Les Légendes prophétiques*, pp. 158ff.]

[31] Ḥājjī Khalīfa, *Kashf al-ẓunūn*, II, 1747.

[i] [C. H. Becker, *Papyri Schott-Reinhardt*, I (Heidelberg, 1906), pp. 1ff. Cf. pp. 132-33 below.]

this fragment does not offer any clear idea of how he structured the *sīra*, or of his attitude towards the *isnād*. The author of the *Ḥilyat al-awliyā'* quoted two fragments from Wahb concerning the *sīra*;[32] these come without *isnāds*, and their style is typical of the style of the storytellers—full of skillful illustration, glorification, and legendary material. The style of the *ayyām* is likewise evident in the fragment discovered by Becker. Wahb's *Maghāzī*, however, is not mentioned in the histories of the Prophet's life, nor did it make any impression on the *maghāzī* literature.

Wahb was particularly interested in the *Isrā'īliyāt*, tales and myths related to the Old Testament, and sought to use them to clarify some of the Qur'ānic references to ancient events. In this way he was able to introduce the *qiṣaṣ* element into Islamic studies. He collected whatever such stories were circulating among the Muslims, especially the tales of Ka'b al-Aḥbār (d. 32-34/652-54) and 'Abd Allāh ibn Salām (d. ca. 40/660),[33] and added to them other lore he had gained through his contacts with the *ahl al-kitāb* and by reading their scriptures. His book *Al-Mubtada'* was the first attempt to write the history of divine mission. Examination of the passages cited from this work by Ibn Qutayba (in his *Ma'ārif*), al-Ṭabarī, and al-Maqdisī (in his *Al-Bad' wa-l-ta'rīkh*) indicate that Wahb began with the Creation, proceeded step by step through Old Testament history to the prophets mentioned in the Qur'ān, and even discussed a number of righteous men, such as Luqmān and the Seven Sleepers.

Wahb's accounts of the history of Yemen are legends taken from *Isrā'īliyāt* tales and popular folklore. They contain an ample measure of fabricated poetry, and are in keeping with

[32] Abū Nu'aym al-Iṣfahānī, *Ḥilyat al-awliyā' wa-ṭabaqāt al-asfiyā'* (Cairo, 1351-57/1932-38), II, 73ff., 79ff.

[33] Al-Dhahabī in August Fischer, "Neue Auszüge aus aḏ-Ḏahabī und Ibn an-Naǧǧār," *ZDMG*, XLIV (1890), p. 439; al-Sakhāwī, *Al-I'lān bi-l-tawbīkh*, p. 49.

the style of the *ayyām*. Wahb produced in prose form a Yemenite folk epic in order to refute the claims to preeminence made by the Arabs of the north.

Wahb was not a scrupulous writer, and was not above making false allegations. For this reason he is to be regarded as no more than a narrator and storyteller; al-Sakhāwī considers his reports to be unworthy of serious historians.[34] He articulated a point of view which, compared to the approach of the *ḥadīth* scholars of Medina, was distorted and weak. But he created from the *Isrā'īlīyāt* material for the history of the pre-Islamic past, and offered a first example of universal history, as represented in his history of divine mission. This perspective found a strong echo in the work of a famous historian of the Medinan school, Ibn Isḥāq.

Let us now return to the Medinan school of history established by al-Zuhrī, in order to consider two historians of particular importance, both of whom were al-Zuhrī's students—Mūsā ibn ʿUqba and Muḥammad ibn Isḥāq.

Mūsā ibn ʿUqba (d. 141/758)[j] strictly adhered to the method of the school of Medina. We find him reflecting the gradually increasing emphasis of the *ḥadīth* scholars on the *isnād*, and evincing a particular emphasis on giving the dates for the events he describes. In addition to documents and oral accounts he

[34] Al-Sakhāwī, *loc. cit.*; Ibn Khallikān, *Wafayāt al-aʿyān wa-anbā' abnā' al-zamān* (Cairo, A.H. 1299); II, 238 [edited by Iḥsān ʿAbbās (Beirut, 1968-72), VI, 35f.].

[j] [On Mūsā ibn ʿUqba, see Fück, *Muḥammad ibn Isḥāq*, pp. 11ff.; Horovitz, "Biographies," II, 164ff.; *GAS*, I, 286f. A manuscript abstract of the contents of his *Maghāzī* was published by Eduard Sachau in his "Das Berliner Fragment des Mūsā ibn ʿUqba; ein Beitrag zur Kenntnis der ältesten arabischen Geschichtsliteratur," in *Sitzungsberichte der Preussischen Akademie der Wissenschaften* (Berlin, 1904), pp. 445ff. Cf. also Joseph Schacht, "On Mūsā ibn ʿUqba's Kitāb al-maghāzī," *Acta Orientalia*, XXI (1953), pp. 288ff.; the English translation and remarks by A. Guillaume, *The Life of Muhammad* (London, 1955), pp. XLIIIff.; Abdu Braimah, "A Reconstruction of the Lost Book *Kitāb al-maghāzī* of Mūsā b. ʿUqba," M.A. thesis (American University in Cairo, 1968).]

made use of written sources, especially the works of his teacher al-Zuhrī, although for such written materials he relied on the narrator transmitting them, the *rāwī*, rather than on the book itself. Mūsā ibn ʿUqba depended primarily on the work of al-Zuhrī and added to it his own special studies, thus adding material to the legacy of the school. It is clear, however, that assessment of the work he produced will require a detailed and rigorous study of all the passages in the works of Ibn Isḥāq, al-Wāqidī, al-Ṭabarī, Ibn Sayyid al-Nās, and Ibn Kathīr where Mūsā's writings are quoted.

When we come to Ibn Isḥāq[k] we notice new lines of development, the most obvious of which are the presence of the folkloric *qiṣaṣ* element and the tendency to exaggerate. We also sense that we have moved on to scholars who were historians first, and scholars of *ḥadīth* second.

Ibn Isḥāq (d. 151/761) has bequeathed to us the oldest *sīra* to survive almost completely intact. His basic design for the *sīra* probably consisted of three parts: the *Mubtada'*, or the history of the period between Creation and Muḥammad's call; the *Mabʿath*, or the mission of the Prophet Muḥammad; and the *Maghāzī*, the Prophet's military campaigns and raids. But in my view the book itself actually consists of two distinct parts, the *Mubtada'* and the *Maghāzī*. It was thus possible to transmit the two together, or each of them separately.[35]

[k] [There is an enormous literature on Ibn Isḥāq. In addition to Fück's study, mentioned above, see Horovitz, "Biographies," II, 169ff.; Guillaume, *Life of Muhammad*, pp. xiiiff.; ʿAbd al-ʿAzīz al-Dūrī, *Dirāsa fī sīrat al-Nabī wa-mu'allifihā Ibn Isḥāq* (Baghdad, 1965); Rudolf Sellheim, "Prophet, Chalif, und Geschichte: die Muhammed-Biographie des Ibn Isḥāq," *Oriens*, XVIII (1967), pp. 33ff.; *EI*², III, 810f. (J.M.B. Jones); *GAS*, I, 288ff. The study of Ibn Isḥāq's historical writing must now be reexamined in light of two recent publications of *sīra* materials transmitted on his authority by Yūnus ibn Bukayr: *Sīra*, edited by Muḥammad Ḥamīd Allāh (Rabat, 1976); *Kitāb al-siyar wa-l-maghāzī*, edited by Suhayl Zakkār (Beirut, 1398/1978).]

[35] See al-Sakhāwī, *Al-Iʿlān bi-l-tawbīkh*, p. 88, also p. 92, where he says, "As for the tales of the prophets, these are included in the *Mubtada'* of Muḥammad ibn Isḥāq ibn Yasār al-Muṭṭalibī, the author of the *Sīra* of the

In both his view of history and his method, Ibn Isḥāq far surpassed the bounds of the school of Medina. In his writings he combined the method of the scholars of *ḥadīth* with that of the storytellers, and made use of various aspects of the interest in the *maghāzī* and the history of the ancient prophets. He thus drew together *ḥadīth* reports, historical accounts, material from the *Isrā'īlīyāt*, and popular *qiṣaṣ* lore, along with a great deal of both genuine and fabricated poetry.[1] As a result, his sources of information are a heterogeneous mixture which calls for considerable caution. In the *Mubtada'*, for example, Ibn Isḥāq cited accounts on the authority of the *ahl al-kitāb* and new converts to Islam, derived much information from Wahb ibn Munabbih[36] and non-Arabs (*'ajam*), and reported ancient Arab tales and fables of Yemenite origin.[37] His accounts of the era of Muḥammad's mission derive substantially from his teachers in Medina, particularly 'Urwa, al-Zuhrī, 'Āṣim ibn 'Umar ibn Qatāda, and 'Abd Allāh ibn Abī Bakr ibn Muḥammad ibn Ḥazm, with further material added from the results of his own studies. In some cases his accounts do no more than provide exegesis for Qur'ānic verses, some transmitted from others and some his own work. But we also find that his information on the Meccan period appears in most cases without an *isnād*, and the frequency with which we find the word *qiṣṣa*, "story," as a heading for his narratives[38]

Prophet." See also al-Khaṭīb al-Baghdādī, *Ta'rīkh Baghdād* (Cairo, 1349/1931), I, 215; al-Maqdisī, *Al-Bad' wa-l-ta'rīkh*, edited and translated by Clement Huart (Paris, 1899-1919), II, 38; Ibn al-'Imād, *Shadharāt al-dhahab fī akhbār man dhahaba* (Cairo, A.H. 1350-51), I, 230; al-Dhahabī/Fischer, p. 419.

[1] [Cf. W. Montgomery Watt, "The Materials Used by Ibn Isḥāq," in *Historians of the Middle East*, edited by Bernard Lewis and P. M. Holt (London, 1962), pp. 23ff.]

[36] Al-Ṭabarī, *Ta'rīkh*, I, 361, 471, 504, 539, 551ff., 562; *idem, Jāmi' al-bayān 'an ta'wīl āy al-Qur'ān (Tafsīr*; Cairo, A.H. 1323-29), XVI, 12, 51; XVII, 45; al-Hamdānī, *Iklīl*, I, 10.

[37] Ibn Hishām (Cairo), I, 73ff., 81ff. [Wüstenfeld ed., I, i, 48f., 52ff.], and similarly, pp. 27, 29 [Wüstenfeld ed., I, i, 16f., 18f.], and the Wüstenfeld edition, I, i, 197.

[38] See Ibn Hishām, I, i, 203, 224.

indicates the influence the *qiṣaṣ* tales had on his work. His accounts of the Medinan period bear a stronger stamp of earnest intent and reveal a clearer attentiveness to the *isnād*, but we nevertheless find along with this the influence of popular folklore, and similarly, the influence of pious devotion in the way Ibn Isḥāq exaggerates.[m] He cites poetry either in the course of his reports or else in aggregate form at the end of the discussion of the event in question, clearly indicating how he has combined the method of the storytellers with that of the scholars of *ḥadīth*. This poetry, in both its fabricated and its genuine varieties, sheds light on contemporary political currents of the day, such as the rivalry between the Anṣār and Quraysh.[39]

Ibn Isḥāq is criticized for his dependence on accounts transmitted by the *ahl al-kitāb*, his many citations of fabricated poetry, his errors in giving genealogies, and because he fails to criticize his sources and passes down information from the books of other living writers (i.e., without actually hearing the reports from their authors).[40] He does, however, express doubt about some of his accounts,[41] and sometimes makes use of Qur'ānic verses to corroborate them. He was not adept at poetry, and acknowledged his shortcomings. In using the *isnād* he was not as rigorous as the scholars of *ḥadīth* would have demanded, but he sufficiently advanced the method of

[m] [On such elements in the *Sīra*, see Josef Horovitz, "Zur Muḥammadlegende," *Der Islam*, V (1914), pp. 41ff.; translated by Emma Agnes Licht as "The Growth of the Mohammed Legend," *Muslim World*, X (1920), pp. 49ff.]

[39] See Dr. Walīd 'Arafāt's dissertation, "A Critical Introduction to the Study of the Poetry Ascribed to Ḥassān b. Thābit." [Now see the introduction to his edition of the *Dīwān* of Ḥassān ibn Thābit (London, 1971), I, 23ff.; also his "Early Critics of the Authenticity of the Poetry of the *Sīra*," *BSOAS*, XXI (1958), pp. 453ff.; "An Aspect of the Forger's Art in Early Islamic Poetry," *BSOAS*, XXVIII (1965), pp. 477ff.]

[40] Yāqūt, *Mu'jam al-udabā'*, edited by D. S. Margoliouth, 2nd ed. (London, 1923-31), VI, 400; Ibn Sayyid al-Nās, *'Uyūn al-athar fī funūn al-maghāzī wa-l-shamā'il wa-l-siyar* (Cairo, A.H. 1356), I, 12.

[41] E.g., Ibn Hishām (Cairo), I, 176, 194, 203f. [Wüstenfeld ed., I, i, 106, 117, 121f. The critical attitude of Ibn Isḥāq is discussed in detail in Guillaume's introduction to his *Life of Muhammad*, pp. xixff.]

using the collective *isnād* so that he was able to offer an engaging story from his accounts.[n] The materials he used were documents, written sources, and oral narratives and reports.

The impact of political and intellectual currents of the day manifests itself in the accusation charging that Ibn Isḥāq was of pro-Shīʿī tendencies, an accusation not devoid of foundation.[42] He is also described as a Qadarite, a believer in freedom of the will. It may also be that he was opposed to the Umayyads, but evidence confirming this is still wanting.

The *Sīra* of Ibn Isḥāq was criticized in Medina; but it was favorably received in the eastern provinces, and apparently its style and content were in keeping with the cultural perspectives of the region. The text that has survived to modern times is a revision made by Ibn Hishām (d. 218/813), who received the text in the recension of al-Bakkā'ī, which in the opinion of al-Sakhāwī offered a better text than the recension of Yūnus ibn Bukayr al-Shaybānī.[43] In his revision of the text Ibn Hishām tried to prune out weak sections, particularly in the *Mubtada'*, to eliminate the fabricated poetry, and to make the text more compatible with the point of view of the *ḥadīth* scholars. It appears that historians generally viewed the *Sīra* of Ibn Isḥāq with favor, especially after Ibn Hishām had revised it.[44]

Another book, a *Ta'rīkh al-khulafā'*, or "History of the Caliphs," has been attributed to Ibn Isḥāq, but only scattered

[n] [See J. Robson, "Ibn Isḥāq's Use of the Isnād," *BJRL*, XXXVIII (1955-56), pp. 449ff.]

[42] See Yāqūt, *Muʿjam al-udabā'*, VI, 400; Ibn Hishām (Cairo), I, 106; III, 234f. [Wüstenfeld ed., I, i, 66; ii, 677f.]; also the Wüstenfeld edition, I, i, 152ff., 435.

[43] Al-Sakhāwī, *Al-Iʿlān bi-l-tawbīkh*, p. 88. [But cf. note k above.]

[44] Ibn Khallikān, *Wafayāt al-aʿyān*, edited by Ferdinand Wüstenfeld (Göttingen, 1835-50), VIII, 7ff. ['Abbās ed., IV., 276f.]; al-Dhahabī, *Tadhkirat al-ḥuffāẓ*, 2nd ed. (Haydarabad, A.H. 1333-34), I, 163f.; Ibn Kathīr, *Al-Bidāya wa-l-nihāya*, X, 109; al-Sakhāwī, *Al-Iʿlān bi-l-tawbīkh*, p. 117; Ibn al-ʿImād, *Shadharāt al-dhahab*, I, 225, 230.

selections from it have come down to us. This work apparently covered the history of the Rāshidūn and Umayyad caliphs.[o]

Ibn Isḥāq both employed and supplemented the approaches of his predecessors. Thus in the *Mubtada'* his plan appears to have been influenced by Wahb ibn Munabbih, which may be one reason for the presence of a special section on Yemen in the work. Although his writings are separate and distinct works, viewed as a whole the *Mubtada'*, the *Maghāzī*, and the *Ta'rīkh al-khulafā'* articulate a definite historical conception, the idea of writing universal history.

Historical studies developed further in the work of Muḥammad ibn 'Umar al-Wāqidī (130-207/748-823).[p] His book *Al-Maghāzī*, or the raids and military campaigns of the Prophet, is limited to the Medinan period, and in content and method is more strictly in keeping with the school of Medina than was the *Sīra* of Ibn Isḥāq. Al-Wāqidī was systematic and selective in his treatment of the material available to him. He first presents a general outline of the topic under discussion, and then follows up by relating the details. He begins with a list of his primary sources, and another of the expeditions of the Prophet and their dates, also giving, when he discusses the expeditions which the Prophet led himself, the names of those who governed Medina in his absence. Then he takes up

[o] [Abbott has published and discussed a papyrus fragment which seems to be a part of this history; see her *Studies*, I, 80ff.]

[p] [On al-Wāqidī, see *EI*[1], IV, 1104f. (J. Horovitz); *GAS*, I, 294ff.; J.M.B. Jones, "Ibn Isḥāq and al-Wāqidī: the Dream of 'Ātika and the Raid to Nakhla in Relation to the Charge of Plagiarism," *BSOAS*, XXII (1959), pp. 41ff.; Petersen, *'Alī and Mu'āwiya*, pp. 83ff.; Rudolf Veselý, "La Bataille d'Uḥud chez al-Wāḳidī," in *Studia semitica philologica necnon philosophica Ioanni Bakoš dicata*, edited by Stanislaus Segert (Bratislava, 1965), pp. 251ff.; Amanullah Khan, "Al-Wāqidī: an Assessment of His Position as an Historian," *Journal of Research (Humanities)*, V (1970), pp. 81ff.; and most importantly, Jones' detailed account of al-Wāqidī and his place in the *sīra-maghāzī* literature in his introduction to his edition of al-Wāqidī's *Kitāb al-maghāzī* (London, 1966), I, 5ff.]

the history of the expeditions one after the other in chronological order, paying particular attention to their dates.[q]

Al-Wāqidī was more rigorous than Ibn Isḥāq not only with respect to method, but also in his use of the *isnād*, in the precision with which he dated events, in his attitude towards poetry (since he used it only in moderation), and in the way he reduced the folkloric *qiṣaṣ* element in his material. He regularly uses the collective *isnād* to present the essential information for each expedition, and then cites individual accounts to present further details or divergent reports. This method clearly demonstrates that al-Wāqidī is presenting accounts of the school of Medina under his collective *isnād*, and then is adding to them whatever else has come to his attention. The contribution made by his own studies is apparent in the supplementary material he furnishes, in the precision of the dates he gives, in his presentation of a clearer outline for the various expeditions, and in his interest in the geographical details relevant to the locations of the various battlefields.

Al-Wāqidī's critical attitude is manifest in several respects: in his travels to various battlefields in order to round out his other material, in his rigorous scrutiny of the sources which had come down to him,[45] in his search for new documents, and in the lists he prepared of the participants in the expeditions, lists which were so much more complete that he later made an excellent compilation of them. Al-Wāqidī very frequently refers to Qur'ānic verses pertaining to the events he describes, and for important cases he mentions the verses as an addendum to his accounts, as, for example, in his discussion of the battles of Badr, Uḥud, and the Ditch. Proceeding in this way allows him to present narrative in smooth sequence. Al-Wāqidī is candid in his accounts, and despite the

[q] [See J.M.B. Jones, "The Chronology of the Maghāzī: a Textual Survey," *BSOAS*, XIX (1957), pp. 245ff.]

[45] Ibn Sayyid al-Nās, *'Uyūn al-athar*, I, 17, 18.

presence of ʿAlid tendencies in his writing, he is far removed from factional partisanship.[46] We do, however, sense the influence of the *qiṣaṣ* lore in his *Maghāzī*.

Al-Wāqidī took nothing from Ibn Isḥāq. This is attributable to the attitude of Medina towards the latter, to the divergence of al-Wāqidī's approach from that of Ibn Isḥāq, and to the prevailing attitude in Medina that historical *ḥadīth* materials were the property of the school of Medina and so were at the disposal of both men.

Al-Wāqidī also undertook the more general study of Islamic history, and wrote books on such important subjects as "The *Ridda*," the day of "The House," or the murder of ʿUthmān, "The Battle of Ṣiffīn," "The Battle of the Camel," and the conquests in Syria and Iraq. Of particular importance to us is his *Al-Taʾrīkh al-kabīr*, or "Great History," which apparently covered the history of the caliphs at least as far as the year 179/795. His *Kitāb al-ṭabaqāt*, a history of the classes of *ḥadīth* scholars in Kufa and Basra, is also important for its illustration of the way *ḥadīth* studies influenced the writing of history, for such works assisted *ḥadīth* scholars in evaluating *isnāds*. This book was probably the prototype and source upon which Ibn Saʿd, al-Wāqidī's secretary, relied in his own *Ṭabaqāt*.[r]

The historical works mentioned above were composed in accordance with the method followed by the scholars of *ḥadīth* in studying Islamic history, but eventually such works broadened in scope to the point where, from the standpoint of subject, they converged with the works of the *akhbāriyūn*

[46] See the complete text of al-Wāqidī's *Maghāzī* edited by J. M. Jones, but still in manuscript form in the library of the School of Oriental Languages, University of London [now published, as noted above. On the question of Shīʿī sympathies in al-Wāqidī's *Maghāzī*, see Jones' introduction, pp. 16ff.]

[r] [On the *ṭabaqāt* literature, see Ibrahim Hafsi, "Recherches sur le genre *ṭabaqāt*," *Arabica*, XXIII (1976), pp. 227ff.; XXIV (1977), pp. 1ff., 150ff.]

and the philologists. When Ibn Saʿd (d. 230/844)[s] wrote his *Kitāb al-ṭabaqāt al-kabīr*, "Great Book of Classes," he set down in the first section (entitled *Akhbār al-Nabī*) the final lines for the structure of the *sīra*, far surpassing al-Wāqidī in the organization and systematic division of his material into chapters, in giving a more extensive collection of documents, and in his markedly stronger interest in the embassies of the Prophet. Similarly, since he discusses some of the prophets who had some connection with the mission of the Prophet Muḥammad, and then gives their line of descent, Ibn Saʿd's section dealing with the pre-Islamic era is tantamount to an introduction to the era of Muḥammad's own mission. Ibn Saʿd dealt at great length with *ḥadīth* material on the virtues of the Prophet, his merits, and the proofs of his prophethood, making of these a special chapter which became the archetype for the *shamāʾil* and *dalāʾil* literature of later times.[47] Ibn Saʿd's work finally and firmly established the structure for the history of the Prophet's life: all subsequent histories of the *sīra* followed the same plan and relied primarily on the materials presented in the works mentioned above.

During the second/eighth century, *sīra* studies spread to other lands beyond Medina—Yemen, Iraq, and Syria. Only a few remnants of these works have survived, but they do indicate the steadily increasing interest in this field of historical studies.

From this brief presentation we can see that interest in the study of *ḥadīth* led to the rise of historical studies, i.e., to an interest in gaining religious knowledge, *ʿilm*, rather than us-

[s] [On Ibn Saʿd, see Otto Loth, *Das Classenbuch des Ibn Saʿd: einleitende Untersuchungen über Authentie und Inhalt* (Leipzig, 1869); *idem*, "Ursprung und Bedeutung der Ṭabaḳāt, vornehmlich der des Ibn Saʿd," *ZDMG*, XXIII (1869), pp. 593ff.; Eduard Sachau, introduction to Ibn Saʿd, III, i (Leiden, 1904), pp. 5ff.; K. V. Zetterstéen, "Ibn Saʿd ock hans arbete Kitāb eṭ-Ṭabaqāt el-Kebīr," *Le Monde Oriental*, I (1906), pp. 66ff.; *EI*², III, 922f. (J. W. Fück), Petersen, *ʿAlī and Muʿāwiya*, pp. 90ff.; *GAS*, I, 300f.]

[47] *EI*¹, Supplement, p. 235 [= Gibb, *Studies on the Civilization of Islam*, p. 113; cf. also Nöldeke, *Geschichte des Qorāns*, II, 135].

ing individual judgment, *ra'y*, for proving a fact or settling a question of law. When *ḥadīth* expanded to include the activities and sayings of the Prophet's Companions, the *ṣaḥāba*, and their descendants, the *tābi'ūn*, and when the experiences of the Islamic community (particularly its consensus, or *ijmā'*) became a source of law, historical studies also expanded to include these subjects. Moreover, political issues, particularly the question of the caliphate, demanded investigation from a historical and topical standpoint. Similarly, other factors, both administrative and social, also made their influence felt.

In line with the basic principles of Islam, there arose historical attitudes which found expression in the study of the *sīra*, in the writing of universal history as expression of a continuous succession of prophetic missions, and in the study of the history of the *umma*. One fundamental concept pervades these attitudes—that it is divine will that created the world, and divine will which directs its activities, although the concept of *qadar*, or freedom of the will, was also present, and the experiences of the Islamic community were similarly regarded as very important. We note that the majority of the early reports on the *sīra* were simple, realistic, and straightforward accounts. But the passage of time, the example of Christian and Jewish tradition, and the activities of the storytellers—inspired either by social factors or by piety—eventually gave rise to a tendency for embellishment and exaggeration.

IV.

The second perspective on historical writing developed out of the persistent interest in the exploits and genealogies of the Arab tribes.[t] The conquests added new feats and great achievements to the tribal topics available for study, and in like manner, the founding of an Islamic empire opened up

[t] [The historical and social background to this and the following sections is discussed in depth in Goldziher, *Muslim Studies*, I, esp. pp. 45ff.]

new horizons for investigation. Among the tribes there quickly developed a spirit of partisanship (*'aṣabīya*) for and pride in the particular garrison towns, or *amṣār*, in which these tribes lived. Moreover, general political developments in the early days served to consolidate tribal alignments, and also to increase the interest in them. Added to this was the fact that information pertaining to the conquests was important for its bearing on the settlement of the tribes in the *amṣār*, and on administrative plans in general. The Umayyads encouraged studies on such topics, which during the period of their rule were an indispensable part of a good education.[48]

The second century A.H. witnessed *akhbārīyūn*, philologists, and genealogists engaged in vigorous activity each in his own field. The *akhbārīyūn*, or narrators of *akhbār*, "accounts" or "stories," represented the line of historical studies, in which the others also had a role to play. But at the same time, the works of such scholars, especially in the early period, indicate that the various aspects of their interests and writings at times intermingled. During the first two centuries A.H., the activities of these scholars were concentrated in Kufa and Basra, two bustling centers of the Arab tribes. This gives the Iraqi accounts a predominant position in this perspective on historical writing.

Qiṣaṣ and *akhbār* on the great deeds of the tribes were told in evening gatherings (*majālis*) of the tribe or governor, or in the mosque, and were customarily regarded as the collective property of the families or tribes. There also appeared transmitters, *ruwāt*, who passed down scattered *akhbār* or poetry. If we know very little about the transmitters of verse, we know a great deal about the *ruwāt* who transmitted reports in prose.

[48] Ibn al-Nadīm, *Fihrist*, edited by Gustav Flügel (Leipzig, 1871-72), p. 89; also Ṣalāḥ al-Dīn al-Munajjid's introduction to 'Umar ibn Yūsuf, *Ṭurfat al-aṣḥāb fī ma'rifat al-ansāb*, edited by K. V. Zetterstéen (Damascus, 1369/1949), pp. 6ff.

At the dawn of the second century A.H. the inclination to collect these *akhbār* and relate them in continuous organized fashion, arranged according to subject or event, emerges into our view in written form. The *akhbārīyūn* were thus the first historians in the tribal perspective. In their gathering of historical materials they consulted family and tribal accounts, and also other accounts in circulation in the garrison town. These they supplemented, especially on matters concerning the Rāshidūn caliphate, with accounts from Medina. There were also government registers in Iraq and Syria, most notably the *Dīwān al-khātam*, or "*Dīwān* of the Seal," and similarly the army *dīwāns* in which the tribes were registered. It is probable that the *akhbārīyūn* made use of these as well. The influence of the Islamic framework on these authors is confirmed by the fact that they could not disregard the *isnād*. Though they used it freely and somewhat carelessly, its gradually increasing importance among the *akhbārīyūn* indicates the continuity of the influence of the Islamic perspective on the writing of history. The collection of *akhbār* was part of a phase of general culture, that of the gathering of *ḥadīth* and other accounts in each individual province.

The writings of the first *akhbārīyūn* have not survived to modern times, thus our assessment of their work is restricted to the extracts which have come down to us by way of such later historians as al-Ṭabarī and al-Balādhurī. Let us now look at some of these *akhbārīyūn*.

Let us begin with Abū Mikhnaf (d. 157/774), a Kufan *akhbārī* with an interest in genealogies.[49] He authored more than thirty books in which he wrote about the Ridda, the conquests in Syria and Iraq, the *shūrā*, Ṣiffīn, on subsequent events

[49] His grandfather was one of the devoted followers of ʿAlī and was killed at Ṣiffīn. See al-Ṭabarī, *Ta'rīkh*, I, 3302f. [Abū Mikhnaf has since been studied in detail in Ursula Sezgin, *Abū Miḫnaf: ein Beitrag zur Historiographie der umaiyadischen Zeit* (Leiden, 1971); cf. also *EI*², I, 140 (H.A.R. Gibb); Petersen, *ʿAlī and Muʿāwiya*, pp. 55ff.; *GAS*, I, 308f.]

in Iraq up until the end of the Umayyad period (especially battles and revolutionary movements), and on the Khārijites. He is esteemed as one of the most distinguished *akhbārīyūn* of Iraq.[50]

Abū Mikhnaf was somewhat indulgent in his use of the *isnād*.[51] He used family accounts, especially on the subject of Ṣiffīn,[52] and relied heavily on the accounts of his own tribe of al-Azd.[53] He also profited from other Kufan accounts, taking material, for example, from al-Sha'bī and from the *ruwāt* of such other tribes as Tamīm, Hamdān, Ṭayyi', and Kinda. All of this he complemented with accounts from Medina.[54] We note that he transmits his accounts through many chains of authority, and that these change with the shifts from one event to another, a feature characteristic of the early *akhbārīyūn*.

Abū Mikhnaf usually presents the Iraqi (Kufan) version of events. He is more favorably inclined to Iraq as opposed to Syria, because of the tendency of the tribes to take pride in their own provinces; and for the same reason he favors the 'Alids as opposed to the Umayyads. Similarly, the tendency of the tribes to boast of their own exploits at times is mirrored in his accounts.[55] Nevertheless, his narratives are generally free of factional bias.

The writing of Abū Mikhnaf shows us a continuous unin-

[50] Ibn Qutayba, *Kitāb al-ma'ārif*, edited by Ferdinand Wüstenfeld (Göttingen, 1850), p. 267 [edited by Tharwat 'Ukāsha (Cairo, 1960), p. 537]; Ibn al-Nadīm, *Fihrist*, p. 93; Yāqūt, *Mu'jam al-udabā'*, VI, 220f.; al-Kutubī, *Fawāt al-wafayāt* (Cairo, A.H. 1283), II, 175 [edited by Iḥsān 'Abbās (Beirut, 1973-74), III, 225f.].

[51] *Ḥadīth* scholars regarded his *isnād* as weak. See Ibn Qutayba, *loc. cit.*; al-Kutubī, *loc. cit.* [cf. also the detailed account of Abū Mikhnaf's use of the *isnād* in Sezgin, *Abū Miḫnaf*, pp. 66ff.].

[52] Al-Ṭabarī, *Ta'rīkh*, I, 3202f., 3266, 3383; II, 122.

[53] *Ibid.*, I, 3276ff., 3283, 3288, 3349, 3396, 3430, 3438; II, 111.

[54] See al-Balādhurī, *Ansāb al-ashrāf*, vol. V, edited by S.D.F. Goitein (Jerusalem, 1936), p. 31 [vol. IV, i, edited by Iḥsān 'Abbās (Wiesbaden, 1979), p. 519]; al-Ṭabarī, *Ta'rīkh*, I, 3403.

[55] Al-Balādhurī, *Ansāb al-ashrāf*, V, 19f. ['Abbās ed., IV, i, 504, 506]; al-Ṭabarī, *Ta'rīkh*, I, 3202f., 3270, 3323ff.

terrupted narrative, although sometimes the account does not hold together very well.[u] At times his writing presents a fascinating and animated image of events, full of speeches and dialogues, and on some occasions it is mixed with poetry.[56] In such manner he reflects the influence of evening story-sessions, and stylistically, somewhat of the approach of the *ayyām* tales.

ʿAwāna ibn al-Ḥakam (d. 147/764), another Kufan *akhbārī*, was well versed in poetry and genealogy.[57] He wrote a book entitled *Sīrat Muʿāwiya wa-banī Umayya*, "Lives of Muʿāwiya and the Umayyads," which in all likelihood was a history of the dynasty dealing with the Umayyad caliphs in consecutive order.[58] His other work, *Kitāb al-taʾrīkh*, dealt with Islamic history in the first century A.H. The quotations taken from him demonstrate that he wrote about the Rāshidūn caliphs, the Ridda, and the conquests—subjects on which he is particularly reliable—the struggle between ʿAlī and his adversaries, the abdication of al-Ḥasan, and the affairs of Iraq and Syria up to the end of the era of ʿAbd al-Malik ibn Marwān.

ʿAwāna's accounts are indicative of inside knowledge of Umayyad affairs.[59] He probably took this information from the pro-Umayyad tribe of Kalb in particular, for he does take pride in his knowledge of this tribe.[60] ʿAwāna most often presents the Umayyad as opposed to the Iraqi version of

[u] [See W. Fischer, "Die Prosa des Abū *Miḥnaf*," in *Islamwissenschaftliche Abhandlungen*, edited by Richard Gramlich (Wiesbaden, 1974), pp. 96ff.]

[56] Al-Balādhurī, *Ansāb al-ashrāf*, V, 34f. [ʿAbbās ed., IV, i, 522f.], 300f.; al-Ṭabarī, *Taʾrīkh*, I, 3296ff., 3303f.

[57] Ibn al-Nadīm, *Fihrist*, p. 134; Yāqūt, *Muʿjam al-udabāʾ*, VI, 94. [Cf. also *EI*², I, 760 (Saleh el-Ali); Petersen, *ʿAlī and Muʿāwiya*, pp. 53ff.; *GAS*, I, 307f.]

[58] See Rosenthal, *Muslim Historiography*, p. 92 [2nd ed., pp. 89f.].

[59] See al-Balādhurī, *Ansāb al-ashrāf*, V, 132ff., 159; al-Ṭabarī, *Taʾrīkh*, II, 197f., 239f., 791ff.

[60] Yāqūt, *Muʿjam al-udabāʾ*, VI, 95.

events,[61] which explains the somewhat pro-Umayyad tone apparent in some of his accounts. This even reaches the point where the Umayyad emphasis on the concept of divine foreordainment, *jabr*, in the interpretation of events, is reflected in his accounts.[62] Nevertheless, he does at times cite Iraqi and Medinan accounts which reflect views of groups opposed to the Umayyads.[63] It can thus be said that ʿAwāna was not partial to any particular side.

The accounts of ʿAwāna have reached us by way of Ibn al-Kalbī, al-Madāʾinī, and al-Haytham ibn ʿAdī, who took them either directly from him or from his books.[64] His design for the writing of general history based on chronological sequence or on the lives of the caliphs represents a pioneering step in the development of historical writing within the tribal perspective. ʿAwāna was erratic in his use of the *isnād*,[65] and the way he cites poetry in his *akhbār* reflects the influence of the style of the *ayyām* tales.[66]

The Kufan Sayf ibn ʿUmar (d. 180/796) wrote two books. The first, a work novel in its historical viewpoint, deals with the Ridda and the conquests and combines the two movements into one; and the second covers the *fitna*, particularly the Battle of the Camel. Sayf basically presents the Iraqi viewpoint, and benefits primarily from the accounts of his own tribe of Tamīm. His *akhbār* on the conquests (especially on the conquest of Iraq) are favorable to Tamīm and tend to be romantic, in line with the *ayyām* style. Sayf did, however, make use of Medinan accounts in his *akhbār*: Hishām ibn ʿUrwa

[61] Al-Ṭabarī, *Taʾrīkh*, II, 420f.

[62] See al-Balādhurī, *Ansāb al-ashrāf*, V, 140, 194ff.; also vol. XI, edited by Wilhelm Ahlwardt (Greifswald, 1883), p. 40.

[63] *Ibid.*, XI, 19ff. (siding with the Zubayrids), 59ff. (against al-Ḥajjāj); al-Ṭabarī, *Taʾrīkh*, II, 9ff. (against Kufa), 309ff. (with the ʿAlids). See Yāqūt, *Muʿjam al-udabāʾ*, VI, 94f.

[64] Al-Ṭabarī, *Taʾrīkh*, II, 113, 189, 421, 424.

[65] See Yāqūt, *Muʿjam al-udabāʾ*, VI, 94.

[66] Al-Balādhurī, *Ansāb al-ashrāf*, XI, 38ff.; al-Ṭabarī, *Taʾrīkh*, II, 463ff.

and Ibn Isḥāq were among the *ruwāt* from whom he took information.[67]

Naṣr ibn Muzāḥim (d. 212/827),[v] another Kufan, was the first Shīʿī *akhbārī*. His books revolved around subjects important to the Shīʿa: "The Battle of the Camel," "The Battle of Ṣiffīn," "The Murder of al-Ḥusayn," "The Murder of Ḥujr ibn ʿAdī," "History (*akhbār*) of al-Mukhtār," and "Merits" (*manāqib*), i.e., of the Shīʿī *imāms*.[68] The printed text of his *Ṣiffīn* could also be reconstructed based on the extant quotations from it, and it is possible for us to examine the work to gain an approximate idea of its character. In *Ṣiffīn* we find that Naṣr ibn Muzāḥim was of Iraqi and Shīʿī inclinations: he cites *ḥadīth* against Muʿāwiya and his faction, and presents *ḥadīth* materials, *akhbār*, and even *qiṣaṣ* in order to buttress the cause of ʿAlī.[69] Nevertheless, in discussing the faults of Muʿāwiya he does not conceal some of the criticism directed against the ʿAlid faction by its adversaries. Some later authors criticized Naṣr severely for his partisan tendencies, while others commended him.[70]

Naṣr gives us a story throbbing with life and vitality on the events which led to the battle of Ṣiffīn and ended with the

[67] See al-Ṭabarī, *Ta'rīkh*, I, 1798f., 1871; Ibn Ḥajar, *Tahdhīb al-tahdhīb* (Haydarabad, A.H. 1325-27), IV, 295f. On Sayf, cf. Wellhausen, *Prolegomena*, pp. 3ff.; [*EI*[1], IV, 73; Petersen, *'Alī and Mu'āwiya*, pp. 78ff.; Rosenthal, *Muslim Historiography*, p. 188; *GAS*, I, 311f.; also the reconstruction of some of his most important narratives in Aḥmad Rātib ʿArmūsh, *Al-Fitna wa-waqʿat al-jamal* (Beirut, 1391/1972)].

[v] [See Carl Brockelmann, "Naṣr ibn Muzāḥim: der älteste Geschichtschreiber der Schia," *ZS*, IV (1926), pp. 1ff.; Petersen, *'Alī and Mu'āwiya*, pp. 104ff.; Rosenthal, *Muslim Historiography*, p. 64; *GAS*, I, 313; Sezgin, *Abū Mikhnaf*, pp. 47f., 123ff.]

[68] Ibn al-Nadīm, *Fihrist*, p. 93; Yāqūt, *Muʿjam al-udabā'*, VII, 210; al-Dhahabī, *Mīzān al-iʿtidāl fī naqd al-rijāl* (Cairo, A.H. 1325), III, 232.

[69] Naṣr ibn Muzāḥim, *Waqʿat Ṣiffīn*, edited by ʿAbd al-Salām Muḥammad Hārūn (Cairo, A.H. 1365), pp. 35, 158, 164f., 246f.

[70] Yāqūt, *Muʿjam al-udabā'*, VII, 210; Ibn Ḥajar, *Lisān al-mīzān* (Haydarabad, A.H. 1329-31), VI, 157; Ibn Abī l-Ḥadīd, *Sharḥ nahj al-balāgha* (Cairo, A.H. 1329), I, 71 [edited by Muḥammad Abū l-Faḍl Ibrāhīm (Cairo, 1959-64), I, 210ff.].

arbitration between ʿAlī and Muʿāwiya. His accounts are full of poetry, dialogue, and speeches. Much of this poetry is fabricated: we see all of the prominent personalities reciting verse, either of their own creation or quoted from others, and even adducing it in correspondence. The book is semi-folkloric, a collection of *akhbār* strung together in a somewhat disjointed fashion. It is worthy of note that Muʿāwiya appears in the book as a tribal *shaykh*, and even some of the statements made by Abū Sufyān in pre-Islamic Mecca are here put in the mouth of Muʿāwiya. It will be noticed that Naṣr was negligent in matters of dating, and extremely careless in his use of the *isnād*.[71] His style of writing is clearly patterned after that of the *ayyām* tales and reflective of evening social gatherings. In keeping with the method of the *ayyām* tales, Naṣr ends his book with a list of the names of the prominent supporters of ʿAlī who died at Ṣiffīn. Finally, however, we should point out that the fact that it is possible to reconstruct the book, primarily from selections taken up by al-Ṭabarī and Ibn Abī l-Ḥadīd, indicates its value in the eyes of the historians.

The studies of the *akhbārīyūn* reach their apogee with al-Madā'inī (d. 135-225/752-839),[w] a Basran who later lived in Baghdad. The *isnād* was of stronger influence on him than on his predecessors because of cultural developments.[72] With him there appears an orientation towards more comprehensive gathering and more extensive organization of historical ac-

[71] *Ṣiffīn*, pp. 42, 43, 158, 167.

[w] [On al-Madā'inī, see *EI*[1], III, 81f. (C.Brockelmann): S.D.F. Goitein's introduction to al-Balādhurī, *Ansāb al-ashrāf*, V, 14ff.; Pellat, *Le Milieu baṣrien*, pp. 144f.; Petersen, *ʿAlī and Muʿāwiya*, pp. 92ff.; Rosenthal, *Muslim Historiography*, pp. 69f.; *GAS*, I, 314f.; Gernot Rotter, "Zur Überlieferung einiger historischer Werke Madā'inīs in Ṭabarīs Annalen," *Oriens*, XXIII-XXIV (1974), pp. 103ff.; Badrī Muḥammad Fahad, *Shaykh al-akhbārīyīn; Abū l-Ḥasan al-Madā'inī* (Najaf, 1975); Lawrence I. Conrad, "Arabic Plague Chronologies and Treatises: Social and Historical Factors in the Formation of a Literary Genre," *Studia Islamica*, LIV (1981), pp. 61ff.]

[72] See Yāqūt, *Muʿjam al-udabā'*, V, 309.

counts, endeavors which had become feasible by al-Madā'inī's time because of the work of earlier authors. We thus see him borrowing from such earlier authors as Abū Mikhnaf, Ibn Isḥāq, and al-Wāqidī, adding to these his own special researches. It appears that he synthesized historical and literary studies. A look at the long list of his compositions and books,[x] totalling about 240, clearly indicates that he occupied himself with studies ranging from the life of the Prophet to ʿAbbāsid history and covered, among other subjects, the conquests, caliphs, tribal notables (*ashrāf*), battles, and poets. One of his works, *Nasab Quraysh wa-akhbāruhā*, "Genealogies and Narratives on Quraysh,"[73] was written along the lines of the books of genealogy. Some of his books, such as those pertaining to the life of the Prophet, comprised nothing more than chapters of the *sīra*. His history of the caliphate, *Akhbār al-khulafā' al-kabīr*, appears to have been his most extensive historical work, in that it covered the period from the caliphate of Abū Bakr up until al-Muʿtaṣim, and was written according to the method of the *akhbāriyūn*.

Al-Madā'inī's research and strictness represent a step above his predecessors. He apparently followed the method of the *ḥadīth* scholars in his criticism of his sources, and thus came to enjoy greater confidence than his predecessors. Moreover, he borrowed more extensively from the Medinan sources than had those who had preceded him, and also used Basran accounts to good advantage, particularly on the subjects of the Khārijites, the city of Basra, and the conquests of Khurāsān and Transoxania. On the events and subjects with which he dealt, al-Madā'inī offered more extensive and more balanced narratives than his predecessors did. Al-Madā'inī became a

[x] [See Fahad, *Shaykh al-akhbāriyīn*, pp. 20ff., for a detailed list of these works; also Pellat's classification in *Le Milieu basrien*, p. 144.]

[73] See Ibn al-Nadīm, *Fihrist*, p. 102.

fundamental source for later historians, and modern research has confirmed the accuracy of his work.

V.

Genealogical studies rendered service to historical writing in both content and compositional format.[y] Interest in genealogies revived in Islam,[74] and establishment of the *dīwān* system introduced a new incentive for interest in them. The Umayyads, beginning with Muʿāwiya, encouraged such studies as these, and it is reported that Walīd II (d. 126/744) commmanded that a complete register of the genealogies of the tribes be made.[75] Administrative exigencies, such as the organization of a system for paying stipends (*ʿaṭāʾ*) and the allotment of residential quarters and lands to the tribes in the *amṣār*, further contributed to the recording of genealogical registers and intensified interest in them. Added to this were tribal disputes, the effect of political circumstances on the status of the tribes, the appearance of a new aristocracy in Islam, and various social factors, all of which spurred the study of tribal genealogies. Finally, disputations with the Shuʿūbīya and the attacks by partisans of the movement on Arab genealogies led to a new Arab emphasis on genealogical studies.

Genealogical information was available in poetry, especially in polemic verse, or the *naqāʾiḍ*, in family and tribal sources, and in the rosters of the army registers. The first genealogists appeared in the Umayyad period, and their concerns were limited to the genealogies of one particular tribe. It was not until later, when accounts were being gathered together in the second/eighth century, that genealogists appeared who were interested in the genealogies of more than one tribe.

[y] [On the evolution and character of Arab genealogical studies, see the important work of Werner Caskel, *Ǧamharat an-Nasab: das genealogische Werke des Hišām ibn Muḥammad al-Kalbī* (Leiden, 1966), I, 23ff.]

[74] See al-Munajjid's introduction to the *Kitāb ṭurfat al-aṣḥāb*.

[75] Ibn al-Nadīm, *Fihrist*, p. 91.

The first to write on the *ansāb* was Abū Yaqẓān al-Nassāba (d. 190/805). None of his works have survived except as quotations in later books, but these fragments provide the first evidence of the gathering of genealogies, primarily from tribal sources.

Cultural developments, and also the strong connections between genealogy, *akhbār*, and literary studies, manifest themselves in the works of two authors from the Arab tribe of Kalb. Muḥammad ibn al-Sā'ib al-Kalbī (d. 146/763)[z] undertook studies in genealogy, philology, and history. His studies on genealogy are indicative of an effort to collect the tribal accounts on the subject, relying, so he claims, on the most learned genealogist of each tribe.[76] In addition, he consulted polemic verse and studied the *naqā'iḍ* of al-Farazdaq under the guidance of the great poet himself. Although scholars of *ḥadīth* criticized him and suspected him of extremist Shī'ī bias, there was general agreement on his ability as a genealogist.[77]

His son Hishām ibn Muḥammad al-Kalbī (d. 204/819)[a] followed up and improved on his father's studies on genealogy. It appears that his book *Jamharat al-nasab*, "Compendium of Genealogy," part of which is found in the British Museum,[b] was an expanded edition of his father's work and contained brief notices, some of them important, on famous men of all

[z] [See Petersen, *'Alī and Mu'āwiya*, pp. 73ff.; Caskel, *Ǧamharat an-Nasab*, I, 72ff.; *EI²*, IV, 495 (W. Atallah).]

[76] Ibn al-Nadīm, *Fihrist*, p. 140. See also Ibn Sa'd, VI, 249; Ibn Khallikān, *Wafayāt al-a'yān* (Cairo), I, 624f. ['Abbās ed., IV, 309ff.]; Ibn Ḥajar, *Tahdhīb al-tahdhīb*, IX, 180.

[77] See Ibn Khallikān, *Wafayāt al-a'yān* (Cairo), I, 625 ['Abbās ed., IV, 309f.]; Ibn Ḥajar, *Tahdhīb al-tahdhīb*, IX, 180.

[a] [See Petersen, *'Alī and Mu'āwiya*, pp. 76ff.; Caskel, *Ǧamharat an-Nasab*, I, 75ff.; *EI²*, IV, 495f. (W. Atallah).]

[b] [MS. Add. 23297; other manuscript material also exists. The contents of the entire work have been exhaustively studied and tabulated by Caskel in the work mentioned above. Cf. also M. J. Kister and M. Plessner, "Notes on Caskel's *Ǧamharat an-Nasab*," *Oriens*, XXV-XXVI (1976), pp. 48ff.; 'Abd al-'Azīz al-Dūrī, "Kutub al-ansāb wa-ta'rīkh al-Jazīra," *Journal of the Jordan Arab Academy*, II (1979), pp. 5ff.]

later times. Al-Hamdānī, however, considers it deficient in the genealogies it gives for the tribes of Yemen.

In his historical studies, Hishām ibn al-Kalbī discussed the history of the ancient prophets, the Arabian peninsula in pre-Islamic times; the battle-days (*ayyām*) of the Arab tribes, Iranian history, and Islamic history. His *akhbār* came from a variety of sources, and some of his evidence was documentary. On the history of the ancient prophets he borrowed from the *ahl al-kitāb*, and for the history of Iran he relied on translations from the Persian and on Arabic *akhbār* and *qiṣaṣ* then in common circulation. He also borrowed from the books of ʿAwāna and Abū Mikhnaf. He displays sound judgment, especially in his use of written sources and of documents from the churches of al-Ḥīra, which pertained to the history of the Arabs of al-Ḥīra and the relations between the Arabs and the Sāsānians. But he was not as rigorous as he should have been, for he took much information from popular *qiṣaṣ* tales (especially on the history of Yemen), legendary sources, and some of the fabricated *akhbār* about pre-Islamic poets.[78]

Also among the genealogists was Muṣʿab al-Zubayrī (d. 233-36/847-50),[c] a descendant of Ibn al-Zubayr. Muṣʿab was a scholar learned in the *ayyām* and in genealogy, and wrote two books: *Al-Nasab al-kabīr*, "Great Book of Genealogy," and *Nasab Quraysh*, "Genealogy of Quraysh." The second of these has survived to modern times and is considered the best book on Quraysh genealogy. The plan of the book indicates that he adhered to a specific framework for writing, one which Ibn al-Kalbī had followed before him, and which al-Balādhurī would follow later on. He refers in the book to al-Zuhrī, to his father, to other genealogists, and sometimes to certain *ru-*

[78] See Ibn al-Nadīm, *Fihrist*, p. 143; *Aghānī*, IX, 19; Yāqūt, *Muʿjam al-udabāʾ*, VI, 259; al-Dhahabī, *Tadhkirat al-ḥuffāẓ*, I, 313.

[c] [On this writer, see *GAS*, I, 271f.; E. Lévi-Provençal's introduction to his edition of al-Zubayrī's *Nasab Quraysh* (Cairo, 1953), pp. 5ff.; also his "Le *Kitāb nasab Quraysh* de Muṣʿab al-Zubayrī," *Arabica*, I (1954), pp. 92ff.]

wāt.[79] He also gives the impression that he relied on various oral accounts. The book sheds particularly strong light on the shifts in tribal alignments and on changes in genealogical lines of descent.[80] In addition to genealogical lines of descent, al-Zubayrī offers *akhbār*, some of them detailed and important, on some of the most important personalities from Jāhilīya times up to his own day.[81] He quotes poetry, especially for the early period, to document or corroborate a prose account. In general the book demonstrates the value of genealogical studies to historical writing.

When we come to al-Haytham ibn ʿAdī (d. 206/821)[d] we see another example of the coalescence of historical and genealogical studies, a synthesis arising from different approaches to the study of history.[82] Al-Haytham's *Ta'rīkh al-ashrāf al-kabīr*, "Great History of the Notables," was a work of history in the genealogical framework which was the antecedent to the *Ansāb al-ashrāf* of al-Balādhurī. He also wrote, in the style of the *ṭabaqāt*, a history of jurists and *ḥadīth* scholars entitled *Ṭabaqāt al-fuqahā' wa-l-muḥaddithīn*; this was probably the first work of its kind in the tribal perspective. Aspects of his interests in regional affairs appear in his two books on the administrative and residential districts, or *khiṭaṭ*, of Kufa and Basra. Each of these gave a history of the city and included topographical and geographical information. Our attention is drawn particularly to his work *Kitāb al-ta'rīkh ʿalā l-sinīn*, "Book of History According to the Years," a book

[79] *Nasab Quraysh*, pp. 229, 246.

[80] *Ibid.*, pp. 5, 7.

[81] *Ibid.*, pp. 4, 128, 145, 147.

[d] [See *EI*², III, 328 (C. Pellat); *GAS*, I, 272.]

[82] Al-Haytham ibn ʿAdī wrote more than fifty books (see Ibn al-Nadīm, *Fihrist*, pp. 99f.; Yāqūt, *Muʿjam al-udabā'*, VII, 265f.) covering the genealogies of the tribes, accounts of their histories and great families, the *mathālib*, or "faults," the governors of the *amṣār*, the quarters of these cities, and other subjects such as the Khārijites and Persian history.

on Islamic history chronologically arranged by year.[83] Al-Haytham ibn ʿAdī is criticized, however, for being somewhat inaccurate and for using the *isnād* loosely.[84]

It was during the second century A.H. that philologists began to play a role in the study of history.[e] Tribal outlooks,

[83] Selections from the works of al-Haytham ibn ʿAdī survive in the histories of al-Ṭabarī and al-Balādhurī as follows: 1. Historical periods (number of years), from Adam to the Hijra (al-Ṭabarī, *Taʾrīkh*, I, 1072); these are probably from his book *Hubūṭ Ādam wa-iftirāq al-ʿarab fī nuzūlihā manāzilahā*, "Fall of Adam and the Dispersal of the Arab Tribes as They Settled in Their Homelands." 2. Names of some of the secretaries of the Prophet, Abū Bakr, and ʿUmar (al-Ṭabarī, II, 836), also names of secretaries of the Umayyad caliphs from Yazīd ibn ʿAbd al-Malik to Ibrāhīm ibn al-Walīd (*ibid.*, II, 838). 3. The Umayyad Period—Here there appear *akhbār* on Yazīd ibn Muʿāwiya (al-Balādhurī, *Ansāb al-ashrāf*, vol. IVB, edited by Max Schloessinger, Jerusalem, 1938, pp. 1, 8 [ʿAbbās ed., IV, i, 286, 295]), the movement of Ibn al-Zubayr and the battle of al-Ḥarra (*Ansāb*, IVB, 21, 30, 39, 40, 42, 49 [ʿAbbās ed., IV, i, 309, 319, 329, 330, 333, 340f.]), ʿUbayd Allāh ibn Ziyād (*Ansāb*, IVB, 81, 83, 84, 101 [ʿAbbās ed., IV, i, 378, 381, 382f., 401]), Marwān ibn al-Ḥakam (*Ansāb*, V, 136, 152, 155, 159), the days of ʿAbd al-Malik and Ibn al-Zubayr (*Ansāb*, V, 191), the affair of the Tawwābūn, or "penitents" (*Ansāb*, V, 212, 231), Ibrāhīm ibn al-Ashtar, Muṣʿab ibn al-Zubayr, and the battle of Ḥarūrāʾ (*Ansāb*, V, 251, 263, 275, 282), the affair of Zufar ibn al-Ḥārith and the murder of Muṣʿab (*Ansāb*, V, 296, 305, 335), other *akhbār* on ʿAbd al-Malik and his entry into Kufa (*Ansāb*, V, 345f., 352), and some *akhbār* on Hishām ibn ʿAbd al-Malik and Khālid al-Qasrī (al-Ṭabarī, II, 1655, 1658, 1668). 4. Al-Haytham also relates *akhbār* on the ʿAbbāsid dynasty which primarily pertain to al-Manṣūr, e.g., his designation as successor, the swearing of allegiance to him, the construction of Baghdad, and his death (al-Ṭabarī, III, 89, 273, 278, 401, 411, 420, 429, 456). There is also some material on al-Mahdī (al-Ṭabarī, III, 532).

It appears that most of his *akhbār* were taken from his written works, since the account given on his authority begins by saying, "Al-Haytham ibn ʿAdī said (*qāla*)," or "related (*dhakara*)." Other accounts do, however, come from him via oral transmission. Also, in the quotations taken from him there appears only a single account or *khabar* on each topic or event; no differing accounts on the same subject appear.

[84] See Ibn al-Nadīm, *Fihrist*, p. 145; Yāqūt, *Muʿjam al-udabāʾ*, VII, 261; Ibn Khallikān, *Wafayāt al-aʿyān* (Cairo), II, 269 [ʿAbbās ed., VI, 106ff.].

[e] [For further details on these developments, see Pellat, *Le Milieu baṣrien*, pp. 128ff.; H. Fleisch, "Esquisse d'un historique de la grammaire arabe," *Arabica*, IV (1957), pp. 1ff.; Abbott, *Studies*, III, 25ff., 153ff.; Muḥammad Ḥusayn Āl Yāsīn, *Al-Dirāsāt al-lughawīya ʿinda l-ʿarab ilā nihāyat al-qarn al-thālith* (Beirut, 1400/1980); Ramzi Baalbaki, "Arab Grammatical Controversies and the Extant Sources of the Second and Third Centuries A.H." in *Studia Arabica et Islamica: Festschrift for Iḥsān ʿAbbās on his Sixtieth Birthday*, edited by Wadād al-Qāḍī (Beirut, 1981), pp. 1ff.]

tribal rivalries, and now philological needs—all these served to focus scholarly attention on poetry. The cultural struggle between the Arabs and non-Arabs, or *ʿajam*, after the emergence of the Shuʿūbīya movement, placed particular emphasis on this field of study.[85]

Poetry was transmitted by bedouin *ruwāt* who customarily prefaced their recitation with a prose introduction explaining the circumstances of its composition and clarifying the historical references it contained. Some philologists, alongside their interest in questions of grammar and philology, began to show interest in the *akhbār* and genealogies which appeared in poetry or to which poets referred, and so began to show an inclination towards the writing of history. Among those representative of this trend was Abū ʿAmr ibn al-ʿAlāʾ, "the most learned of men on the Arab tribes, the Arabic language, variant readings of the Qurʾān, poetry, and the battle-days of the Arabs."[86]

Representative of the same perspective was Abū ʿUbayda (110-211/728-826),[f] a student of Abū ʿAmr ibn al-ʿAlāʾ. Abū ʿUbayda based his work on that of his teachers (such as Abū ʿAmr and Yūnus ibn Ḥabīb). He also directed his attention to the bedouin *ruwāt* and gathered together the accounts they were transmitting, which for the most part pertained to their own tribes. Interest in the accounts of these *ruwāt* encouraged them to come to the towns—especially to the Mirbad of Basra—where some of them settled down.[g] Abū ʿUbayda undertook wide-ranging studies which extended over almost the entire

[85] Al-Jāḥiẓ, *Al-Bayān wa-l-tabyīn*, edited by ʿAbd al-Salām Muḥammad Hārūn (Cairo, 1367-70/1948-50), III, 366. [Cf. Goldziher, *Muslim Studies*, I, 98ff.; ʿAbd al-ʿAzīz al-Dūrī, *Al-Judhūr al-taʾrīkhīya li-l-shuʿūbīya* (Beirut, 1962).]

[86] Ṭāhā al-Ḥājirī, "Abū ʿUbayda," *Majallat al-kātib al-miṣrī*, II (1946), p. 280. [Cf. also Pellat, *Le Milieu baṣrien*, pp. 76ff.; *EI*², I, 105f. (R. Blachère).]

[f] [See Pellat, *Le Milieu baṣrien*, pp. 141ff.; *EI*², I, 158 (H.A.R. Gibb); Āl Yāsīn, *Al-Dirāsāt al-lughawīya*, pp. 108ff., 206ff., 388ff.]

[g] [The Mirbad was the vast marketplace and social forum of early Basra. See Pellat, *Le Milieu baṣrien*, pp. 11f.]

range of the accounts transmitted by the northern Arabs. These were not only accounts transmitted by the *ruwāt*, but also those handed down in families, tribes, and local areas. Abū l-Faraj accordingly ranks Abū ʿUbayda "among the most knowledgeable men on the battle-days, history, poems, genealogies, and dialects of the Arab tribes,"[87] while al-Jāḥiẓ considers him one of the most learned men of his time, saying, "In all the earth there was no one, either orthodox or non-orthodox, more learned in all fields of knowledge than he was."[88] Ibn al-Nadīm refers to the broad scope of his studies in saying, "He possessed the learning of both Islam and the Jāhilīya."[89]

Abū ʿUbayda wrote a great number of books on the history of the Arab tribes and of early Islamic times. In writing, his approach was that of the philologists, i.e., he gathered the accounts pertaining to a particular event or subject together in book form. In this way he wrote about the cities and *amṣār*, the "boasts" (*mafākhir*) and "faults" (*mathālib*) of the tribes, history (*akhbār*), historical personalities, battles, factions (the Khārijites), judges, and the *mawālī*, in addition to other studies on *ḥadīth*, the Qur'ān, and poetry. He was so renowned for his learning on the battle-days of the Arab tribes that Abū l-ʿAbbās al-Mubarrad dubbed him the most learned of all his peers "on the *ayyām* and *akhbār* of the Arab tribes," a distinction also accorded to him by Ibn Qutayba.[90] In later times, his studies on the *ayyām* became a fundamental source for historians.[91]

Abū ʿUbayda made an effort to be a rigorous scholar, spec-

[87] Al-Ḥājirī, "Abū ʿUbayda," p. 285.

[88] Al-Khaṭīb al-Baghdādī, *Taʾrīkh Baghdād*, XIII, 252; Yāqūt, *Muʿjam al-udabāʾ*, VI, 165.

[89] *Fihrist*, p. 53.

[90] Yāqūt, *Muʿjam al-udabāʾ*, VI, 165.

[91] See Maḥmūd Ghannāwī, *Naqāʾiḍ Jarīr wa-l-Farazdaq: dirāsa adabīya taʾrīkhīya* (Baghdad, 1954), Chapter I.

ifying his *ruwāt*, giving different accounts of a given subject, and sometimes offering a succession of mutually complementary accounts for the sake of clarity. In his *akhbār* on the battle-days he faithfully reflects both the spirit and the literary style of the bedouin *ruwāt*. Abū ʿUbayda relied primarily on his written notes and records, not on memory, and in this respect was representative of the level of culture in the era in which he lived. Indeed, it was said of him, "Abū ʿUbayda was a scholar as long as he was left with his books to read"; also that "the register (*dīwān*) of the Arab tribes rests in his house."[92]

Abū ʿUbayda assumed a position unfavorable to the Arabs in the cultural conflict between the Arabs and the Shuʿūbīya. He wrote a *Kitāb al-mawālī* in which he apparently discussed the non-Arab Muslims, and also an *Akhbār al-furs* (or "Merits of the Persians," *Faḍāʾil al-furs*, as Ibn al-Nadīm calls it) in which he presented pro-Persian *akhbār*. Similarly, he wrote a great deal on the *mathālib*, or "faults," of the Arabs. All of this is consistent with the cultural line of the Shuʿūbīya movement. He is not suspected of retouching his accounts and his scholarly reputation is very high, but his *akhbār* bring to light some repugnant personal faults.[93] It is probable that Abū ʿUbayda was one of those Shuʿūbīs referred to as the *Ahl al-taswiya*, "proponents of equality"; this is consistent with statements linking him to the Khārijites.[94]

[92] Ibn al-Nadīm, *Fihrist*, p. 53; al-Khaṭīb al-Baghdādī, *Taʾrīkh Baghdād*, XIII, 252; Yāqūt, *Muʿjam al-udabāʾ*, VI, 164; al-Yāfiʿī, *Mirʾāt al-janān wa-ʿibrat al-yaqẓān* (Haydarabad, A.H. 1337-39), II, 44, 46; Ibn al-ʿImād, *Shadharāt al-dhahab*, II, 24. [The first of these two quotations compares Abū ʿUbayda unfavorably with al-Aṣmaʿī, who had no need of books to demonstrate his learning.]

[93] See Ibn al-Nadīm, *Fihrist*, p. 53; al-Thaʿālibī, *Laṭāʾif al-maʿārif*, edited by P. de Jong (Leiden, 1867), p. 63 [edited by Ibrāhīm al-Abyārī and Ḥasan Kāmil al-Ṣayrafī (Cairo, 1960), p. 99, mentioning Abū ʿUbayda in a list of notorious sodomists].

[94] Ibn Qutayba, *Maʿārif*, p. 269 [ʿUkāsha ed., p. 543]; *idem, Kitāb al-ʿarab*, edited by Muḥammad Kurd ʿAlī in his *Rasāʾil al-bulaghāʾ*, 3rd ed.

The Shuʿūbīya movement had a definite impact on historical studies, since its partisans schemed against the Arabs and made a special effort to distort their history. This in turn caused the Arabs to react unequivocally by addressing themselves to a broad-ranging study of their own history and literature.[95]

The Shuʿūbīya and the secretarial class, or *kuttāb*, were responsible for the broadening interest in the culture and heritage of the Persians, and the second century A.H. witnessed a widespread popular movement to translate works from Persian. Books both historical and pseudo-historical were translated, the most important of these being the *Khodāy-nāmag*, which Ibn al-Muqaffaʿ (d. 144/760) translated from the Pahlavi (Middle Persian) and entitled *Siyar al-mulūk*, "Lives of the Kings." Other direct translations were made of the same book, which likewise appeared in other forms as translations with additions of myths and historical *akhbār* from other Pahlavi works. Other literary works on the same subject relied on these translations.[96]

The *Khodāy-nāmag* presents the story of Iranian national history as viewed by the nobility and religious authorities. It contains fabulous tales and legends from the Avesta, religious

(Cairo, 1365/1946), p. 346; Yāqūt, *Muʿjam al-udabāʾ*, VI, 164; al-Ḥājirī, "Abū ʿUbayda," p. 414. Also see Ignaz Goldziher, *Muhammedanische Studien* (Halle, 1889-90), I, 194ff. [=*Muslim Studies*, I, 179ff.]; Pellat, *Le Milieu baṣrien*, p. 142ff.; H.A.R. Gibb, "The Social Significance of the Shuʿūbīya," in *Studia orientalia Ioanni Pedersen dicata* (Copenhagen, 1953), pp. 105ff. [reprinted in Gibb's *Studies on the Civilization of Islam*, pp. 62ff.].

95 See Gibb, "Significance of the Shuʿūbīya"; ʿAbd al-ʿAzīz al-Dūrī, *Muqaddima fī taʾrīkh ṣadr al-Islām* (Baghdad, 1949), pp. 2ff. [also, in addition to the studies cited in the previous note, Roy P. Mottahedeh, "The Shuʿūbīyah Controversy and the Social History of Early Islamic Iran," *IJMES*, VII (1976), pp. 161ff.].

96 Ḥamza al-Iṣfahānī found eight different translations of the *Khodāy-nāmag*, and the *mōbedh* Bahrām ibn Mardānshāh made use of twenty translations; Mūsā ibn ʿĪsā al-Kisrawī found no two copies which could be collated together. See Ḥamza al-Iṣfahānī, *Taʾrīkh sinī mulūk al-arḍ wa-l-anbiyāʾ*, edited by J.M.E. Gottwaldt (Leipzig, 1844-48), I, 8f.; al-Bīrūnī, *Al-Āthār al-bāqiya*, edited by Eduard Sachau (Leipzig, 1878), p. 99.

traditions, the story of Alexander (taken from outside sources), and fanciful genealogies; and it does not distinguish between that which is completely incredible, that which is semi-mythical, and information of a truly historical nature. The image it gives of the Sāsānians is probably more historical than any other it contains, but the information known about the Sāsānian period up to Yazdagird I was scanty at best; thus the gap was filled by extravagant literary pieces and resounding speeches.

Books other than the *Khodāy-nāmag* were also translated, such as the *Ā'īn-nāmag*, "Conventions and Decrees," the *Gāh-nāmag*, "The Book of Ranks," as well as historical and folk tales, and historical works based on the contents of the *Khodāy-nāmag* but rearranged in a new order.[97] These books introduced a dubious folkloric element, full of mythical content, into the corpus of historical material. As the Persians had no fixed calendar, there was no chronological year-by-year sequence in these works. On the other hand, the method of writing history based on a succession of biographies, or *siyar*, was known and followed among the Arabs prior to the appearance of these translations—it was for this reason that the *Khodāy-nāmag* was called *Siyar al-mulūk*, whereas the term *ṭabaqāt* designated successive generations of descendants.[98] Books of *akhbār* on the ruling families thus consisted of a series of biographies, *siyar*, of the successive caliphs. For these reasons

[97] Al-Mas'ūdī, *Al-Tanbīh wa-l-ishrāf*, edited by M. J. de Goeje (Leiden, 1893), pp. 106ff.; Arthur Christensen, *L'Iran sous les Sassanides* (Copenhagen, 1936), pp. 52ff.; translated by Yaḥyā al-Khashshāb as *Īrān fī 'ahd al-Sāsānīyīn* (Cairo, 1957), pp. 52ff.; also West, *Grundriss*, II, 117; Theodor Nöldeke, *Geschichte der Perser und Araber zur Zeit der Sasaniden* (Leiden, 1879); *idem, Das iranische Nationalepos*, 2nd ed. (Berlin and Leipzig, 1920); [translated by Leonid T. Bogdanov as *The Iranian National Epic* (Bombay, 1930)]; K. A. Inostrantsev, *Iranian Influence on Moslem Literature*, translated by G. K. Nariman (Bombay, 1918).

[98] Ḥamza al-Iṣfahānī, *Ta'rīkh*, I, 8; al-Mas'ūdī, *Al-Tanbīh wa-l-ishrāf*, pp. 85ff.

available confused historical material for the period prior to Islam, but offered no conception or new design for the writing of history. The motivating factors behind the translations were apparently political and cultural ones.[99]

Translations were also made from Greek and Syriac. But these too were of cultural inspiration, and they contain nothing to indicate that they had any effect on historical writing.

It is thus clear that the tribal perspective on historical writing arose from persistent tendencies and antecedent foundations which in Islam found new incentives, new horizons, and a new structural framework. The motivating factors were primarily social and political, and to a limited extent, spiritual and administrative. Thus the appeal to divine foreordainment as an explanation for events, the appeal embraced by the Umayyads, found no significant endorsement in such centers of opposition to the regime as Kufa and Basra, while the spirit of *ʿaṣabīya* for the various provinces, factional politics, and tribal fervor all reflected their influence into historical writing. Likewise, cultural associations and developments explain the shift from individual accounts transmitted by the *ruwāt* to books composed by the *akhbārīyūn* and the genealogists, and from oral accounts to written works. The third century A.H. had no sooner dawned than we find the two historical perspectives—that of Medina, and that of Kufa and Basra—joining together in common fields of interest in historical studies, and in common historical views.

VI.

The above-mentioned historical studies produced extensive historical material of various degrees of critical rigor. The trend towards employment of the critical method of the *ḥadīth* scholars gained strength and established itself in Iraq. There

[99] Al-Jāḥiẓ, *Al-Bayān wa-l-tabyīn*, III, 3, 14.

emerged, for example, an enthusiasm for travel in search of learning, the *riḥla fī ṭalab al-ʿilm*,[h] in order to pursue one's subject for study and collect as much information as possible. The *ḥadīth* scholars initiated this practice, and the historians followed after them. Likewise, cultural developments made people more acutely aware of and attentive to the importance of the collective experiences of the Islamic community and the importance of the *ijmāʿ* over a wide range of topics. Finally, the fundamental principles and perspectives of Islam gained the decisive advantage over the tribal perspectives in society. Together, these factors affected both the scope of historical studies and the outlook on the writing of history.

The second half of the third century A.H. witnessed the appearance of historians who were not restricted by any of the schools or perspectives mentioned above. Instead, they tried to make use of *sīra* materials, the "books" of the *akhbārīyūn*, genealogical works, and the other available sources. Their studies comprehended the entire *umma* in systematic fashion. Their task was to criticize and then select materials for their works, and their horizons were of general, or universal dimensions.

The first representative of this new development was Aḥmad ibn Yaḥyā ibn Jābir al-Balādhurī (d. 279/892),[i] who wrote two important books: the *Futūḥ al-buldān*, "Conquests of the Provinces," and the *Ansāb al-ashrāf*, "Genealogies of the Notables." The *Futūḥ al-buldān* studies the history of the Islamic conquests and presents a continuous story for the conquest of each province. Al-Balādhurī took his material from books specifically pertaining to the conquests in each province, from

[h] [Important research on the *riḥla fī ṭalab al-ʿilm* has been done by Goldziher, *Muslim Studies*, II, 164ff.; and by Abbott, *Studies*, II, 40ff.]

[i] [See Goitein's very important introduction to al-Balādhurī's *Ansāb al-ashrāf*, V, 9ff.; and more recently, *EI*², I, 971f. (C. H. Becker/F. Rosenthal); Muhammad Hamidullah, "Le 'Livre des Généalogies' d'al-Balāduriy," *BEO*, XIV (1952-54), pp. 197ff.; Petersen, *ʿAlī and Muʿāwiya*, pp. 136ff.; Caskel, *Ǧamharat an-Nasab*, I, 115; Rosenthal, *Muslim Historiography*, index; *GAS*, I, 320f.; Sezgin, *Abū Miḥnaf*, pp. 48ff.; al-Dūrī, "Kutub al-ansāb," pp. 21ff.]

materials he was able to collect during his travels to these regions, and from other sources available to him. His method of writing consisted of selecting material after he had sifted and criticized it, and presenting a balanced image of events while refraining from citing multiple accounts of the same event. He relied heavily on the accounts of Medina, which were known, more than others, for their impartiality and accuracy, and likewise used primarily regional accounts. In this book al-Balādhurī offers much valuable information on cultural, economic, and administrative affairs.

The *Ansāb al-ashrāf* is a general work on Islamic history within a genealogical framework. In both design and content it constitutes an unusual mixture. Its design combines the methodologies of the *ṭabaqāt*, *akhbār*, and genealogical works. The biography of each caliph comprehends the events which occurred in his reign, including the activities of the political factions, with subtitles for important events which are similar to the titles of the "books" of the *akhbārīyūn*. Al-Balādhurī usually adheres to chronological order, although there do appear exceptions dictated by the need to follow genealogical succession (e.g., the discussion of Yazīd appears before that of ʿUthmān ibn ʿAffān).

Al-Balādhurī subjects his sources to criticism before taking material from them. We do notice, however, that views on earlier historians had finally stabilized in his era. This is reflected by such phrases of his as "al-Wāqidī in his *isnād*," "Abū Mikhnaf in his *isnād*," and so forth.[100] Also, some accounts were apparently accepted by most historians, as is evident from some of al-Balādhurī's *akhbār* which begin by saying *qālū*, "They said."[101] It seems that in his selection of historical material al-Balādhurī placed particular importance on the accounts attributable to the province in which the event occurred, and complemented them with other reports on the subject. In his

[100] *Ansāb al-ashrāf*, V, 3, 36 [ʿAbbās ed., IV, i, 484, 524].
[101] *Ibid.*, XI, 283ff., 287ff.

discussion of the *shūrā*, for example, he relies primarily on al-Wāqidī and al-Zuhrī (from Medina), adds to that accounts on the authority of Abū Mikhnaf (which are closer to the ʿAlid position), and takes material pertaining to genealogy from al-Zubayr ibn Bakkār. In his *akhbār* on ʿAbd al-Malik ibn Marwān, he relies heavily on al-Madāʾinī (from ʿAwāna ibn al-Ḥakam), ʿAwāna ibn al-Ḥakam himself (from Damascus), and al-Wāqidī (from Medina), and supplements these with some Iraqi accounts. And on the battle of al-Ḥarra, he essentially bases his discussion on al-Madāʾinī, al-Wāqidī, ʿAwāna, and "teachers" from Medina, thus giving Medinan and Umayyad versions of the event.

Al-Balādhurī's sources were both written works and oral accounts. Such expressions as *ḥaddathanī*, "he told me," and *qāla lī*, "he said to me," indicate directly received oral accounts, while *rawā*, "he reported," generally refers to written works. *Qāla*, "he said," can imply borrowing from either an oral or a written source.[102] Al-Balādhurī uses the *isnād* as a matter of course in certain of his accounts pertaining to events in Medina in the time of the Rāshidūn, and also in some individual accounts. But when he takes information from a source the *isnād* of which is well known, he considers it sufficient to give only the name of the source. Very frequently he uses the collective *isnād* to indicate the consensus on basic points of fact, then gives minor additions.[103] It sometimes happens that al-Balādhurī cites a number of accounts among which there is a certain degree of contradiction on the same subject.[104] In his work there are also some isolated accounts with no *isnād* at all.[105]

Despite his affiliations with the ʿAbbāsids, al-Balādhurī is

[102] *Ibid.*, IVB, 54; V, 24f., 28 [ʿAbbās ed., IV, i, 347, 510ff., 514f.], 135. [On the medieval Islamic terminology used in the transmission of reports and texts, see *GAS*, I, 237ff.]

[103] *Ibid.*, V, 34 [ʿAbbās ed., IV, i, 522].

[104] *Ibid.*, V, 19f., 24 [ʿAbbās ed., IV, i, 504ff., 510f.]; XI, 59.

[105] As the author says, "Some learned men said," *qāla baʿḍ ahl al-ʿilm*.

Despite his affiliations with the ʿAbbāsids, al-Balādhurī is impartial and balanced in the *akhbār* he gives. He thus gives free play to all the accounts and makes a serious effort to be objective in selecting narratives for presentation.

In the *Ansāb al-ashrāf*, al-Balādhurī gives expression to the concept of the unity of the Islamic community and the continuity of its experiences in Islamic history. The *Futūḥ al-buldān*, on the other hand, indicates the value of the *umma*'s experiences for administrative and judicial purposes.

Coming now to al-Yaʿqūbī (d. 284/897),[j] we find a scholar expressing a conception of universal history. Al-Yaʿqūbī was a historian from the secretarial class who combined wide erudition with professional experience in the administration. Beginning in the days of his youth, he traveled widely and succeeded in gathering large collections of historical and geographical information.[106] He also wrote a book, *Kitāb al-buldān*, "Book of the Provinces," on historical geography, the first work of its kind in Arabic.[k] All this had an influence on both the style and content of his history.

The *Ta'rīkh* of al-Yaʿqūbī consists of a comprehensive synopsis of universal history prior to Islam, and of Islamic history up to the year 259/872. In his writing al-Yaʿqūbī adheres to the chronological sequence of periods and events. He begins with Creation (this section is missing from the printed edition), and does not confine himself to discussion of the history of the prophets, Iranian history, and the history of the Arabs prior to Islam. Instead, he also includes the history of such other ancient nations as the Assyrians, Babylonians, Indians, Greeks, Romans, Egyptians, Berbers, Abyssinians, Blacks (*zunūj*), Turks, and Chinese, thus applying in its fullest sense his

[j] [See *EI*[1], IV, 1152f. (C.Brockelmann); Petersen, *ʿAlī and Muʿāwiya*, pp. 169ff.; Rosenthal, *Muslim Historiography*, pp. 133f.]

[106] *Kitāb al-buldān*, edited by M. J. de Goeje (Leiden, 1892), p. 233.

[k] [See André Miquel, *La Géographie humaine du monde musulman jusqu'au milieu du 11e siècle* (Paris, 1967-80), I, 102ff., 285ff.]

conception of universal history. It appears that his interest in this part of his history, and to the extent permitted by the information available to him, was focused on its cultural aspects. It could be said that the material he sets forth in his book reflects the intermingling of cultures in Islamic society. We also note the influence his interest in geography had on his writing.[107] Similarly, his predilection for astronomy manifests itself in the passages he wrote in this section concerning the Persian and Roman calendars,[108] and in the astrological information he offers in the second section in specifying the beginning of the reign of each caliph.

In the first part of the history al-Yaʿqūbī maintains a critical attitude towards his sources. In his writing on the history of the prophets he goes back to the primary sources, and does so with remarkable rigor. When he discusses Iranian history he makes it clear that the materials for this history prior to the Sāsānian period are legendary and unworthy of our confidence. He also uses Greek sources (in translation) when he writes on Greek culture.

In the Islamic history al-Yaʿqūbī follows the method of selecting material from accounts he has already subjected to critical examination. He specifies that he based his work on "what has been reported by past authorities from among the scholars, *ruwāt*, biographers, *akhbārīyūn*, and chronologists," and that he found that these sources "disagreed in their *ḥadīth* and *akhbār*, and in giving dates and life-spans." He therefore tried to sift through them, take "the reports and accounts enjoying the greatest consensus of approval," and compile these together to write his history. He considered it unnecessary to give *isnāds*, since the attitude towards the important historical *isnāds* had already been fixed before his time. He is thus content to mention his basic sources in the introduction to the

[107] *Ta'rīkh*, I, 207.
[108] *Ibid.*, I, 178, 199f.

second section,[109] and thereafter we only rarely find references to a source or chain of authorities.[110] We note that his sources were ʿAlid, ʿAbbāsid (such as Sulaymān ibn ʿAlī al-Hāshimī),[111] and Medinan (e.g., al-Wāqidī and Ibn Isḥāq); similarly, he took material from such *akhbāriyūn* as al-Madāʾinī, al-Haytham ibn ʿAdī, and Ibn al-Kalbī (on genealogy), and from certain astronomers like al-Khwārizmī and the mathematician Mā Shāʾ Allāh.

We also notice that al-Yaʿqūbī is balanced in his *akhbār* and generally accurate in the information he presents. At times he provides information found in no other source.[112] This does not, however, prevent certain aspects of his own inclinations from manifesting themselves in points of detail. Thus, in his discussion of the Rāshidūn and Umayyad caliphs he sometimes reveals ʿAlid sympathies, goes to great lengths in relating the sayings and speeches of the *imāms*, and gives their biographies in conjunction with accounts of their deaths.[113] It would probably be most accurate for us to describe his point of view as Imāmī, since he treats the rebellion of Zayd ibn ʿAlī with casual brevity.[114]

In his account of the ʿAbbāsids, he reveals a certain penchant for indulgence or sycophancy. He refers to the *daʿwa* as the *daʿwa* of the Hāshimites,[115] and to the era of the ʿAb-

[109] *Ibid.*, II, 3f.

[110] *Ibid.*, II, 27, 32f., 126, 159.

[111] See al-Jāḥiẓ, *Al-Bayān wa-l-tabyīn*, III, 367.

[112] Al-Yaʿqūbī, *Taʾrīkh*, II, 479.

[113] *Ibid.*, II, 52, on ʿAlī's conversion to Islam; 125, on his reputation; 35, on Abū Ṭālib; 125, on Ghadīr Khumm; 126f., on the virtues of the Prophet's family; 137, on al-Saqīfa; 220f., on the attitude of Ṭalḥa and al-Zubayr; 225f., on al-Ḥasan ibn ʿAlī; 315f., 318, 320, on his view of the Zubayrids. See also pp. 191f., 195ff., 256f., 261f., 302f., on the Umayyad period. [Cf. William G. Millward, "Al-Yaʿqūbī's Sources and the Question of Shīʿa Partiality," *Abr-Nahrain*, XII (1971-72), pp. 47ff.; Yves Marquet, "Le Šīʿisme au IXe siècle à travers l'histoire de Yaʿqūbī," *Arabica*, XIX (1972), pp. 1ff., 101ff.]

[114] *Ibid.*, II, 391.

[115] *Ibid.*, II, 318, 392, 408.

bāsids as *al-dawla*, "the dynasty." He also cites ʿAbbāsid accounts in his *akhbār*.[116] Likewise, his discussion of the ʿAbbāsid caliph al-Mahdī subtly reflects something of the ʿAbbāsid propaganda claiming that this caliph was the messianic *mahdī* come to spread justice in the world.[117] He offers a similar presentation when he takes up certain events embarrassing to the ʿAbbāsids, such as the murders of Ibn Hubayra and Abū Muslim and the fall of the Barmakids. Even when he comes to the death of the *imām* Mūsā al-Kāẓim he is content to relate the ʿAbbāsid explanation for it. But these points do not limit the value of his work, its importance, or its position in the development of historical writing among the Arabs.

Al-Yaʿqūbī laid out his study of Islamic history according to the order of the caliphs, although at the same time he adhered to the plan of presenting events in chronological order according to year.[118] As he draws closer to his own time, he begins to restrict himself to recording *akhbār* in concise form; thus, for example, we see him devoting only slight notices to the perilous Zanj rebellion. This can perhaps be explained in light of al-Yaʿqūbī's plan. He sought to write a concise condensed history based on the extensive and variegated materials before him, and by doing so to explicate the development of the *umma* on the one hand, and to fill a cultural need [on the other]. For such tasks, contemporary history was not of much assistance.

Let us now turn to Ibn Qutayba (d. 270/883).[1] His book *Al-Maʿārif* is an encyclopedic compendium in which various

[116] *Ibid.*, II, 409, 429ff., 433.

[117] *Ibid.*, II, 432ff., 475ff., 479.

[118] See, in particular, what he has to say in *Ta'rīkh*, II, 167.

[1] [The studies of Gérard Lecomte are of particular importance to our understanding of Ibn Qutayba. See his *Ibn Qutayba: l'homme, son oeuvre, ses idées* (Damascus, 1965), esp. pp. 121ff.; *EI*², III, 844ff. (G. Lecomte); also Charles Pellat, "Ibn Qutayba wa-l-thaqāfa al-ʿarabīya," in *Mélanges Taha Husain*, edited by Abdurrahman Badawi (Cairo, 1962), pp. 29ff.; Conrad, "Arabic Plague Chronologies and Treatises," pp. 59ff.]

lines of historical writing are blended together. We find in it a conception of writing universal history, beginning with the Creation and ending in the days of al-Mu'taṣim. It also displays the approach of the *akhbārīyūn* and genealogists to the writing of history, and briefly discusses the *ayyām al-'arab*. There also appears in it the jurist's interest in how places were conquered, by treaty of submission (*ṣulḥan*) or by force of arms (*'anwatan*). It is believed that the work was composed in order to fill the need of the secretarial class, or *kuttāb*, for fundamental historical information.

In writing the *Ma'ārif*, Ibn Qutayba benefited from both written sources and oral accounts, and followed the method of selecting his historical information after he had subjected his sources to critical evaluation. One will notice that those of his sources whom he mentions by name were scholars of lofty reputation in their fields of study (e.g., Ibn Isḥāq, al-Wāqidī, and Ibn al-Kalbī). Ibn Qutayba was the first to consult the Old Testament to take information directly from it about the beginning of Creation and the history of the prophets.[119] His historical material is distinguished for its impartiality and emphasis on matters of historical fact. At times he presents the prevailing view of events,[120] but at others he offers his own novel judgments.[121]

Al-Dīnawarī (d. 282/891)[m] wrote *Al-Akhbār al-ṭiwāl*, "Book of Long Narratives," another exemplar of universal history. Although he adheres to chronological order in his writing, he concentrates on certain events and movements and discusses

[119] Ibn Qutayba, *Ma'ārif*, pp. 6ff.['Ukāsha ed., pp. 9ff.; cf. also Georges Vajda, "Judéo-Arabica: Observations sur quelques citations bibliques chez Ibn Qutayba," *REJ*, IC (1935), pp. 68ff.; Gérard Lecomte, "Les Citations de l'Ancien et du Nouveau Testament dans l'oeuvre d'Ibn Qutayba," *Arabica*, V (1958), pp. 134ff.; *idem, Ibn Qutayba*, pp. 192ff.].

[120] *Ibid.*, pp. 183, 186 ['Ukāsha ed., pp. 359ff., 366ff.].

[121] *Ibid.*, pp. 273f., on al-Hajjāj ['Ukāsha ed., p. 397].

[m] [On him, see *EI*[2], II, 300 (B. Lewin); Petersen, *'Alī and Mu'āwiya*, pp. 159ff.; Rosenthal, *Muslim Historiography*, pp. 92, 133.]

them in some detail. This makes his history more of a series of *akhbār* linked together by the author. For the pre-Islamic period he tried to present parallel corresponding sketches of events in Iran, Yemen, the Arabian peninsula, and Byzantium, although Iranian history is predominant and holds a place of fundamental importance in this period. He shows no interest in the history of the prophets, and passes over the mission of Muḥammad in a few lines. For the Islamic period, his topic of interest is primarily events in Iraq and Iran.

Al-Dīnawarī shows little aptitude for criticism in his book, and in his *akhbār* reveals something of an inclination towards the ʿAbbāsids. He shows no interest in the *isnād*, since he sought to present a summary derived from other works. Examination of his historical material indicates that he brought together the *Isrāʾīliyāt*, Persian sources, and accounts from Iraq and Medina.

Finally, we come to the *Taʾrīkh al-rusul wa-l-mulūk*, "History of the Prophets and Kings," of al-Ṭabarī (d. 310/923),[n] which represents the highest point reached by Arab historical writing during its formative period. Al-Ṭabarī was an indefatigable student of learning. He studied under teachers in al-Rayy, Baghdad, Kufa, Basra, Syria, and Egypt, and finally settled to live in Baghdad. In his knowledge of historical and juridical sources he gained a reputation unrivaled by any other.

Al-Ṭabarī's view of history and style of writing were influenced by his studies and education as a scholar of *ḥadīth* and jurisprudence. Thus his method for criticizing accounts is directed towards the *isnād*, while his sources are historians with reliable reputations in their fields, or in the subjects on which they wrote. In his history he gives expression to two funda-

[n] [There is an enormous literature on this historian. See Goldziher, *Richtungen*, pp. 85ff.; *EI*¹, IV, 578f. (R. Paret); Petersen, *ʿAlī and Muʿāwiya*, pp. 149ff.; Rosenthal, *Muslim Historiography*, pp. 134f.; *GAS*, I, 323ff.; Marshall G. S. Hodgson, *The Venture of Islam* (Chicago, 1974), I, 354ff.]

mental historical conceptions: on the one hand, the essential oneness of prophetic mission, and on the other, the importance of the experiences of the *umma* and the continuity of these experiences through time. It was of equally great importance to follow the community through times of both unity and discord, its experiences in both situations serving to elucidate how the *umma* was faring through the course of its history.

In al-Ṭabarī's view, the value of an account depended on the strength of its *isnād*: the closer the first link in an *isnād* came to the event itself, the better the report was. Thus early historical writings and accounts preserved nowhere else have survived to modern times by virtue of the method al-Ṭabarī used in compiling his history. The accounts themselves may already have been influenced by various factors, such as memory, personal inclinations and predilections, and so forth, and even after criticizing and evaluating them it was impossible to be absolutely sure of their accuracy and integrity. This is what made *ra'y*, or individual judgment, so unreliable and sometimes confusing. To al-Ṭabarī it therefore sufficed to pass along the accounts of trustworthy *ruwāt* and historians, who themselves bore the responsibility for the integrity of their work. In the material he presents, then, the *ra'y* of al-Ṭabarī manifests itself in his evaluation of accounts and narratives and in his selection of some rather than others. He avoids passing judgment, rarely shows preference for one account over another (all the more so since he gives those which are generally accepted), and displays a manifest impartiality in the ones he cites.

His style of writing was influenced by his attitude towards the sources. Striving to give the different accounts concerning an event or subject, he could not proffer a continuous history of it. It appears that he sought to compile the entire corpus of Arabic historical accounts into his work—a goal to which earlier scholars in the field of *ḥadīth* had aspired—and this explains the enormous number of his sources.[o] This was a great service on the part of al-Ṭabarī, and with it the first era in the development of historical writing draws to a close, since in later times we find no one who tried to reevaluate the historical sources for the periods on which al-Ṭabarī had written.

Al-Ṭabarī's history begins with the Creation, covers the prophets and kings of antiquity, proceeds to the history of the Sāsānians and the Arab tribes,[p] and then discusses Islamic history up to al-Ṭabarī's own time (A.H. 302). His view of history as an expression of divine will and a depository for experiences probably explains the brevity or weakness of the last section of the history, which deals with contemporary history.

VII.

Regional history appeared in the third/ninth century. Some of these works, such as the *Futūḥ Miṣr*, or "Conquest of Egypt," by Ibn ʿAbd al-Ḥakam (d. 257/870),[q] were histories of one particular province; others were histories of cities, like the *Ta'rīkh Wāsiṭ*, "History of Wāsiṭ," by Bahshal (d. 288/900),[r] and the *Ta'rīkh Baghdād*, "History of Baghdad," by Ṭayfūr (d. 280/893).[s] The composition of some of these books was an outgrowth of the regional studies in *ḥadīth*; these give the

[o] [These have been examined in detail in Jawād ʿAlī, "Mawārid ta'rīkh al-Ṭabarī," *Majallat al-majmaʿ al-ʿilmī al-ʿIrāqī*, I (1950), pp. 143ff.; II (1951), pp. 135ff.; III (1954), pp. 16ff.; VIII (1961), pp. 425ff.]

[p] [This section of al-Ṭabarī's history was translated, with a detailed and important commentary, in Nöldeke's *Geschichte der Perser und Araber*.]

[q] [Edited by Charles C. Torrey (New Haven, 1922); cf. also the important study by Robert Brunschvig, "Ibn ʿAbdalḥakam et la conquête de l'Afrique du Nord par les Arabes," *AIEO*, VI (1942-47), pp. 110ff.; Ibrāhīm Aḥmad al-ʿAdawī, *Ibn ʿAbd al-Ḥakam: rā'id al-mu'arrikhīn al-ʿarab* (Cairo, 1963); *EI*², III, 674f. (F. Rosenthal).]

[r] [Edited by Gurgis ʿAwwād (Baghdad, 1387/1967). See *EI*², I, 949 (F. Rosenthal); *GAS*, I, 349.]

[s] [Ibn Abī Ṭāhir Ṭayfūr, *Kitāb Baghdād*, edited by Hans Keller (Leipzig, 1908). Cf. *EI*², III, 692f. (F. Rosenthal); *GAS*, I, 348f.]

biographies of the *ḥadīth* scholars who grew up in these cities or lived there for a length of time, and present these biographies in *ṭabaqāt* form. Others were written out of a sense of devotion and pride for the city or province. These histories usually contain some geographical or topographical information.[t]

From our review of the above, we find that historical writing among the Arabs was a natural development in Islam. The new religion, the formation of an empire, and the establishment of a fixed system of dating—all these laid the foundation. The Islamic perspectives represented in the interest in the biography of the Prophet, the consensus (*ijmāʿ*) and collective experiences of the *umma*, the views and judgments of its learned men, and the great events which had defined the course of its history, were then the principal factors motivating the study of history in Medina. On the other hand, the tribal perspectives oriented towards interest in genealogies, poetry, and the battle-days, persisted in the new tribal centers in Kufa and Basra, though within a new framework, and found fresh incentives in the new political, social, and cultural currents. Behind these two perspectives there was the awareness among all of a historical mission, and this to a certain extent explains the diversity and breadth of historical works.

The development of historical writing was a vital part of cultural development. Scattered accounts—in *akhbār, ḥadīth*, and genealogical form—came to be gathered together in oral form by *akhbāriyūn* or *ḥadīth* scholars, but history did not emerge in any definite form until the beginning of the use of writing for preserving narratives and accounts. The first stage in the rise of history was primarily regional and somewhat

[t] [Cf. further on such works, Ṣāliḥ Aḥmad al-ʿAlī, "Al-Muʾallafāt al-ʿarabīya ʿan al-Madīna wa-l-Ḥijāz," *Majallat al-majmaʿ al-ʿilmī al-ʿIrāqī*, XI (1964), pp. 118ff.; Rosenthal, *Muslim Historiography*, pp. 150ff.; *GAS*, I, 339ff.]

limited in scope: in Medina, the cradle of Islam, interest was directed at the *sīra* and the age of the Rāshidūn caliphs, and in Kufa and Basra it turned towards the activities of the tribes and the conquests. This phase also made its appearance in other aspects of culture, in the development of the concept of *ijmā'*, and in the study of *ḥadīth*, for in this first stage, the attention these two fields of study received was confined to the scope of a single city or province (e.g., Medina, Kufa). But the continuous influence of the fundamental principles and ideas of Islam, and their infusion into society at the expense of tribal views and regional social ideas, explains the appearance of such new cultural developments as the gradually increasing importance of the *isnād* and the expansion of its use in reporting events, and the focusing of communal awareness on the unity of the *umma* and the importance of its continuous experiences. There then developed a kind of systematic gathering of historical narratives and accounts (and similarly, of *ḥadīth*) from the different provinces, and the inclination for writing general histories, some of which involved a universal view of the history of the pre-Islamic past.

From its earliest days history was regarded as a form of *'ilm*, or formal learning, as opposed to *ra'y*, an exercise in individual judgment; and the emphasis was on the evaluation and criticism of the sources according to the method of the *isnād*. Since accounts and narratives were exposed to the influence of personal predilections, factional tendencies, and various forms of *'aṣabīya*, assuring oneself of the trustworthiness of the chain of *ruwāt* who had transmitted the report was the way to confirm the integrity of the report itself. Beyond this, it can be said that the inclinations of the historian manifest themselves in the kinds of accounts and narratives he offers and quotes. Personal judgment could be expressed after the text of the account or narrative had been cited, but not before. A historian developed a reputation for trustworthiness when he presented varying accounts, or when he presented well-known impartial accounts. Thus the level of a given author's strictness and criticism emerges when we examine his accounts in light of the above remarks.

Islam takes an interest in life in general. So for this reason the affairs of this life are important, and likewise, experiences and examples are essential to proper personal conduct. Here history is the best source of guidance. It provides examples enabling the individual to live a better life and serving to enlighten the ruling authorities; history was thus important for a proper education. Moreover, the *ijmāʿ* was an important source of legislation, and a fundamental guide for taking the proper course of action. In its broad lines, history was an expression of the will of God. For particular events or individual actions, however, mankind was no doubt accountable, and opinions about such events were therefore bound to differ. Thus history was generally helpful in understanding the development of the *umma*, and also useful to Islamic religious studies when it offered histories of the Prophet's life, provided practical precedents for administration, and shed light on the community's experiences and on the *ijmāʿ*. On the other hand, much history was written for political or social reasons. This holds true of most of the "books" of the *akhbāriyūn*, and similarly of some of the general histories, since it is hardly possible to find any motive for the writing of al-Dīnawarī's *Al-Akhbār al-ṭiwāl* or Ibn Qutayba's *Maʿārif* other than the motives of general culture.

Let us mention here that, with the help of speculative theologians and the Muʿtazila, the principle of free will met with broad acceptance in the early ʿAbbāsid period. Although the *ḥadīth* scholars triumphed over the Muʿtazila politically in the first half of the third century A.H., their cultural ascendancy did not come until later. It is therefore impossible to speak with certainty—as some have done—of the supremacy of the principle of divine foreordainment and the impact it had on the writing of history in this period. Causation was found in man's activities in accordance with God's will in the world.

In historical writing there appears a strong emphasis on the element of time, and chronological order is generally followed in historical works. This manifests itself in the writing of history based on the succession of the caliphs, the order of events, or the series of *ṭabaqāt*, and culminates in the writing of annalistic history. Dates and *isnāds* were fundamental elements for assuring accuracy. In books of genealogy and *ṭabaqāt*, attention is paid to time in the records of death dates and lifespans (these latter were mentioned in order to compensate for uncertainty over birth dates). History thus consisted of the activities of mankind over specific spans of time. This view of time is an Islamic one.

The various forms of historical writing developed from the methods of the *sīra*, *akhbār*, and genealogies, and the concept of the *umma*; the element of time pervaded them all. In such manner, historical "books" derive from the *akhbār* style, and the *sīra*, *ṭabaqāt*, and biographies derive from the *sīra* style; while general or annalistic history is founded on the idea of the *umma*. Finally, the genealogical style appears in certain works of general history—even histories of families influenced by the *akhbār* style—and in other historical works.

These three centuries were the formative period of historical writing among the Arabs, the age in which the lines and methods for the writing of history were established. The era which followed witnessed other cultural elements, such as geography, philosophy, and astronomy, which had their effects on the writing of history. But no change worthy of note overtook the early historical ideas and methods.

CHAPTER TWO

Origins of the Historical School of Medina: ʿUrwa—al-Zuhrī

Studies both historical and otherwise began as common endeavors represented by academic circles, or *ḥalaqāt*, each gathered around a teacher, and when a superior student had surpassed a certain academic level it was possible for him to establish his own circle. Instruction was available to anyone who sought it, and the teacher's lecture, or *riwāya*, circulated from one student to the next. In this way, and with the passage of time, there arose a school of history, *ḥadīth*, and jurisprudence. The first school of history was the *maghāzī* school of Medina,[1] the growth and orientation of which was closely linked to the efforts of two authorities on jurisprudence and *ḥadīth*: ʿUrwa ibn al-Zubayr and his student al-Zuhrī.

I.

ʿUrwa was one of the notables of Quraysh.[a] His father was al-Zubayr ibn al-ʿAwwām, and his mother was Asmāʾ bint Abī Bakr; ʿĀʾisha was his maternal aunt, Khadīja bint Khuwaylid was his grandmother, and his brother was ʿAbd Allāh ibn al-Zubayr. His wife was Umm Yaḥyā, the youngest child of al-Ḥakam ibn Abī l-ʿĀṣ. He prided himself on his ancestry on both his father's and mother's sides,[2] which consequently

[1] The word *maghāzī* usually signifies battles and military expeditions. This is correct from a linguistic standpoint, but in the sense intended here, and in the early Islamic period, the meaning of the word comprehends the entire era of the Prophet's mission. [Cf. p. 24, n. e above.]

[a] [On ʿUrwa ibn al-Zubayr, see Horovitz, "Biographies," I, 542ff.; *EI*[1], IV, 1047 (V. Vacca); *GAS*, I, 278f.]

[2] See al-Jāḥiẓ, *Al-Bayān wa-l-tabyīn*, I, 180; al-Balādhurī, *Ansāb al-ashrāf*, V, 160, 371; al-Ṭabarī, *Taʾrīkh*, II, 2313; al-Dhahabī, *Tarājim*, p. 40.

had an influence both on his upbringing and on the accounts he produced.

The sources differ on the year of his birth, with various authorities saying that he was born in A.H. 22, 26, or 29.[3] According to one report he was born in 23/643; this seems to be the most accurate account, since it is confirmed by another report stating that he was thirteen years old at the time of the Battle of the Camel (in A.H. 36), and is supported by ʿUrwa's own statement that on his way to the battlefield that day he was turned back because of his tender age.[4] Numerous reports on the year of his death are available to us; al-Ṭabarī places it in A.H. 94, as also do "Ibn Saʿd and his colleagues,"[5] while Ibn Qutayba, as also Ibn Khallikān, makes it either A.H. 93 or 94.[6] There are also other accounts placing his death in A.H. 92, 95, 99, 100, or 101,[7] but the earliest and most reliable is that placing his death in the year 94/712.

ʿUrwa grew up and studied in Medina. He then lived for the seven years between A.H. 58 and 65 in Egypt, where he also married,[8] and visited Damascus several times. ʿUrwa's aspirations differed from those of his father and his two brothers ʿAbd Allāh and Muṣʿab, and he clearly voiced his own outlook in saying, "My wish is to be abstinent in this world, to gain [Paradise] in the next, and to be among those from whom learning is handed down."[9] This attitude manifested itself in

[3] Ibn Khallikān, *Wafayāt al-aʿyān* (Cairo), I, 399 [ʿAbbās ed., III, 258]; al-Dhahabī, *Tarājim*, p. 48.

[4] Ibn Saʿd, V, 133; al-Dhahabī, *Tarājim*, p. 48; Ibn Ḥajar, *Tahdhīb al-tahdhīb*, VII, 183f.

[5] Ibn Saʿd, V, 135; al-Ṭabarī, *Taʾrīkh*, II, 1266; al-Dhahabī, *Tarājim*, pp. 42, 48.

[6] Ibn Qutayba, *Maʿārif*, edited by Muḥammad al-Ṣāwī (Cairo, 1353/1934), p. 98 [ʿUkāsha ed., p. 222]; Ibn Khallikān, *Wafayāt al-aʿyān* (Cairo), I, 399 [ʿAbbās ed., III, 258].

[7] Al-Nawawī, *Tahdhīb al-asmāʾ*, edited by Ferdinand Wüstenfeld (Göttingen, 1842-47), p. 331; al-Dhahabī, *Tarājim*, p. 48; Ibn Ḥajar, *Tahdhīb al-tahdhīb*, VII, 184.

[8] Al-Balādhurī, *Futūḥ al-buldān* (Cairo, 1932), p. 219 [de Goeje ed., p. 217]; Horovitz ["Biographies," I, 543ff.], *Al-Maghāzī al-ūlā*, p. 13.

[9] Ibn Khallikān, *Wafayāt al-aʿyān* (Cairo), I, 399 [ʿAbbās ed., III, 258].

the way he lived: Ibn Hishām says of him, "He used to fast all the time except on the feast days of ʿĪd al-Fiṭr and ʿĪd al-Aḍḥā, and when he died he was fasting."[10] His love of learning is evident from a report by his son Hishām stating, "On the day of the battle of al-Ḥarra, my father burned some books of jurisprudence which belonged to him, and afterwards he used to say, 'Having them back would be dearer to me than to have such things as my family and fortune.' "[11] ʿUrwa did not participate in the successive political events of his time. As al-ʿIjlī said of him, "He was a trustworthy upright man who took no part in discords."[12] He was opposed to the policies of the Umayyads, but decided only to dissociate himself from the "oppressors."[13]

ʿUrwa passed his life between studying and teaching. He sought out *ḥadīth* and other sources of learning, and passed down reports from such eminent men and women of Medina as ʿĀ'isha, ʿAmra, Usāma ibn Zayd, ʿAbd Allāh ibn ʿAmr ibn al-ʿĀṣ, Abū Hurayra, and ʿAbd Allāh ibn ʿAbbās.[14] He became one of the "seven jurists of Medina" and one of its most outstanding scholars of *ḥadīth*, such that ʿUmar ibn ʿAbd al-ʿAzīz said of him, "There was no one more learned than ʿUrwa ibn al-Zubayr," and al-Zuhrī once remarked, "ʿUrwa was a sea the buckets never muddied."[15] It is important to us here that we study ʿUrwa as a historian, leaving aside his role in jurisprudence and *ḥadīth*.

[10] Ibn Saʿd, V, 134; al-Dhahabī, *Tarājim*, p. 42, also see p. 43.
[11] Ibn Saʿd, V, 133; al-Dhahabī, *Tarājim*, p. 41.
[12] Al-Dhahabī, *Tarājim*, p. 45.
[13] Ibn Saʿd, V, 135; al-Dhahabī, *Tarājim*, pp. 43f.
[14] See Ibn Saʿd, V, 133; al-Dhahabī, *Tarājim*, p. 45.
[15] See Abū l-Faraj al-Iṣfahānī, *Kitāb al-aghānī* (Cairo, 1345-94/1927-74), VIII, 89, 93 [(Bulaq, A.H. 1285), VIII, 92, 97; also Abū Zurʿa al-Dimashqī, *Ta'rīkh*, edited by Shukr Allāh ibn Niʿmat Allāh al-Qawajānī (Damascus, 1400/1980), I, 418;] al-Dhahabī, *Tarājim*, pp. 45.; Ibn Ḥajar, *Tahdhīb al-tahdhīb*, VII, 182. Al-Jāḥiẓ says (*Al-Bayān wa-l-tabyīn*, II, 202), "ʿUrwa exhorted his sons, saying, 'Seek to gain in learning, for if you are the lowliest of men now, you may become the most renowned of men later.' " Also see Ibn Saʿd, V, 134.

Before taking up his historical studies, we should indicate that ʿUrwa had ties with the Umayyads. He knew ʿAbd al-Malik in his youth in Medina and used to meet with him in the mosque of the city. He came to see ʿAbd al-Malik in Damascus after the death of ʿUrwa's brother ʿAbd Allāh, and similarly, later came to visit the caliph al-Walīd. He met with difficulty at the hands of the Syrians, and the reports available to us indicate that although they esteemed him for his learning, he was wary in his dealings with them. All that concerns us here is that the Umayyad court asked him questions about events pertaining to the mission of the Prophet. He responded to these queries in essays, some of which have come down to us in al-Tabarī and are among the earliest and most trustworthy fragments to survive to modern times.[16] In the following pages we will try to describe ʿUrwa's historical works in order to form a tentative idea of what they were like:

1. Muhammad's call (*baʿth*) at the age of forty;[17] the first signs of prophecy: "the first sign with which the prophethood of the Apostle of God was begun . . . was . . . true vision (*al-ru'yā al-ṣādiqa*). . . . God evoked in him a desire for seclusion, so that nothing was dearer to him than to be isolated by himself";[18] beginning of revelation (*nuzūl al-waḥy*) while he was performing his devotions in a cave on Ḥirā', and the first Qur'ānic verses, "Recite, in the name of thy Lord . . .";[b] the fear which overcame the Prophet as a result; he tells Khadīja of his anxiety, so she quickly takes him to Waraqa ibn Nawfal, who prophesies that something great will happen to him.[19]

ʿUrwa also offers an essay explaining how the Prophet

[16] On ʿUrwa's relations with the Umayyads, see al-Jāḥiẓ, *Al-Bayān wa-l-tabyīn*, II, 70; *Aghānī*, IV, 118, 123; IX, 147; XVI, 44f.; Ibn Khallikān, *Wafayāt al-aʿyān* (Cairo), I, 398f. [ʿAbbās ed., III, 255ff.].

[17] Al-Tabarī, *Ta'rīkh*, I, 1140, 1835.

[18] Ibn Hishām (Cairo), I, 249 [Wüstenfeld ed., I, 1, 151].

[b] [Sūrat al-ʿAlaq (XCVI), 1.]

[19] Al-Ṭabarī, *Ta'rīkh*, I, 1147; *Aghānī* (Cairo), II, 15 [Bulaq ed., III, 16].

came to realize that he was destined for a mission of the greatest importance. This is the account of the two angels who met him in the *Baṭḥā'* of Mecca,[c] split open his abdomen and heart, removed the blemish of Satan and a clot of blood from inside him, and set the seal of prophecy between his shoulder blades.[20]

2. The Hijra to Abyssinia—This appears in a letter from ʿUrwa to ʿAbd al-Malik ibn Marwān in which he discusses the beginning of Muḥammad's appeal and the attitude of Quraysh at that time, saying, "They did not shy away from him when he first summoned them, and almost listened to him, until he made references to their idols. . . ." They then began to treat him harshly, and all but a few of the people broke away from him. "So thus matters remained, for as long as God decided that they should remain so." He then states that a group of Quraysh coming from al-Ṭā'if to Mecca rejected the Prophet's message, and incited his people against him so that they persecuted the Muslims. Moreover, they conspired together to lure away his followers, "so that there was severe trial and upheaval. . . . Some were led astray, but God vouchsafed those whom he willed." When the Prophet saw what had befallen his Companions, he ordered them to emigrate to Abyssinia. ʿUrwa explains that Abyssinia was chosen because over it there ruled a righteous king in whose domain no one suffered injustice, and similarly, because Abyssinia was a place where Quraysh conducted trade. Many of the Muslims thereupon emigrated, while Muḥammad remained in Mecca; "and so matters remained for years."[21] He also mentions ʿUbayd Allāh ibn Jaḥsh's conversion to Christianity in Abyssinia.[22]

[c] [The hollow where the oldest part of Mecca, including the Kaʿba, is located.]

[20] Al-Ṭabarī, *Ta'rīkh*, I, 1154.

[21] *Ibid.*, I, 1180f.

[22] Ibn Hishām, IV, 6 [Wüstenfeld ed., I, ii, 783f.].

3. The increasing Quraysh opposition to the Prophet's mission and what he suffered at their hands. They even threw filth into his house, and one sprinkled dust over his head.[23] ʿUrwa also gives the names of those members of Quraysh who mocked the Prophet.[24] Quraysh meets at al-Ḥijr[d] to deliberate on the matter of the Prophet: "He has belittled our customs, reviled our forefathers, denounced our religion, divided our ranks, and cursed our gods." The next day, as the Prophet passed by them, they rushed at him all at once. One of their men seized hold of the seam of his robe, but Abū Bakr stepped in front of him and, crying, said, "Woe unto you! Would you kill a man for saying, 'God is my Lord'?" With that they withdrew.[25] Departure of Abū Bakr from Mecca after seeing how the polytheists were joining ranks against the Prophet, and his return to Mecca under the protection of Ibn al-Dughunna.[26]

4. The Hijra—ʿUrwa begins with an introduction on the circumstances leading up to the Hijra. He mentions the return of most of those who had emigrated to Abyssinia, and says that this "caused the adherents of Islam to increase and multiply in numbers. There were many conversions among the Anṣār in Medina and Islam began to gain ground there, so that the people of Medina began to come to visit the Apostle of God—may the blessing and peace of God be upon him." The Quraysh were troubled by this and conspired together to persecute the Muslims. "They thus suffered severe hardship, and that was the latter persecution." ʿUrwa reports the contacts the Medinans made with the

[23] Ibn Hishām, II, 57f. [Wüstenfeld ed., I, i, 277]; al-Ṭabarī, *Ta'rīkh*, I, 1199.
[24] Ibn Hishām, II, 50f. [Wüstenfeld ed., I, i, 271f.].
[d] [The area just beyond the northern corner of the Kaʿba.]
[25] Ibn Hishām, I, 309 [Wüstenfeld ed., I, i, 183]; al-Ṭabarī, *Ta'rīkh*, I, 1185.
[26] Ibn Hishām, I, 309; II, 11ff. [Wüstenfeld ed., I, i, 183, 245f.].

Prophet, saying, "Then there came to the Apostle of God—may the blessing and peace of God be upon him—seventy representatives, leaders of those who had accepted Islam, who appeared before him during the pilgrimage, then pledged their loyalty to him at al-ʿAqaba and offered him their oaths providing that 'we are of you and you are of us.' Quraysh thereupon became harsher in their treatment of the Muslims in Mecca, so the Prophet gave the order for the emigration (*hijra*) to Medina. It was concerning this that God revealed the verse, 'Fight them until persecution (*fitna*) is no more, and all religion is God's.' "[27]

This fragment completes the discussion of the first persecution and the Hijra to Abyssinia. We do not know whether this was part of ʿUrwa's letter to ʿAbd al-Malik, as Horovitz believes, or whether it was an independent account, since it is probable that ʿUrwa related the contents of the latter and this supplement separately.[28]

Account of the Prophet's own Hijra to Medina—ʿUrwa begins by referring to the Hijra of the Muslims to Medina while the Prophet remained in Mecca waiting for the appropriate moment to depart. He gives the details on the preparations for the Hijra, on the Prophet and Abū Bakr hiding for three days in the cave of Thawr, and on other related events, and describes the remainder of the journey to Medina.[29] This fragment bears the same *isnād* as the two previous fragments, and contains a reference to the Qur'ānic verse, "Fight them until persecution is no more," all of which points to the conclusion that its discussion was meant to supplement that of the two previous accounts.[30]

[27] Al-Ṭabarī, *Taʾrīkh*, I, 1224f. [citing Sūrat al-Anfāl (VIII), 39].

[28] See Horovitz ["Biographies," I, 548f.], *Al-Maghāzī al-ūlā*, p. 20.

[29] Al-Ṭabarī, *Taʾrīkh*, I, 1234ff. There is another account giving the story of the Hijra which is similar to the above, but bears a different chain of authorities. See al-Ṭabarī, *Taʾrīkh*, I, 1237.

[30] This caused Horovitz to consider this and the two preceding fragments

In another account 'Urwa tells of the Prophet's arrival at Qubā' on the way to Medina, and how the Muslims were every day awaiting his arrival.[31] He also reports the affliction of some of the Prophet's companions by fever after their arrival in Medina,[32] and gives an account of the attitude of 'Abd Allāh ibn Ubayy towards the appeal of the Prophet, a narrative in which there appears dissatisfaction and antipathy to the Prophet.[33]

5. A report on the expedition of 'Abd Allāh ibn Jaḥsh— The account contains details on the sending of the expedition, the Prophet's orders to 'Abd Allāh, the attack on the Quraysh caravan, its capture by the Muslims and the killing of two of the Quraysh guards, and the misgivings which arose on the question of fighting during the sacred month, until the revelation of the verse, "They will ask thee about the sacred month . . . ," after which the Prophet agrees to take possession of the caravan.[34]

6. The expedition of Badr—'Urwa's account appears in a letter he sent to 'Abd al-Malik ibn Marwān, and begins, "To wit: You wrote to me about Abū Sufyān and his departure. . . ." A long continuous account, it begins by recounting Abū Sufyān's return from Syria at the head of a Meccan caravan, his appeal to the Quraysh for help, and the Prophet's capture of a young slave water-carrier of Quraysh and his efforts to learn the enemy's numbers. 'Urwa refers to the Prophet's preparations for the battle, the clash between the two forces, and the Muslim victory. He does not discuss the fighting in detail, but rather is content to

to comprise a single letter to 'Abd al-Malik, but I do not believe this to be the case.

[31] Ibn Hishām, II, 137ff. [Wüstenfeld ed., I, i, 333ff.]; al-Ṭabarī, *Ta'rīkh*, I, 1242.

[32] Ibn Hishām, II, 238 [Wüstenfeld ed., I, i, 413f.]; al-Balādhurī, *Futūḥ al-buldān*, p. 25 [de Goeje ed., p. 11].

[33] Ibn Hishām, II, 236f. [Wüstenfeld ed., I, i, 412f.].

[34] Al-Ṭabarī, *Ta'rīkh*, I, 1273ff. [citing Sūrat al-Baqara (II), 217].

say, "They (Quraysh) and the Prophet—may the blessing and peace of God be upon him—clashed, and God granted his Apostle victory, disgraced the leaders of disbelief, and restored from their affliction the hearts of the Muslims." The letter also contains some novel features, among them an explanatory introduction stating, "There had been fighting between them before that. Some were killed in battle, Ibn al-Ḥaḍramī was killed among others at Nakhla, and some of the Quraysh were taken prisoner. . . . ʿAbd Allāh ibn Jaḥsh attacked them. . . . That conflict provoked war between the Apostle of God and Quraysh, and was the first time war broke out among them." We should also note his description of the Muslim frame of mind when they set out for Badr: "They regarded the caravan as no more than an opportunity for them to plunder, and they did not think there would be any serious fighting when they encountered Quraysh."[35]

In another account by ʿUrwa there are further references to Badr, among them one in which the Prophet instructs the Muslims, "This is the Quraysh caravan bearing their wealth; so set out to attack it, and God may deliver it up to you as spoils."[36] Another describes Quraysh's fear of what the clan of Bakr might do should Quraysh set out, and the alleged role of Satan (Iblīs) in convincing them to do so.[37] ʿUrwa also relates that when the Prophet saw the Quraysh forces approaching on the day of the battle, he called out, "O God, you have revealed to me the Book [ordered me to fight,] and promised me, you who does not break a promise, one of the two parties.[c] O God, these Quraysh have

[35] Al-Ṭabarī, *Ta'rīkh*, I, 1284ff.

[36] Ibn Hishām, II, 257f. [Wüstenfeld ed., I, i, 457f.].

[37] Ibn Hishām, II, 263 [Wüstenfeld ed., I, i, 432]; al-Ṭabarī, *Ta'rīkh*, I, 1296.

[c] [Alluding to Sūrat al-Anfāl (VIII), 7: "And when God promised you that one of the two parties will be yours . . . ," taken in Qur'ānic exegesis to mean

come in their conceit and pride, turning away from you and denouncing your Apostle as a liar. O God, this is your victory which you promised me. O God, destroy them in the early morning!"[38] After the battle, the polytheists who had been killed were thrown into a pit.[39]

7. The campaign against Qaynuqā'—After Badr, the clan of Qaynuqā' began to manifest feelings of envy and disloyalty. 'Urwa mentions the revelation of the verse, "If thou fearest treachery at the hands of a people, then cast them out in like measure";[f] the Prophet's siege of their quarters; their submission to his judgment; mediation by 'Abd Allāh ibn Ubayy; their expulsion from Medina, and the property confiscated from them by the Prophet;[40] a report on the expedition to Bi'r Ma'ūna;[41] also a passing reference to the expedition to al-Rajī'.[42]

8. The expedition of the Ditch—The effort of the Jews to rally the various parties against the Prophet; the inducements they offered to Quraysh and Ghaṭafān; departure of Quraysh under the leadership of Abū Sufyān, followed by Ghaṭafān, Fazāra, Banū Murra, and a clan from Ashja'; the Prophet hears of this and digs a ditch around Medina.[43]

9. The campaign against Banū Qurayẓa—After the departure of Quraysh and their allies, the Prophet attacked and besieged Qurayẓa; they submitted to his judgment, and

---

that Muḥammad was guaranteed either capture of the Quraysh caravan, or victory over the Meccan force (defeated at Badr) sent to relieve it. See al-Wāqidī, *Maghāzī*, I, 131f.]

[38] Al-Wāqidī, *Kitāb al-maghāzī*, edited by 'Abbās al-Shirbīnī (Cairo, 1947), p. 43 [Jones ed., I, 59].

[39] Ibn Hishām, II, 291f. [Wüstenfeld ed., I, i, 453f.]; al-Ṭabarī, *Ta'rīkh*, I, 1331.

[f] [Sūrat al-Anfāl (VIII), 58.]

[40] Al-Wāqidī, *Maghāzī*, pp. 139, 141 [Jones ed., I, 177ff., 180]; al-Tabarī, *Ta'rīkh*, I, 1360.

[41] Al-Wāqidī, *Maghāzī*, p. 270 [Jones ed., I, 347].

[42] *Ibid.*, p. 275 [Jones ed., I, 354].

[43] Al-Ṭabarī, *Ta'rīkh*, I, 1463.

Saʿd ibn Muʿādh, appointed to decide their fate, ordered that their warriors be killed, their children enslaved, and their property divided.[44]

10. The expedition of Banū l-Muṣṭaliq—Reference to the apportionment of the captives from Banū l-Muṣṭaliq; the Prophet's marriage to Juwayriya bint al-Ḥārith;[45] account of the Lie, *Al-Ifk*, during this expedition.[46]

11. Truce of al-Ḥudaybiya—The Prophet sets out in the year of al-Ḥudaybiya to visit the Kaʿba, and not seeking a fight, takes along camels for sacrifice; the number of those accompanying him; his arrival at al-Ḥudaybiya and negotiations with Quraysh; the call for cessation of hostilities, the truce and treaty for four years providing "that anyone can enter into alliance with anyone else, so long as there is no treachery or bad faith. . . ."; the Prophet makes Banū Kaʿb party to the pact, and Quraysh does likewise with their allies of Banū Kināna; the remainder of the provisions and the postponement of the Muslim entry into Mecca until the following year.[47]

12. The expedition to Mu'ta—Its date, organization of its leadership, and number of participants; the Muslim arrival at Maʿān, the approach of Heraclius, the numbers of his troops, and his confederates; the steadfastness of the Muslims after the conference;[48] return of the Muslims, at-

[44] Ibn Hishām, III, 252f. [Wüstenfeld ed., I, ii. 690]; al-Balādhurī, *Futūḥ al-buldān*, p. 35 [de Goeje ed., p. 22]; Abū ʿUbayd, *Kitāb al-amwāl* (Cairo, A.H. 1353), p. 129; al-Ṭabarī, *Ta'rīkh*, I, 1494.

[45] Ibn Hishām, III, 307 [Wüstenfeld ed., I, ii, 729]; al-Ṭabarī, *Ta'rīkh*, I, 1517. Also see Ibn Hishām, IV, 295 [Wüstenfeld ed., I, ii, 1002], for another account by ʿUrwa about the Prophet's marriage to Juwayriya.

[46] Ibn Hishām, III, 309ff. [Wüstenfeld ed., I, ii, 731ff.]. There is a reference to the Affair of the Lie in al-Ṭabarī, *Ta'rīkh*, I, 1518.

[47] Al-Balādhurī, *Futūḥ al-buldān*, p. 49 [de Goeje ed., p. 36]; Abū ʿUbayd, *Amwāl*, pp. 157, 158; al-Ṭabarī, *Ta'rīkh*, I, 1534.

[48] Ibn Hishām, IV, 15ff. [Wüstenfeld ed., I, ii, 791ff.]; al-Ṭabarī, *Ta'rīkh*, I, 1610.

titude of the people and young boys towards them, and the Prophet's praise for their courage.[49]

13. The conquest of Mecca—An account reporting some of the terms of the truce of al-Ḥudaybiya, and Quraysh's violation of them through their role in the fighting between their tribal ally, Bakr, and the Prophet's ally, Khuzāʿa;[50] Ḥāṭib ibn Abī Baltaʿa writes to Quraysh of the Prophet's intention to set out in their direction.[51]

ʿUrwa gives a detailed account of the conquest of Mecca in a letter he sent to ʿAbd al-Malik. In it he clarifies the reason for the campaign, its organization, the Quraysh representatives (Abū Sufyān and those accompanying him) who came to the Prophet, the Muslim entry into Mecca, the fighting led by Khālid against the *aḥābīsh*, and his victory over them, along with some other individual details.[52]

14. The expedition of Ḥunayn—The Prophet remains in Mecca about two weeks; the tribes of Thaqīf and Hawāzin, as soon as they receive word of Muḥammad's campaign against Mecca, unite their forces, fearing that the campaign will continue against them; their subsequent arrival at Wādī Ḥunayn; the Prophet meets them, puts them to flight, seizes as booty the animals they had brought with them, and takes the women and children as captives;[53] a Hawāzin delegation accepts Islam after the expedition to al-Ṭā'if, and the Prophet releases their children and women.[54]

15. The expedition to al-Ṭā'if—The Prophet sets out for al-Ṭā'if after Ḥunayn; Thaqīf fights the Muslim force be-

[49] Ibn Hishām, IV, 24 [Wüstenfeld ed., I, ii, 797f.]; al-Ṭabarī, *Ta'rīkh*, I, 1617.

[50] Ibn Hishām, IV, 32 [Wüstenfeld ed., I, ii, 803f.]; al-Ṭabarī, *Ta'rīkh*, I, 1619.

[51] Ibn Hishām, IV, 40f. [Wüstenfeld ed., I, ii, 809f.].

[52] Ibn Hishām, IV, 60 [Wüstenfeld ed., I, ii, 825f.]; al-Ṭabarī, *Ta'rīkh*, I, 1634ff.

[53] Al-Ṭabarī, *Ta'rīkh*, I, 1654.

[54] *Ibid.*, I, 1770.

sieging the fortress; the people in the surrounding area accept Islam; the siege lasts for two weeks; the Prophet returns to al-Jiʿrāna, where the prisoners taken at Ḥunayn had been left; after releasing them he returns to Medina; a Thaqīf delegation comes to Medina and pays homage to the Prophet.[55]

16. Letters from the Prophet to various places—A letter to the people of Hajar;[56] letter to al-Ḥārith ibn ʿAbd Kulāl, Shurayḥ ibn ʿAbd Kulāl, and Nuʿaym ibn ʿAbd Kulāl;[57] his letter to al-Mundhir ibn Sāwā;[58] his letter to the people of Yemen;[59] his letter to Thaqīf;[60] his letter to the people of Ayla;[61] his letter to Khuzāʿa;[62] his letter to Zurʿa ibn Dhī Yazan;[63] his letter to ʿAbd Allāh ibn Jaḥsh.[64]

17. Final days of the Prophet's life—He gives orders to make preparations for the campaign of Usāma ibn Zayd; beginning of his illness; he urges the Muslims to carry out Usāma's mission;[65] intensification of his illness, his death, and his age;[66] reference to the rebellion of al-Aswad al-ʿAnsī, who is defeated and killed in the Prophet's lifetime.[67]

18. Personal matters—A letter to ʿAbd al-Malik relates the death of Khadīja and the Prophet's marriage to ʿĀ'isha.[68]

[55] *Ibid.*

[56] Al-Balādhurī, *Futūḥ al-buldān*, p. 60 [de Goeje ed., pp. 79f.]; Abū ʿUbayd, *Amwāl*, p. 199.

[57] Abū ʿUbayd, *Amwāl*, p. 13.

[58] *Ibid.*, p. 20.

[59] *Ibid.*, p. 27.

[60] *Ibid.*, p. 190.

[61] *Ibid.*, p. 200.

[62] *Ibid.*

[63] Al-Balādhurī, *Futūḥ al-buldān*, p. 81 [de Goeje ed., pp. 69f.]; Abū ʿUbayd, *Amwāl*, p. 201.

[64] Al-Ṭabarī, *Ta'rīkh*, I, 1273.

[65] Ibn Hishām, IV, 299f. [Wüstenfeld ed., I, ii, 1006ff.]; al-Ṭabarī, *Ta'rīkh*, I, 1808f.

[66] Ibn Hishām, IV, 304f. [Wüstenfeld ed., I, ii, 1011]; al-Ṭabarī, *Ta'rīkh*, I, 1814; Ḥusaynīya ed., II, 447, 454 [de Goeje ed., I, 1824, 1835].

[67] Al-Ṭabarī, *Ta'rīkh* (Ḥusaynīya), II, 431 [de Goeje ed., I, 1798].

[68] Al-Ṭabarī, *Ta'rīkh*, I, 1770.

In a letter to al-Walīd, ʿUrwa explains that the Prophet married neither the sister of al-Ashʿath nor a woman of Kinda; he did marry a woman of Banū Jawn, but divorced her before consummating the marriage.[69]

ʿUrwa did not limit his interest to the *maghāzī*, but rather took up the period of the Rāshidūn as well. This is clear from some of the quotations which have come down to us from him. To form a general idea of his studies we can briefly refer to them here:

1. ʿUrwa mentions Abū Bakr's decision to carry out Usāma's mission, despite the apostasy (*ridda*) of the tribes and the critical situation of the Muslims.[70] He relates the story of the apostasy of the tribes briefly, yet adequately and comprehensively,[71] and provides details on the Ridda in al-Yamāma because of the great danger it posed.[72] He also tells of Mutammam ibn Nuwayra coming to Abū Bakr to seek satisfaction for his brother's death, ask that the captives be released, and complain about Khālid ibn al-Walīd; ʿUrwa then speaks of Abū Bakr's refusal to accept ʿUmar's advice that he dismiss Khālid.[73]

2. Abū Bakr fits out the armies and sends them to Syria, explaining the route each leader is to take;[74] account of Ajnadayn, the date of the battle, the Muslim victory, and the names of some of those who were killed.[75]

3. Al-ʿAbbās and Fāṭima's request that Abū Bakr grant them their inheritance from the Prophet—Fadak and the Prophet's share of Khaybar; Abū Bakr's refusal; the request by the wives of the Prophet that Abū Bakr grant them their

[69] *Ibid.*, III, 2458.
[70] Al-Ṭabarī, *Ta'rīkh* (Cairo: Maṭbaʿat al-Istiqāma, 1358/1939), II, 461 [de Goeje ed., I, 1848].
[71] *Ibid.*, II, 475 [de Goeje ed., I, 1871].
[72] Al-Balādhurī, *Futūḥ al-buldān*, p. 99 [de Goeje ed., p. 89].
[73] Al-Ṭabarī, *Ta'rīkh*, I, 2085; II, 503.
[74] *Ibid.*, I, 2085.
[75] *Ibid.*, I, 2125.

inheritances from the Prophet's share of Khaybar and Fadak, and the view of 'Ā'isha.[76]

4. Abū Bakr gives up trade to devote his attention to the affairs of the Muslims, and is allotted a stipend from the treasury (*bayt al-māl*);[77] illness of Abū Bakr and the date of his death.[78]

5. Reference to the battle of al-Yarmūk;[79] another to the battle of al-Qādisīya.[80]

6. A report on 'Umar ibn al-Khaṭṭāb's journey to Ayla on his way to Jerusalem.[81]

7. A report on the Battle of the Camel.[82]

It is hardly possible for us to formulate any idea of 'Urwa's view of history based on his accounts concerning the period of the Rāshidūn, for he goes into relative detail only on the Ridda, and except for this topic offers us only tidbits and passing references. From his *akhbār* on the Ridda, we notice that he follows the same method he used in the *Maghāzī*, and since we find more material extant from this latter work we can derive from it an approximate idea of 'Urwa's writing.

In his *Maghāzī* we find 'Urwa touching upon the beginning of Qur'ānic revelation, on the beginning of Muḥammad's call, and on the two Hijras to Abyssinia and Medina. He then covers some of the activities of the Medinan period, such as the expedition of 'Abd Allāh ibn Jaḥsh, the great battle of Badr, the conflict with Qaynuqā', the Battle of the Ditch, the conflict with Banū Qurayẓa, the truce of al-Ḥuday-

[76] Al-Balādhurī, *Futūḥ al-buldān*, p. 44 [de Goeje ed., p. 30]; al-Ṭabarī, *Ta'rīkh*, I, 1825.

[77] Abū 'Ubayd, *Amwāl*, p. 211.

[78] Al-Ṭabarī, *Ta'rīkh*, I, 2128, 2130.

[79] *Ibid.*, I, 2348.

[80] *Ibid.*, I, 2251.

[81] *Ibid.*, I, 2522.

[82] *Ibid.*, I, 3208. 'Urwa also gives a report on the killing of his brother Muṣ'ab and the role of 'Abd al-Malik ibn Marwān in the affair; *ibid.*, II, 811.

biya, the expedition to Mu'ta, the conquest of Mecca, the expeditions to Ḥunayn and al-Ṭā'if, some of the letters sent by the Prophet, and his final days. Some of his accounts provide replies to queries of the Umayyad court, while others are narratives he related to his students.

It appears that his accounts were little more than basic sketches in varying degrees of detail. While some amount to nothing more than passing references, others provide us with continuous narratives, as in his discussions of Badr, al-Ḥudaybiya, and the conquest of Mecca. We note that he presents [only scattered notices] on the battle of Uḥud,[83] [yet he carefully notes the dates of such other expeditions as those of Ibn Jaḥsh, the Ditch, Banū Qurayẓa, Banū l-Muṣṭaliq, al-Ḥudaybiya, Ḥunayn, and Mu'ta.[84] We can] see that 'Urwa covered the *maghāzī* in the course of his studies, and that rather than limit himself to the military campaigns, he treated other aspects of the *sīra* ranging from the beginning of revelation to the death of the Prophet. A reference to the *Maghāzī* of 'Urwa appears in al-Sakhāwī,[85] and Ḥājjī Khalīfa corroborates this in saying, "It is said that the first to compose a book on (the *maghāzī*) was 'Urwa ibn al-Zubayr."[86] All we can deduce from the selections available to us is that 'Urwa did discuss the *maghāzī*; we cannot distinguish in his accounts any clear plan for the *sīra*.[g]

'Urwa was a trustworthy scholar of *ḥadīth*, and in his ac-

[83] See al-Ṭabarī, *Ta'rīkh* (Istiqāma), II, 194f. [de Goeje ed., I, 1397; also al-Wāqidī, *Maghāzī* (Jones ed.), I, 286f.; Ibn Kathīr, *Al-Bidāya wa-l-nihāya*, IV, 46, 49].

[84] [Ibn Sa'd, III, ii, 6; Ibn Kathīr, *Al-Bidāya wa-l-nihāya*, III, 249; IV, 156, 164, 322.]

[85] *Al-I'lān bi-l-tawbīkh*, p. 88. [Cf. also Ibn Kathīr, *Al-Bidāya wa-l-nihāya*, IV, 55f.]

[86] *Kashf al-ẓunūn*, II, 1747.

[g] [On the *Maghāzī* of 'Urwa ibn al-Zubayr, see now *Maghāzī Rasūl Allāh li-'Urwa ibn al-Zubayr*, compiled and edited by Muḥammad Muṣṭafā l-A'ẓamī (Riyad, 1981); also Salwā Mamdūḥ Mursī, "'Urwa ibn al-Zubayr wa-bidāyat madrasat al-maghāzī," M.A. thesis (Jordan University, 1979).]

counts he adhered to the method of his colleagues. His social position and connections enabled him to take accounts directly from their sources, thus in some of his accounts we find mention of the *isnād*,[87] while in others he provides none at all.[88] It appears that in his written replies to ʿAbd al-Malik, ʿUrwa incorporated a number of *ḥadīths* into a single continuous narrative, and that for such accounts he provided no *isnād*. And let us recall that ʿUrwa was among the foremost of the *tābiʿūn*, that rules on the *isnād* had not yet crystallized, and that it was deemed a reliable course of action to take an account—particularly a historical one—directly from a *tābiʿ*.

Alongside oral narratives, ʿUrwa also paid heed to written documents, quoting many of the letters, cited above, which the Prophet sent to various places—this is an important aspect of ʿUrwa's approach to historical writing. Similarly, he cites the Qur'ānic verses pertaining to the events he describes, as in his discussion of the Hijra,[89] his explanation of the Muslims' frame of mind as they set out for Badr,[90] and his exposition on the conflict with Qaynuqāʿ.[91] Likewise, he explains for Ibn Abī Hunayda, the secretary of al-Walīd, the historical circumstances behind the Qur'ānic verse, "O ye who believe, when believing women come to you as emigrants . . . (it is to God) to judge among you, and God is knowing and wise." He elucidates an important aspect of this passage, the emigration of certain women, desirous of converting to Islam, from Mecca to Medina after the negotiations at al-Ḥudaybiya, and the Prophet's position concerning them.[92] This attests to the early connection between history and Qur'ānic exegesis;

[87] Al-Ṭabarī, *Ta'rīkh*, I, 1147, 1154, 1185, 1237, 1331, 1454, 1534, 1808, 1809, 1813, 1825, 1835, 2128, 2251.

[88] *Ibid.*, I, 1140, 1167, 1173, 1199, 1296, 1360, 1463, 1518, 1610, 1617, 1654, 1670, 1836, 2085, 2125, 2307, 2522.

[89] *Ibid.*, I, 1224.

[90] *Ibid.*, I, 1284.

[91] *Ibid.*, I, 1360.

[92] Ibn Hishām, III, 340f. [Wüstenfeld ed., I, ii, 754f. The verse is Sūrat al-Mumtaḥana (LX), 10.]

eventually it became common practice to cite Qur'ānic verses as evidence in *maghāzī* writings.

The worth of an account depended on the reliability of the narrator, or *rāwī*, who transmitted it. 'Urwa took material from the most trusted authorities. His best-known source, and the one from whom most of his *ḥadīth* derive, was 'Ā'isha, the importance of whose *ḥadīth*s was well known to him.[93] He also gives reports on the authority of the Zubayrids,[94] and of such others as Usāma ibn Zayd,[95] 'Abd Allāh ibn 'Amr ibn al-'Āṣ,[96] and Abū Dharr.[97] This emphasis on the *ḥadīth* scholar accounts for the presence of only a faint folkloric echo in what he reported. For example, he relates on the authority of 'Ā'isha that "when the Negus died it was said that there would always be light on his tomb."[98] In this case we see 'Urwa's concern for accuracy in his account, since he exercises caution and says *kāna yutaḥaddathu*, "it was said." Another example we find when he tells of the Muslims' capture and questioning of the Quraysh water-bearers before Badr, saying, "They alleged (*za'amū*) that the Prophet said . . . , etc."[99]

In his accounts 'Urwa does quote some poetry, albeit little, recited by participants in the events concerned, such as the verses spoken by Waraqa ibn Nawfal when he saw Bilāl being tortured in the burning heat,[100] and by Abū Bakr and Bilāl when they were afflicted by fever after the Hijra.[101] Poetry being a fundamental element of both culture and narrative, it appears that this was characteristic of the Medinan milieu. And

[93] See al-Dhahabī, *Tarājim*, p. 46. Cf. also al-Ṭabarī, *Ta'rīkh*, I, 1147, on the beginning of revelation; I, 1334ff., on the Hijra; I, 1262, 1547, on some of the marriages of the Prophet.

[94] Al-Ṭabarī, *Ta'rīkh*, I, 2348, 3207; II, 811.

[95] Ibn Hishām, II, 236, 237 [Wüstenfeld ed., I, i, 412, 413].

[96] Al-Ṭabarī, *Ta'rīkh*, I, 1185.

[97] *Ibid.*, I, 1154.

[98] See Ibn Hishām, II, 51 [Wüstenfeld ed., I, i, 271f.], on the story of those who mocked the Prophet.

[99] Al-Ṭabarī, *Ta'rīkh*, I, 1288.

[100] *Aghānī*, III, 15 [Bulaq ed., III, 14].

[101] Al-Balādhurī, *Futūḥ al-buldān*, p. 25 [de Goeje ed., pp. 11f.].

as Abū l-Zinād said of him, "I never saw anyone who related more poetry than ʿUrwa."[102]

ʿUrwa's style is a lucid and direct one, vigorous and smooth, and far removed from exaggeration or effort to influence the reader's opinion. He sometimes leads into an event with an introduction which places it in its historical context and produces a continuous, uninterrupted narrative. We see him doing this in his discussion of the battle of Badr, which he prefaces by calling attention to the beginning of hostilities between the Muslims and Quraysh,[103] and also in his account of the Hijra to Abyssinia, which he introduces by recalling the development of relations between the Muslims and Quraysh since the beginning of the Prophet's call.[104] He gives a similar introduction for his account of the Hijra to Medina.[105] It is noteworthy that the continuity of his discussion, in both its vitality and its fluid style, proceeds without interruption in his written essays.

We can see from the foregoing that historical studies began with very close ties to the study of *ḥadīth*, even derived from it, and that in both form and structure the style of the historical account was that of the *ḥadīth*. It can be said that ʿUrwa offered us a vital realistic image, without exaggeration, of Muslim experiences and accomplishments. It appears that the historical conception behind such study was to set out the important historical circumstances and events in the lives of the Prophet and the early Muslims, and involved a recognition of the importance of both the *sīra* and the experience of the *umma*. By the same token, we sense from the queries set by the Umayyad court that interest in the *maghāzī* was not lim-

[102] Al-Dhahabī, *Tarājim*, p. 46. When it was said to ʿUrwa, "What a great amount you recite, O Abū ʿAbd Allah!" he replied, "What is mine compared to that of ʿĀʾisha? No subject ever passed her way without her reciting poetry about it."

[103] Al-Ṭabarī, *Taʾrīkh*, I, 1284.

[104] *Ibid.*, I, 1180f.

[105] *Ibid.*, I, 1224f.

ited to the learned, but rather was representative of a more general social and cultural appeal.

ʿUrwa's work was extremely important, for by gathering so many historical *ḥadīth*s into the *maghāzī*, laying part of the groundwork for historical studies, and articulating a historical conception of considerable influence, he placed the study of history on its own firm and independent foundations. As one might expect, neither the course followed by historical research, nor its structure, are clear at this early stage. But what ʿUrwa began al-Zuhrī brought to fruition, in a way which now calls for our attention.

II.

The primary role in the rise of the historical school of Medina belongs to Abū Bakr Muḥammad ibn Muslim ibn ʿUbayd Allāh ibn ʿAbd Allāh ibn Shihāb al-Zuhrī, for it was he who placed it on solid foundations and elaborated its approach to the study of history. Studying him is thus important from this point of view; and from another, it enables us to establish whether the origins of the *maghāzī* go back to the folkloric *qiṣaṣ* tales, as some believe,[106] or to the serious studies undertaken by *ḥadīth* scholars and their students.

The date of al-Zuhrī's death is almost certain, since the sources consistently give it as 17 Ramaḍān 124/742.[107] As one might expect, the date of his birth is disputed. According to various reports it was A.H. 50, 51, 56, or 58;[108] but both al-Zubayr

[106] See *EI*[1], IV, 441 (G. Levi Della Vida).

[107] Al-Bukhārī, *Al-Taʾrīkh al-kabīr*, I, i, 221; Ibn Qutayba, *Maʿārif*, p. 239 [ʿUkāsha ed., p. 472]; Ibn al-Jawzī, *Ṣafwat al-ṣafwa*, II, 79; al-Yāfiʿī, *Mirʾāt al-janān*, I, 260; al-Dhahabī/Fischer, p. 435. Both al-Dhahabī (*Tarājim*, p. 73) and Ibn Kathīr (*Al-Bidāya wa-l-nihāya*, IX, 344) give the alternative dates of A.H. 123 and 125, but confirm 124. Cf. also *Aghānī*, VI, 106.

[108] Ibn al-Jawzī, *Ṣafwat al-ṣafwa*, II, 79; Ibn Khallikān, *Wafayāt al-aʿyān* (Cairo, A.H. 1310), I, 452 [ʿAbbās ed., IV, 178]; al-Dhahabī, *Tarājim*, p. 73; *idem, Tadhkirat al-ḥuffāẓ*, I, 102; Ibn Kathīr, *Al-Bidāya wa-l-nihāya*, IX, 344 (al-Wāqidī making it A.H. 58).

ibn Bakkār[109] and al-Wāqidī, in one of his reports,[110] state that he lived to the age of 72, making it probable that he was born about 51/671.[111]

Al-Zuhrī studied under some of the foremost scholars of *ḥadīth*, four of whom—Saʿīd ibn al-Musayyab,[112] Abān ibn ʿUthmān,[113] ʿUbayd Allāh ibn ʿAbd Allāh ibn ʿUtba,[114] and ʿUrwa ibn al-Zubayr—he held in special esteem and regard and very frequently quoted. He considered them the "four seas" of knowledge,[115] and it is reported that he mastered their learning and added to it studies of his own.[116]

Al-Zuhrī was renowned for his strong memory—a very important asset in his day—and tried to fortify it by taking honey syrup.[117] More important to us is his concern to record his notes and the *ḥadīth* he heard on slates (*alwāḥ*) and sheets (*ṣuḥuf*) in order to aid his memory. Indeed, his contemporaries were acutely aware of this point and considered his habit of setting material down in writing to be a fundamental reason for his ascendancy in learning over the other men of his age. One account has it that he used to write down everything he heard, and according to another he used to write down

[109] Ibn Kathīr, *Al-Bidāya wa-l-nihāya*, IX, 344.

[110] Al-Dhahabī/Fischer, p. 435.

[111] For general information on al-Zuhrī, see Ibn Saʿd, IV, i, 92; V, 158; Ibn Qutayba, *Maʿārif*, p. 239 [ʿUkāsha ed., p. 472]; Abū Nuʿaym, *Ḥilyat al-awliyāʾ*, I, 370f.; Ibn al-Jawzī, *Ṣafwat al-ṣafwa*, II, 78; Ibn Khallikān, *Wafayāt al-aʿyān*, I, 451 [ʿAbbās ed., IV, 178]; Ibn al-Athīr, *Al-Kāmil fī l-taʾrīkh*, II, 119 [Tornberg ed., V, 195]; al-Dhahabī, *Tarājim*, pp. 64ff.; *idem, Tadhkirat al-ḥuffāẓ*, I, 105; Ibn Kathīr, *Al-Bidāya wa-l-nihāya*, IX, 340ff.; [Horovitz, "Biographies," II, 33ff.; *EI*[1], IV, 1239ff. (J. Horovitz); Petersen, *ʿAlī and Muʿāwiya*, pp. 36f.; Rosenthal, *Muslim Historiography*, pp. 130ff.; Abbott, *Studies*, I, 17ff.; II, 21ff.; *GAS*, I, 280ff.; Azmi, *Studies*, pp. 278f.].

[112] He attended Saʿīd's sessions for 6-10 years. See al-Dhahabī, *Tarājim*, p. 67; [Abū Zurʿa, *Taʾrīkh*, I, 411, 412].

[113] See al-Bukhārī, *Al-Taʾrīkh al-kabīr*, I, i, 451.

[114] See *Aghānī*, VIII, 92, 93.

[115] *Ibid.*, VIII, 93; [Abū Zurʿa, *Taʾrīkh*, I, 407].

[116] *Ibid.*, VIII, 92; Ibn Ḥajar, *Tahdhīb al-tahdhīb*, VII, 65.

[117] Al-Dhahabī, *Tarājim*, p. 70. Cf. also al-Bukhārī, *Al-Taʾrīkh al-kabīr*, I, i, 221; Ibn al-Jawzī, *Ṣafwat al-ṣafwa*, II, 77f.

traditions (*sunan*) of the Prophet and "what came down concerning his Companions."[118]

For his studies on the *maghāzī* al-Zuhrī depended primarily on ʿUrwa ibn al-Zubayr. He studied with him, apparently for a fairly long time, regarded him with particular esteem, and referred to him as "an inexhaustible sea."[119] Al-Bukhārī refers to al-Zuhrī's composition of a work on the *maghāzī* in saying, "We were told by . . . Mūsā ibn ʿUqba from Ibn Shihāb, who said, 'These are the *maghāzī* of the Apostle of God,' and then related the *ḥadīth*."[120] Al-Sakhāwī further reports that al-Zuhrī reported the *maghāzī* from ʿUrwa.[121] Ḥājjī Khalīfa spoke of the *Maghāzī* of al-Zuhrī, and said, "And among them (i.e., *maghāzī* works) was the *Maghāzī* of Muḥammad ibn Muslim al-Zuhrī."[122] We might additionally note that in those parts of al-Zuhrī's *Maghāzī* that have come down to us, the accounts of ʿUrwa figure as the primary source. He also frequently quotes Saʿīd ibn al-Musayyab,[123] ʿUbayd Allāh ibn ʿAbd Allāh ibn ʿUtba,[124] and many others as well.[125]

[118] Al-Samʿānī, *Kitāb al-ansāb*, published in facsimile by D. S. Margoliouth (Leiden, 1912), p. 281; al-Dhahabī, *Tarājim*, p. 68; Ibn Ḥajar, *Tahdhīb al-tahdhīb*, VII, 68; Ibn Kathīr, *Al-Bidāya wa-l-nihāya*, IX, 342; [and much earlier, Abū Zurʿa, *Ta'rīkh*, I, 412].

[119] Al-Bukhārī, *Al-Ta'rīkh al-kabīr*, IV, 32; Abū Nuʿaym, *Ḥilyat al-awliyā'*, III, 360; al-Dhahabī, *Tarājim*, p. 45; Ibn Ḥajar, *Tahdhīb al-tahdhīb*, VII, 65.

[120] Al-Bukhārī, *Ṣaḥīḥ* (Cairo, A.H. 1296), V, 14.

[121] *Al-Iʿlān bi-l-tawbīkh*, p. 88; see also Ibn Sayyid al-Nās, *ʿUyūn al-athar*, I, 81.

[122] *Kashf al-zunūn*, II, 1747.

[123] Al-Wāqidī, *Maghāzī* (the complete but unpublished text edited by Professor Jones from the British Museum manuscript), pp. 151, 219, 421, 436, 562, 828, 869, 1025 [Jones ed., I, 103, 110, 111, 250; II, 477, 491, 505, 621, 696, 715, 865; III, 890, 945]; al-Balādhurī, *Ansāb al-ashrāf*, V, 25, 27, 67, 96 [ʿAbbās ed., IV, i, 512, 514, 556, 590]; al-Ṭabarī, *Ta'rīkh*, I, 1815.

[124] Al-Wāqidī, *Maghāzī* (Jones MS), pp. 383, 519, 657, 816 [Jones ed., II, 435, 576, 695, 717, 871; III, 890]; al-Ṭabarī, *Ta'rīkh*, I, 1834.

[125] E.g., Ibn Kaʿb ibn Mālik (al-Wāqidī, *Maghazi*, Jones MS, pp. 162, 208 [Jones ed., I, 184, 236; II, 509, 535]; Ibn Sayyid al-Nās, *ʿUyūn al-athar*, I, 231), Anas ibn Mālik (al-Ṭabarī, *Ta'rīkh*, I, 1829), Muḥammad ibn Jubayr ibn Muṭʿim (al-Wāqidī, Jones MS, p. 381 [Jones ed., I, 110; II, 795]; Ibn

It seems that in Medina al-Zuhrī undertook a wide-ranging study of the *ḥadīth* of the Prophet and his Companions, aided in this endeavor by his social position, his strong memory, and his reliance on writing. Rather than limit his studies and queries to *ḥadīth* scholars, he questioned anyone who might have known *ḥadīth* materials or other accounts and who had a reputation for being trustworthy. To this end he used to attend sessions and visit people in their homes. Al-Dhahabī says, "Ibrāhīm ibn Saʿd said, 'I once said to my father, "In what respects did al-Zuhrī surpass the rest of you?" He replied, "He used to come to the sessions by the front way rather than from the back, and there would remain in the session not a single man, old or young, whom he had not queried. He would also come to the house of one of the Anṣār, and again, there would remain not a soul, old man or young, aged woman or younger, whom he had not queried. He even tried to ask questions of young ladies in their private quarters." ' "[126]

An investigation of his great reputation as a jurist and scholar of *ḥadīth* is not what concerns us here;[127] rather we will confine our inquiry to his work as a historian. It will suffice for us to recall some of what was said concerning him. He was "the depository of the learning of the seven jurists" and "had no equal among men," as Mālik ibn Anas said. ʿUmar ibn ʿAbd al-ʿAzīz said that "there remained no one more learned

---

Sayyid al-Nās, *ʿUyūn al-athar*, I, 30), Ibn ʿAbbās (al-Ṭabarī, *Taʾrīkh*, I, 1569; Ibn Sayyid al-Nās, *ʿUyūn al-athar*, II, 145), ʿAbd Allāh ibn ʿAmr ibn al-ʿĀṣ (Ibn Hishām, I, i, 412), Abū Salama ibn ʿAbd al-Raḥmān ibn ʿAwf (al-Wāqidī, Jones MS, p. 754 [Jones ed., II, 865; III, 1103]; al-Ṭabarī, *Taʾrīkh*, I, 1019; Ibn Sayyid al-Nās, *ʿUyūn al-athar*, I, 142), Mālik ibn Aws al-Ḥadathān (al-Wāqidī, Jones MS, pp. 249, 363 [Jones ed., I, 413]).

[126] Al-Dhahabī, *Tarājim*, p. 69.

[127] Ibn al-Jawzī, *Ṣafwat al-ṣafwa*, II, 77ff.; Abū Nuʿaym, *Ḥilyat al-awliyāʾ*, III, 360f.; al-Dhahabī, *Tarājim*, pp. 68, 70; *idem, Tadhkirat al-ḥuffāẓ*, I, 104, 105; Ibn Kathīr, *Al-Bidāya wa-l-nihāya*, IX, 342, 343; Horovitz ["Biographies," II, 33ff.], *Al-Maghāzī al-ūlā*.

than he on Islamic practice (*sunna*)," and Ibrāhīm ibn Saʿd related from his father that al-Zuhrī gathered together knowledge which no one before him had ever collected. ʿAbd al-Raḥmān ibn Abī l-Zinād said that in his father's opinion, al-Zuhrī was "the most learned of all men."[128] This serves to indicate his enormous prestige and influence.

Al-Ṭabarī summarizes the role of al-Zuhrī the historian by saying, "Muḥammad ibn Muslim al-Zuhrī was foremost in knowledge of the *maghāzī* of the Apostle of God—may the blessing and peace of God be upon him—and *akhbār* about Quraysh and the Anṣār, a great transmitter of narratives about the Apostle of God—may the blessing and peace of God be upon him—and his Companions."[129] We will now turn to his historical studies, beginning with the *Maghāzī*.

It appears that al-Zuhrī's studies dealt with the life of the Prophet, beginning with certain events preceding the rise of Islam, some of them concerning the Prophet, then continuing on to his life in Mecca and later Medina. Al-Sakhāwī (d. 902/1497) states that Ḥajjāj ibn Abī Manīʿ (d. after 216/831) transmitted the *maghāzī* on the authority of al-Zuhrī,[130] and Ḥājjī Khalīfa confirms that al-Zuhrī did write a book on this subject.[131] Al-Zuhrī used the term *sīra*[132] as well as *maghāzī*,[133] but the former does not appear as a title for his work.

Of al-Zuhrī's *Maghāzī* we have only selections, found primarily in the works of Ibn Isḥāq, al-Wāqidī, al-Ṭabarī, al-Balādhurī, and Ibn Sayyid al-Nās. The pages below attempt

[128] See al-Bukhārī, *Al-Taʾrīkh al-kabīr*, I, i, 621; [Abū Zurʿa, *Taʾrīkh*, I, 411]; Ibn al-Jawzī, *Ṣafwat al-ṣafwa*, II, 77; al-Yāfiʿī, *Mirʾāt al-janān*, I, 261; al-Dhahabī, *Tarājim*, pp. 68, 72; Ibn Kathīr, *Al-Bidāya wa-l-nihāya*, IX, 342.

[129] Al-Ṭabarī, *Al-Muntakhab min kitāb dhayl al-mudhayyal* (Cairo, A.H. 1336), p. 97.

[130] *Al-Iʿlān bi-l-tawbīkh*, p. 88.

[131] *Kashf al-ẓunūn*, II, 1747.

[132] *Aghānī*, XIX, 59.

[133] Al-Ṭabarī, *Muntakhab*, p. 97.

to place these selections within their historical framework so that we may formulate an approximate idea of the structure of this *maghāzī* work:[h]

I. THE PRE-ISLAMIC ERA

1. The day (Friday) on which Adam was created, the day he entered Paradise, and the day he was expelled from it; an account of various dates from Adam's fall to earth until the call of the Prophet.[134]

2. An account of Noah, the propagation of his sons and descendants on the earth, and its division among them.[135]

3. Chronology of the descendants of Ishmael (i.e., the Arabs), beginning with the fire of Abraham, to the Year of the Elephant, and ending with the establishment of the Hijra dating system.[136]

4. *Akhbār* on some of the Prophets;[137] God's call to Moses, His mention of Muḥammad and his *umma* to him;[138] Moses and Khaḍir;[139] the sickness of Job;[140] account (from Ka'b al-Aḥbār) of Abraham's vow to sacrifice his son Isaac, and Satan's effort to thwart the plan.[141]

These fragments indicate al-Zuhrī's interest in narratives on past prophets. We do not know whether they were actually part of his *Maghāzī*, but this seems unlikely.

[h] [Cf. also al-Ṣan'ānī, *Al-Musannaf*, edited by Ḥabīb al-Rahmān Al-A'zamī (Beirut, 1390-92/1970-72), III, 311ff. This very long section reports the *Maghāzī* of al-Zuhrī in the recension of Ma'mar ibn Rāshid and adds much to our knowledge.]

[134] Al-Ṭabarī, *Ta'rīkh*, I, 112.

[135] *Ibid.*, I, 200f.

[136] *Ibid.*, I, 1253.

[137] Abū Nu'aym, *Ḥilyat al-awliyā'*, III, 372; Ibn Kathīr, *Al-Bidāya wa-l-nihāya*, IX, 348.

[138] Abū Nu'aym, *Ḥilyat al-awliyā'*, III, 375.

[139] Al-Bukhārī, *Ṣaḥīḥ*, I, 27; al-Ṭabarī, *Ta'rīkh*, I, 419.

[140] Abū Nu'aym, *Ḥilyat al-awliyā'*, III, 374.

[141] Al-Ṭabarī, *Ta'rīkh*, I, 293.

5. Some accounts concerning Āmina bint Wahb when she was pregnant with the Prophet;[142] the death of ʿAbd Allāh ibn ʿAbd al-Muṭṭalib while staying with his maternal uncles in Yathrib.[143]

6. Al-Sakhāwī[144] mentions that Yūnus ibn Yazīd (d. 159/775) transmitted from al-Zuhrī the *mashāhid al-Nabī*, or the events the Prophet witnessed prior to Islam, such as the rebuilding of the Kaʿba and the *Ḥilf al-fuḍūl*.[1] Al-Zuhrī rejects the claim that Muḥammad participated in the war of al-Fijār,[145] and this account in essence confirms the testimony of al-Sakhāwī.

7. Khadīja bint Khuwaylid concludes an agreement with Muḥammad ibn ʿAbd Allāh for him to lead her caravan to Syria; their marriage and Muḥammad's age at the time.[146]

8. Al-Zuhrī also gives accounts on the signs, *dalā'il*, of Muḥammad's prophethood, among them accounts of an angel warning Chosroes,[147] and of a soothsayer relating a warning from his master about the end of paganism. Similarly, he attributes to ʿUmar ibn al-Khaṭṭāb a report concerning one of these supernatural phenomena.[148]

II. ERA OF MUḤAMMAD'S PROPHETIC MISSION

A. The Meccan Period

1. The beginning of Qur'ānic revelation—the first signs, "true vision" (*al-ru'yā al-ṣādiqa*), devotions (*taḥannuth*) in

[142] Ibn Sayyid al-Nās, *ʿUyūn al-athar*, I, 25.
[143] *Ibid.*; Ibn al-Athīr, *Al-Kāmil fī l-ta'rīkh*, II, 6 [Tornberg ed., II, 6].
[144] *Al-Iʿlān bi-l-tawbīkh*, p. 88.
[1] [A famous pact concluded between a number of Quraysh clans, probably about A.D. 605. The specific details concerning this pact are much disputed; see *EI*[2], III, 389 (C. Pellat).]
[145] Ibn al-Athīr, *Al-Kāmil fī l-ta'rīkh*, I, 443.
[146] Al-Ṭabarī, *Ta'rīkh*, I, 1154; Ibn Sayyid al-Nās, *ʿUyūn al-athar*, I, 47, 50.
[147] Al-Ṭabarī, *Ta'rīkh*, I, 1014.
[148] *Ibid.*, I, 1145.

seclusion, descent of first revelation (*nuzūl al-waḥy*); the Prophet's agitation and his return to Khadīja, who takes him to Waraqa ibn Nawfal, Waraqa's words; how the Prophet first knew that God had chosen him for His mission;[149] the first and last verses of the Qur'ān to be revealed;[150] interruption of revelation for a time, and the Prophet's anxiety over this;[151] the first Muslims.[152]

2. An idea of the Quraysh attitude towards the Prophet's preaching and other activities;[153] he tries during festivals to spread his message among such other tribes as Kinda and Banū ʿĀmir ibn Ṣaʿṣaʿa, but without success.[154]

3. The Night Journey (*Al-Isrāʾ*) and Muhammad's ascent through the seven heavens (*Al-Miʿrāj*).[155]

4. The Hijra to Abyssinia—the first to emigrate; attitude of the Negus towards the Muslims; Quraysh sends a delegation to persuade the Negus to hand over the Muslims; failure of the delegation; other details concerning the Negus.[156]

5. The Quraysh boycott of Banū Hāshim and Banū ʿAbd al-Muṭṭalib (al-Zuhrī under a collective *isnād*);[157] death of Abū Ṭālib.[158]

149 Ibn Hishām, I, 249 [Wüstenfeld ed., I, i, 150f.]; al-Bukhārī, *Ṣaḥīḥ*, I, 115; al-Ṭabarī, *Taʾrīkh*, I, 1147f., 1154; Ibn Sayyid al-Nās, *ʿUyūn al-athar*, I, 84f.

150 Al-Ṭabarī, *Taʾrīkh*, I, 1155; Ibn al-Nadīm, *Fihrist*, p. 25; Ibn Sayyid al-Nās, *ʿUyūn al-athar*, I, 88.

151 Al-Ṭabarī, *Taʾrīkh*, I, 1155; Ibn Sayyid al-Nās, *ʿUyūn al-athar*, I, 85.

152 Al-Ṭabarī, *Taʾrīkh*, I, 1167; Ibn Sayyid al-Nās, *ʿUyūn al-athar*, I, 91.

153 Ibn Hishām, I, i, 203. See Ibn Sayyid al-Nās, *ʿUyūn al-athar*, I, 111f.

154 Ibn Hishām, I, i, 282, 283; al-Ṭabarī, *Taʾrīkh*, I, 1205f., 1213.

155 Ibn Hishām, II, 41 [Wüstenfeld ed., I, i, 266]; al-Bukhārī, *Ṣaḥīḥ*, IV, 99, 116, 130; Ibn Sayyid al-Nās, *ʿUyūn al-athar*, I, 142, 145, 148.

156 Ibn Hishām, I, i, 217ff., 222f.; Ibn Sayyid al-Nās, *ʿUyūn al-athar*, I, 115, 126, 292.

157 Ibn Sayyid al-Nās, *ʿUyūn al-athar*, I, 126f.

158 *Ibid.*, I, 131f.

6. The pledge of al-ʿAqaba—text of the pledge; beginnings of Islam in Medina.[159]

B. The Medinan Period

1. Discussion of the Hijra to Medina and the affair of Surāqa ibn Jasham;[160] the Muslims await the Prophet; circumstances and date of his arrival; building of the mosque of Medina;[161] effect of the city's weather on the Muhājirūn and the affliction of some of them by fever.[162]

2. The expedition of ʿAbd Allāh ibn Jaḥsh; number and identity of the participants;[163] the Prophet's view of the attack on the caravan.[164]

3. Some information on the Jews' view of the Prophet;[165] attitude of ʿAbd Allāh ibn Ubayy (rude and hostile);[166] reorientation of the *qibla* towards the Kaʿba;[167] fasting enjoined as a religious obligation, and the date for this; *zakāt al-fiṭr* also enjoined.[168]

4. Expedition of Badr—al-Zuhrī's account appears under a collective *isnād*;[169] other details pertaining to Badr: the vision of ʿĀtika bint ʿAbd al-Muṭṭalib about the Quraysh

[159] Al-Bukhārī, *Ṣaḥīḥ*, IV, 243; al-Ṭabarī, *Taʾrīkh*, I, 1213; Ibn Sayyid al-Nās, *ʿUyūn al-athar*, I, 157f.

[160] Ibn Hishām, I, i, 231f.

[161] Al-Ṭabarī, *Taʾrīkh*, I, 1250, 1256; Ibn Sayyid al-Nās, *ʿUyūn al-athar*, I, 185f. See also al-Bukhārī, *Ṣaḥīḥ*, IV, 245f., 256ff.; V, 43.

[162] Ibn Hishām, I, i, 414f.

[163] Al-Ṭabarī, *Taʾrīkh*, I, 1273.

[164] Al-Wāqidī, *Maghāzī* (Cairo), p. 10 [Jones ed., I, 18]; Ibn Sayyid al-Nās, *ʿUyūn al-athar*, I, 229.

[165] Ibn Hishām, I, i, 393f.

[166] *Ibid.*, I, ii, 591.

[167] Ibn Sayyid al-Nās, *ʿUyūn al-athar*, I, 221, 236.

[168] *Ibid.*, I, 239. [The *zakāt al-fiṭr* is an obligatory charitable donation of provisions to be made at the end of the fasting month of Ramaḍān. See *EI*[1], IV, 1204 (J. Schacht).]

[169] Al-Ṭabarī, *Taʾrīkh*, 1291ff.; *Aghānī*, IV, 170ff. [Bulaq ed., IV, 17ff.].

caravan;[170] Īmā' ibn Raḥḍa offers Quraysh ten camels and indicates his willingness to render further assistance; ʿUmayr ibn Wahb, a Quraysh spy, reports on the discipline of the Muslims and advises Quraysh to avoid a fight, but although ʿUtba ibn Rabīʿa supports this, Abū Jahl interrupts and rejects the advice, and the encounter with the Muslims begins; Abū Jahl's curse upon seeing the Muslims; the Prophet sees Quraysh approaching, his prayers and curse upon them;[171] other details,[172] including mention of the first Muslim martyr and the first martyr from each Muslim group; the Prophet inspects the field of battle; the numbers of those killed among the Muslims and Quraysh; the time when the Quraysh prisoners were brought forth, and the Prophet's inclination to deal leniently with them.[173].

5. The raid of al-Sawīq and its date.[174]

6. Deterioration of relations with the Jews and the outbreak of conflict with them; al-Aws kill Kaʿb ibn al-Ashraf;[175] al-Aws and al-Khazraj compete to gain the Prophet's favor, and al-Khazraj kill the Jew Ibn Abī l-Ḥuqayq;[176] fearfulness of the Jews, and the implementation of the famous *kitāb*.[177]

7. The conflict with Banū Qaynuqāʿ as a result of the revelation of the verse, "And if thou fearest treachery from

[170] Al-Ṭabarī, *Ta'rīkh*, I, 1212.

[171] Al-Wāqidī, *Maghāzī* (Cairo), pp. 43, 45f., 50, also the Jones MS, pp. 52f., 56f., 131; al-Ṭabarī, *Ta'rīkh*, I, 1322f.

[172] Al-Wāqidī, *Maghāzī* (Cairo), pp. 62, 82, and the Jones MS, p. 101.

[173] *Ibid.*, pp. 89, 109, 110f., and the Jones MS, pp. 107f. [For al-Wāqidī's quotations from al-Zuhrī on Badr, see now Jones' edition of the *Maghāzī*, I, 34f., 59f., 60, 62ff., 70, 91ff., 103, 110, 110f., 116, 119, 144, 145f., 152f., 156.]

[174] *Ibid.*, p. 142, and the Jones MS, pp. 159f. [Jones ed., I, 181f.].

[175] *Ibid.*, pp. 144f., and the Jones MS, p. 162 [Jones ed., I, 184ff.].

[176] Al-Ṭabarī, *Ta'rīkh*, I, 1378f.

[177] Al-Wāqidī, *Maghāzī* (Cairo), p. 151 [Jones ed., I, 191f.].

a people, cast them out in like measure"; details on the campaign, its date, and the treatment of Banū Qaynuqā'.[178]

8. Other raids and expeditions—the raid to Qarārat al-Kudr against Banū Sulaym and Ghaṭafān 22 months after the Hijra;[179] the dispatch of an expedition against Banū Sulaym in Buḥrān 27 months after the Hijra.[180]

9. Battle of Uḥud—al-Zuhrī's account under a collective *isnād*;[181] Muslim deliberations on whether to stay in Medina or set out to meet Quraysh;[182] opinion of 'Abd Allāh ibn Abī Salūl (Ibn Ubayy);[183] withdrawal of the "hypocrites" (*munāfiqūn*) and the numbers of the Muslims; the fighting, circulation of the rumor that the Prophet had been killed, then one of the Muslims sees him after the battle;[184] Ubayy ibn Khalaf, of Quraysh, tries to kill the Prophet, but Muḥammad outfights and kills him;[185] details on the martyrdom of Ḥamza ibn 'Abd al-Muṭṭalib;[186] the Prophet inspects the field of battle.[187]

10. Expulsion of Banū l-Naḍīr, a Jewish tribe, from Medina—circumstances of the affair, its date, and the conditions Muḥammad imposed; the possessions of Banū l-Naḍīr

178 *Ibid.*, pp. 139ff., and the Jones MS, pp. 156ff. [Jones ed., I, 177ff.]; al-Ṭabarī, *Ta'rīkh*, I, 1360. [The relevant verse is from Sūrat al-Anfāl (VIII), 58.]

179 Al-Wāqidī, *Maghāzī* (Cairo), p. 143, and the Jones MS, p. 124 [Jones ed., I, 182].

180 *Ibid.*, p. 159 [Jones ed., I, 196f.].

181 Al-Wāqidī, *Maghāzī* (Jones MS), p. 185 [Jones ed., I, 199ff.]; al-Ṭabarī, *Ta'rīkh*, I, 1384ff.; Ibn Sayyid al-Nās, *'Uyūn al-athar*, II, 2ff.

182 Al-Wāqidī, *Maghāzī* (Cairo), pp. 164ff., and the Jones MS, pp. 185f.

183 Ibn Hishām, I, ii, 591.

184 Al-Wāqidī, *Maghāzī* (Cairo), pp. 184ff., and the Jones MS, p. 208; al-Ṭabarī, *Ta'rīkh*, I, 1406; Ibn Sayyid al-Nās, *'Uyūn al-athar*, II, 5, 11f.

185 Al-Wāqidī, *Maghāzī* (Cairo), pp. 185f., and the Jones MS, p. 219; al-Ṭabarī, *Ta'rīkh*, I, 1406f.

186 Al-Wāqidī, *Maghāzī* (Cairo), p. 212.

187 Ibn Hishām, I, ii, 576; al-Wāqidī, *Maghāzī* (Cairo), p. 239 [for the Uḥud accounts from al-Zuhrī, see the Jones ed., I, 209, 236, 250, 286, 310]; Ibn Sayyid al-Nās, *'Uyūn al-athar*, II, 21.

and their variety; the Prophet divides the booty seized from them among the Muslims.[188]

11. Battle of the Ditch—al-Zuhrī's account under a collective *isnād*;[189] difficulty of the Muslim position; the Prophet negotiates with some of the groups besieging Medina, the Anṣār viewpoint opposed to any bargaining; the sole Quraysh attempt to break the Medinan line of defense, and its failure;[190] the Prophet uses the conspiracy of Banū Qurayẓa against the Muslims as a means of provoking suspicions among his enemies; the storms and the end of the siege.[191]

12. The attack on Banū Qurayẓa (the third Jewish tribe of Medina) immediately after the Battle of the Ditch,[192] and the terms to which they submitted;[193] other details.[194]

13. Dispatch of an expedition against Banū Liḥyān (al-Zuhrī in a collective *isnād*).[195]

14. The "Affair of the Lie" (*Ḥadīth al-ifk*).[196]

15. The expedition of Zayd ibn Ḥāritha against Umm Qirfa.[197]

16. The truce of al-Ḥudaybiya—intentions of the Prophet; number of Muslims who set out from Medina with him

[188] Al-Wāqidī, *Maghāzī* (Jones MS), pp. 158ff., 331ff. [Jones ed., I, 180, 378]; Yaḥya ibn Ādam, *Kitāb al-kharāj*, edited by Aḥmad Muḥammad Shākir (Cairo, A.H. 1347), p. 33; al-Balādhurī, *Futūḥ al-buldān*, pp. 18, 20; al-Ṭabarī, *Ta'rīkh*, I, 1451; Ibn Sayyid al-Nās, *'Uyūn al-athar*, II, 48.

[189] Al-Wāqidī, *Maghāzī* (Jones MS), pp. 387ff. [Jones ed., II, 441f.]; al-Ṭabarī, *Ta'rīkh*, I, 1462; Ibn Sayyid al-Nās, *'Uyūn al-athar*, II, 58ff.

[190] Al-Wāqidī, *Maghāzī* (Jones MS), pp. 421ff. [Jones ed., II, 477ff.]; al-Ṭabarī, *Ta'rīkh*, I, 1473.

[191] Al-Wāqidī, *Maghāzī* (Jones MS), pp. 431f., 436 [Jones ed., II, 486f., 491]. See also al-Ṭabarī, *Ta'rīkh*, I, 1475f.

[192] Al-Ṭabarī, *Ta'rīkh*, I, 1485; Ibn Sayyid al-Nās, *'Uyūn al-athar*, II, 68.

[193] Al-Balādhurī, *Futūḥ al-buldān*, p. 22.

[194] Ibn Sayyid al-Nās, *'Uyūn al-athar*, II, 73.

[195] Al-Wāqidī, *Maghāzī* (Jones MS), pp. 480ff. [Jones ed., II, 535ff.].

[196] Al-Bukhārī, *Ṣaḥīḥ*, V, 54, 55f.; al-Ṭabarī, *Ta'rīkh*, I, 1517ff.; Ibn Sayyid al-Nās, *'Uyūn al-athar*, II, 387ff.

[197] Al-Wāqidī, *Maghāzī* (Jones MS), p. 508 [Jones ed., II, 565]; Ibn Sayyid al-Nās, *'Uyūn al-athar*, II, 105f.

(also the number of camels for sacrifice);[198] the Prophet determines the line of march, the Muslims stop at al-Ḥudaybiya; the Prophet indicates a desire for conciliation with Quraysh; reaction of Quraysh and their point of view; the Khuzāʿa, on friendly terms with the Muslims, convey the latter's position to Quraysh;[199] movement of messengers between the two parties, most of them from the Quraysh side, and their impressions of the Muslims; the Prophet speaks in a diplomatic tone, stresses his good intentions, and proposes a truce; Suhayl ibn ʿAmr finally arrives to negotiate for Quraysh, argument over certain words, the final text of the pact and names of the witnesses; other details, including the reluctance of some of the Companions to slaughter the sacrificial animals at al-Ḥudaybiya; al-Zuhrī's comment on the importance and consequences of the truce of al-Ḥudaybiya.[200]

17. Conquest of Khaybar—circumstances and date of the conquest; the agreement with Khaybar and its legal implications; viewpoint of Abū Bakr and ʿUmar on this;[201] an incident on the way to Khaybar;[202] disposal of Fadak; expedition of Mu'ta;[203] some minor expeditions.[204]

198 Ibn Hishām, III, 322 [Wüstenfeld ed., I, ii, 740]; al-Ṭabarī, *Ta'rīkh*, I, 1529; Ibn Sayyid al-Nās, *'Uyūn al-athar*, II, 113.

199 Ibn Hishām, III, 324f. [Wüstenfeld ed., I, ii, 742f.]; al-Wāqidī, *Maghāzī* (Jones MS), pp. 519, 529f. [Jones ed., II, 576f., 586ff.]; al-Ṭabarī, *Ta'rīkh*, I, 1531, 1537; Ibn Sayyid al-Nās, *'Uyūn al-athar*, II, 115.

200 Ibn Hishām, I, ii, 740ff., 747ff.; al-Wāqidī, *Maghāzī* (Jones MS), pp. 565ff., 572f. [Jones ed., II, 621ff., 631ff.]; al-Ṭabarī, *Ta'rīkh*, I, 1549f.; Ibn Sayyid al-Nās, *'Uyūn al-athar*, II, 115ff., 121, 122.

201 Ibn Hishām, I, ii, 779; al-Wāqidī, *Maghāzī* (Jones MS), pp. 634, 657 [Jones ed., II, 695, 696, 697, 715]; al-Balādhurī, *Futūḥ al-buldān*, p. 26; Ibn Sayyid al-Nās, *'Uyūn al-athar*, II, 136, 137.

202 Al-Ṭabarī, *Ta'rīkh*, I, 1575.

203 Ibn Hishām, IV, 25 [Wüstenfeld ed., I, ii, 766f.]; al-Balādhurī, *Futūḥ al-buldān*, p. 59; Ibn Sayyid al-Nās, *'Uyūn al-athar*, II, 138.

204 Raid of al-Qaḍīya, al-Wāqidī, *Maghāzī* (Jones MS), pp. 670ff. (al-Zuhrī in a collective *isnād*) [Jones ed., II, 731]; raid of Ibn Abī l-ʿAwjā' al-Sulamī, *ibid.*, p. 680 [Jones ed., II, 741]—Both of these expeditions occurred in A.H.

18. Conquest of Mecca—al-Zuhrī explains the role of Khuzāʿa as allies and spies for the Prophet,[205] their formal alliance with him after al-Ḥudaybiya, and how the aggression of Bakr and its ally Quraysh against Khuzāʿa created the immediate cause for the campaign;[206] Abū Sufyān goes to Medina to negotiate, but fails; the Prophet's preparations for the campaign;[207] he leaves a deputy in Medina and leads the campaign himself; date of the campaign, numbers in the army, and the Prophet's triumphant entry into Mecca;[208] the rubbing out of the images found inside the Kaʿba, and other decisions; the length of time the Muslims stayed in Mecca after the conquest.[209]

19. Subsequent campaigns—the expedition against Hawāzin; Muslim confidence in their great numbers; story of Dhāt Anwāṭ;[210] confusion of the Muslims during the battle, the Prophet's appeal to the Anṣār and their response, critical period in the fighting and the Prophet's prayer, the victory;[211] division of the spoils and release of the captives;[212] the expedition against Tabūk—al-Zuhrī in a collective *isnād*;[213] individual details;[214] the *jizya* imposed on Ayla, Adhruḥ, Adhriʿāt,[215] Tabāla, and Jurash;[216] the expedition

7; a raid on Dhāt al-Aṭlāḥ in A.H. 8, Ibn Sayyid al-Nās, *'Uyūn al-athar*, II, 152; [al-Wāqidī, *Maghāzī*, Jones ed., II, 752f.].

205 Ibn Hishām, I, ii, 747ff.

206 Al-Ṭabarī, *Ta'rīkh*, I, 1620; Ibn Sayyid al-Nās, *'Uyūn al-athar*, II, 120.

207 Al-Wāqidī, *Maghāzī* (Jones MS), p. 731 [Jones ed., II, 795f.].

208 Ibn Hishām, I, ii, 810; al-Bukhārī, *Ṣaḥīḥ*, V, 90; al-Wāqidī, *Maghāzī* (Jones MS), p. 818 [Jones ed., II, 889], giving the date of the conquest; al-Ṭabarī, *Ta'rīkh*, I, 1628.

209 Al-Wāqidī, *Maghāzī* (Jones MS), pp. 766, 795 [Jones ed., II, 834, 864, 865], also see pp. 765ff. [II, 834]; al-Ṭabarī, *Ta'rīkh*, I, 1565f.

210 Ibn Hishām, I, ii, 844; al-Wāqidī, *Maghāzī* (Jones MS), pp. 818, 819 [Jones ed., II, 890f.]; Ibn Sayyid al-Nās, *'Uyūn al-athar*, II, 191f.

211 Al-Wāqidī, *Maghāzī* (Jones MS), pp. 826ff. [Jones ed., II, 898ff.]; al-Ṭabarī, *Ta'rīkh*, 1661, 1662; Ibn Sayyid al-Nās, *'Uyūn al-athar*, I, 191.

212 Al-Wāqidī, *Maghāzī* (Jones MS), pp. 869f. [Jones ed., II, 945ff.].

213 Al-Ṭabarī, *Ta'rīkh*, I, 1692. Cf. also al-Bukhārī, *Ṣaḥīḥ*, IV, 99ff., 104f.

214 Ibn Hishām, I, ii, 798; Ibn Sayyid al-Nās, *'Uyūn al-athar*, II, 218.

215 Al-Balādhurī, *Futūḥ al-buldān*, p. 68.

216 *Ibid.*, p. 59.

against Dūmat al-Jandal, and imposition of the *jizya* upon it.[217]

20. Letters and embassies—the visit of Kinda's delegation;[218] the Prophet sends a letter to Heraclius with Diḥya al-Kalbī, details on the subject; al-Zuhri also tells a story about Heraclius' vision and his secret inclination towards Islam, and quotes a bishop to confirm this;[219] the Prophet sends a letter to Chosroes, who tears it up, the Prophet's comment upon hearing the news;[220] Chosroes asks Bādhān, governor of Yemen, to go to the Prophet and demand that he either repent or be killed; Bādhān exchanges letters with the Prophet, and the correspondence ends with Bādhān and the *abnā'* (Persians)[j] accepting Islam when the Prophet's prediction concerning the end of Chosroes is fulfilled.[221]

21. Incidents of unrest—Khālid ibn al-Walīd sent against Banū l-Ḥārith in Najrān and their acceptance of Islam;[222] Tamīm refuses to pay the alms tax (*ṣadaqa*), they are subdued by the Muslims and their delegation comes to Medina.[223]

22. Personal details concerning the Prophet—references to his marriages,[224] and clarification of some of his names.[225]

23. Reference to the Farewell Pilgrimage (*Ḥijjat al-wadā'*) and some information concerning it;[226] perparations for the campaign of Usāma ibn Zayd.[227]

[217] *Ibid.*, p. 63.
[218] Al-Ṭabarī, *Ta'rīkh*, I, 1739.
[219] Al-Bukhārī, *Ṣaḥīḥ*, IV, 2ff.; al-Ṭabarī, *Ta'rīkh*, I, 1565f.
[220] Al-Ṭabarī, *Ta'rīkh*, I, 1572.
[j] [On the *abnā'*, see p. 123, n. b below.]
[221] Ibn Hishām, I, 71f. [Wüstenfeld ed., I, i, 46f.].
[222] Ibn Sayyid al-Nās, *'Uyūn al-athar*, II, 244f.
[223] Al-Wāqidī, *Maghāzī* (Jones MS), pp. 896ff. [Jones ed., III, 973ff.].
[224] Al-Bukhārī, *Ṣaḥīḥ*, V, 17; al-Ṭabarī, *Ta'rīkh*, I, 1776.
[225] Al-Ṭabarī, *Ta'rīkh*, I, 1788. See also al-Bukhārī, *Ṣaḥīḥ*, IV, 162; Ibn Sayyid al-Nās, *'Uyūn al-athar*, I, 30.
[226] Al-Wāqidī, *Maghāzī* (Jones MS), pp. 1001, 1005f. [Jones ed., III, 1092, 1097f.].
[227] *Ibid.*, p. 1025 [Jones ed., III, 1118].

24. Last illness of the Prophet—he senses that the end is near, alludes to this in an address from the *minbar*, and urges the dispatch of Usāma's campaign; al-ʿAbbās asks ʿAlī ibn Abī Ṭālib to accompany him to ask the Prophet who should succeed him, but ʿAlī declines; other details;[228] the Prophet observes the Muslims in the mosque during his last days on earth, and delegates Abū Bakr to lead them in prayer;[229] the last charge of the Prophet and his passage into eternity, date and Muḥammad's age;[230] impact of his death; burial of the Glorious Prophet's mortal remains.[231]

It is clear from this summary review that al-Zuhrī provided the *sīra* with its first distinct framework and clearly sketched out the lines it would follow, leaving his successors to fill out this framework in detail only. His plan for the *Maghāzī* (or *Sīra*) begins with some materials relevant to the life of the Prophet before his mission began, and within this probably gave his genealogy.[232] After referring to some of the signs of the impending prophethood, he passes on to the beginning of Qur'ānic revelation. He then discusses the period of Muḥammad's prophetic career, recounting some of the most important aspects of the Meccan period, the Hijra, the raids and expeditions, such other activities as the embassies and delegations, and finally the Prophet's illness and death.

It appears that al-Zuhrī generally observed the chronological sequence of events. He gives some dates, such as the date of the Hijra, possibly the dates for the battles of Badr, Uḥud, and the Ditch (since his accounts for these appear under collective *isnāds*), and the dates for such expeditions as Qarārat

[228] [Ibn Hishām, I, ii, 1000, 1006, 1007, 1008, 1010f.]; al-Bukhārī, *Ṣaḥīḥ*, IV, 45; V, 137, 139f., 140f.; al-Ṭabarī, *Ta'rīkh*, I, 1800, 1809, 1810; Ibn Sayyid al-Nās, *ʿUyūn al-athar*, II, 336f.

[229] Ibn Hishām, I, ii, 1008ff.; al-Ṭabarī, *Ta'rīkh*, I, 1813.

[230] Al-Bukhārī, *Al-Ta'rīkh al-kabīr*, I, i, 8; al-Ṭabarī, *Ta'rīkh*, I, 1814, 1834f.

[231] Ibn Hishām, IV, 305f. [Wüstenfeld ed., I, ii, 1012f.]; al-Bukhārī, *Ṣaḥīḥ*, IV, 163; al-Ṭabarī, *Ta'rīkh*, I, 1831.

[232] See al-Ṭabarī, *Ta'rīkh*, I, 1116; also pp. 113-14 below.

al-Kudr, Banū Sulaym, Qaynuqā', Banū l-Naḍīr, and Khaybar, the conquest of Mecca, the arrival of the delegation of Kinda, and the death of the Prophet.[233] This concern for providing dates served to stabilize al-Zuhrī's framework for the *sīra*.

Al-Zuhrī's approach is basically that of a scholar of *ḥadīth*.[234] His concern was to acquire *'ilm*, or *ḥadīth* materials, of which historical *ḥadīth* were a part. *'Ilm*, in his view, fills social and spiritual needs, in addition to being an act of faith.[235] Consequently, the one who knows it gains nobility and lofty social status.[236]

Al-Zuhrī's method of verifying *ḥadīth* materials and other accounts relies on the *isnād*.[237] His attitude towards the *isnād* is that of a committed *ḥadīth* scholar of his day: he sometimes considers it sufficient to cite the account of one of the *tābi'ūn*, and allows greater leeway with historical *ḥadīth*s. But al-Zuhrī did make an important contribution when he adopted the collective *isnād*, collecting numerous accounts into a smooth, uninterrupted story preceded by a list of the authorities from whom the original accounts were taken. In this way he took an important step towards continuous historical narrative.[238] Moreover, al-Zuhrī makes many references to Qur'ānic verses pertaining to the narratives he presents.[239] Indeed, the ac-

233 See above, pp. 103-10ff.

234 Al-Dhahabī/Fischer, p. 431; Ibn Kathīr, *Al-Bidāya wa-l-nihāya*, IX, 343.

235 Al-Dhahabī (*Tarājim*, p. 72) quotes al-Zuhrī as saying, "Security lies in adherence to the *sunna*." Cf. Ibn Hishām, I, 79 [Wüstenfeld ed., I, i, 51]; also al-Dhahabī, *Tarājim*, p. 78, where al-Zuhrī says, "There is no way to serve God more virtuously than through learning (*'ilm*),"

236 There is a saying attributed to him and to 'Urwa ibn al-Zubayr, "Learn *'ilm*, and through it become the masters of your people"; al-Bukhārī, *Al-Ta'rīkh al-kabīr*, I, i, 32; al-Dhahabī, *Tarājim*, p. 45.

237 'Amr ibn Dīnār said, "I never saw anyone more precise in transmitting *ḥadīth* than al-Zuhrī"; al-Dhahabī/Fischer, p. 431.

238 See al-Ṭabarī, *Ta'rīkh*, I, 1517; Ibn Sayyid al-Nās, *'Uyūn al-athar*, II, 96.

239 See al-Wāqidī, *Maghāzī* (Jones MS), pp. 156f., 562ff. [Jones ed., I, 177; II, 621ff.]; Ibn Sayyid al-Nās, *'Uyūn al-athar*, II, 96ff., 121.

counts of al-Wāqidī quoted from al-Zuhrī clearly demonstrate that the study of the Qur'ān, which is full of references to Muslim affairs in Medina, was another factor in the emergence of historical studies.[240]

In al-Zuhrī's accounts we can see activities attributed to divine inspiration, and also activities based on human initiative, particularly in the details of military campaigns.[241] The concept of divine foreordainment had not yet become the dominant one, and in fact, al-Zuhrī's judgment on the truce of al-Ḥudaybiya implies endorsement of an action which in its own time did not meet with the approval it deserved.[242]

It can be said that al-Zuhrī's accounts generally provide realistic, balanced information on the events they describe, and do so in a style which can be described as candid, unaffected, and concise.[243] In them there are few of the attempts to glorify or exaggerate which are so common among historians of later times. We do sense, however, that the first indications of this tendency are already present in his work.[244] But on the whole, al-Zuhrī's historical data is drawn from *ḥadīth*; popular *qiṣaṣ* tales he regarded as material for entertainment and enjoyment.[245]

It appears that other materials did seep into his historical *akhbār*, but only to a limited extent. The presence of these materials indicates the beginnings of developments which only emerged after the age of al-Zuhrī. There is something of a

240 See al-Wāqidī, *Maghāzī* (Jones MS), pp. 562ff., 572f. [Jones ed., II, 621ff., 631ff.]; Ibn Sayyid al-Nās, *'Uyūn al-athar*, I, 222.

241 Al-Wāqidī, *Maghāzī* (Jones MS), pp. 421f. [Jones ed., II, 486f.]; al-Ṭabarī, *Ta'rīkh*, I, 1473.

242 Al-Ṭabarī, *Ta'rīkh*, I, 1594.

243 See Ibn Hishām, I, ii, 844, on Dhāt Anwāṭ.

244 See al-Ṭabarī, *Ta'rīkh*, I, 1154, 1360, 1485.

245 Al-Dhahabī, *Tarājim*, p. 73, where the author says, "Al-Zuhrī used to relate *ḥadīth*s and then say, 'Tell me your poetry and stories, for the ear is weary, but the soul is still eager.' " See also p. 74; and Ibn Kathīr, *Al-Bidāya wa-l-nihāya*, IX, 343.

trace of popular *qiṣaṣ* lore in certain places, such as his account of Heraclius' view of the new faith,[246] the warning heard by Chosroes,[247] the story of the soothsayer warned by Satan,[248] and details on what happened to Surāqa.[249] Similarly, al-Zuhrī's interest in *akhbār* about past prophets and in the *ahl al-kitāb*[250] left a faint echo of the *Isrā'īliyāt* in his writing, and in such passages Kaʿb al-Aḥbār figures as a source.[251] He also quotes fragments of verse from time to time in his *akhbār*,[252] and this is to be expected when we recall that people were generally very fond of poetry, which was a fundamental element of culture. Al-Zuhrī himself was extremely fond of poetry[253] and renowned for his wide knowledge of it;[254] but there is only a limited amount of it in his *Maghāzī*, and his citation of it provides no indication of any trace of the style of the *ayyām* tales.

The historical studies of al-Zuhrī were not limited to the *maghāzī*, but included genealogy and early Islamic history as well. He was well known for his knowledge of genealogy.[255] Khālid al-Qasrī asked him to set Arab genealogy down in writing, so he began with the genealogies of Muḍar, but never

[246] Al-Ṭabarī, *Ta'rīkh*, I, 1565f.

[247] *Ibid.*, I, 1014.

[248] *Ibid.*, I, 1145.

[249] Ibn Hishām, I, i, 331f.

[250] Ibn al-Jawzī, *Ṣafwat al-ṣafwa*, II, 88: "When he related accounts about the prophets and the *ahl al-kitāb*, you said he excelled in nothing but that. . . ." Cf. also Abū Nuʿaym, *Ḥilyat al-awliyā'*, III, 362; Ibn Kathīr, *Al-Bidāya wa-l-nihāya*, IX, 342.

[251] See al-Tabari, *Ta'rikh*, I, 112, 200f., 293. It seems, however, that such *akhbār* as these were not part of al-Zuhrī's *Maghāzī*.

[252] See al-Wāqidī, *Maghāzī* (Cairo), p. 94, and the Jones MS, pp. 569ff. [Jones ed., II, 586f.]; al-Ṭabarī, *Ta'rīkh*, I, 1652f.

[253] Al-Dhahabī, *Tarājim*, p. 73; Ibn Kathīr, *Al-Bidāya wa-l-nihāya*, IX, 343.

[254] See *Aghānī*, IV, 49.

[255] Abū Nuʿaym, *Ḥilyat al-awliyā'*, III, 361; al-Dhahabī/Fischer, p. 343. Also see Ibn Hishām, I, 7f. [Wüstenfeld ed., I, i, 5]; Ibn al-Jawzī, *Ṣafwat al-ṣafwa*, II, 78, saying, "When he related accounts about the bedouins and genealogies, you said he excelled in nothing but that."

finished the work.[256] Muṣʿab al-Zubayrī cites him in his book *Nasab Quraysh*,[257] and this corroborates Qurra ibn ʿAbd al-Raḥmān's statement that he wrote a book on the genealogy of his people (i.e., Quraysh).[258]

Al-Zuhrī also dealt with the period of the Rāshidūn caliphs, for the great events which played a fundamental role in the development of the *umma*, as also in Medinan tradition, were still live issues when al-Zuhrī studied them. He provides detailed information on the election of Abū Bakr and explains the effect the election had.[259] He then gives Abū Bakr's first address, as well as an idea of his conduct as caliph.[260] After this he presents ʿAlī's view of the election, then his later oath of allegiance, and the request of Fāṭima to inherit Fadak.[261] Of the events associated with the era of ʿUmar ibn al-Khaṭṭāb, he deals in detail with the establishment of the *dīwān* (i.e., of the army), its organization and the stipends paid,[262] and most probably with the *shūrā*.[263] He also gives ʿUmar's age and some of his speeches.[264] He then discusses the caliphate of ʿUthmān in detail. First he takes up the collection of the Qur'ān,[265] and then presents a minutely detailed discussion of the *fitna*—his account of this is important because it represents the Medinan point of view on the subject. In al-Zuhrī's account, ʿUthmān appears as a ruler popular for the first

[256] *Aghānī*, XIX, 59.
[257] *Nasab Quraysh*, p. 3.
[258] Al-Dhahabī, *Tarājim*, p. 68, where Qurra ibn ʿAbd al-Raḥmān is quoted as saying, "Al-Zuhrī had no book other than a book on the genealogy of his people." [This statement is also cited in Abū Zurʿa, *Ta'rīkh*, I, 410.]
[259] Al-Ṭabarī, *Ta'rīkh*, I, 1820ff.; Ibn Hishām, I, ii, 673ff. On the outburst of emotion arising from the death of the Prophet, see al-Ṭabarī, *Ta'rīkh*, I, 1816f.
[260] *Ibid.*, I, 1828f., 2142f.
[261] *Ibid.*, I, 1825ff., and on the death of Abū Bakr, I, 2128.
[262] Al-Balādhurī, *Futūḥ al-buldān*, pp. 450ff., 455.
[263] See al-Balādhurī, *Ansāb al-ashrāf*, V, 21 [ʿAbbās ed., IV, i, 507].
[264] Al-Ṭabarī, *Ta'rīkh*, I, 2731, 2757f.; also see I, 2798.
[265] Ibn al-Nadīm, *Fihrist*, p. 24.

six years of his caliphate, after which complaints began to appear and accumulate.[266] Al-Zuhrī gives a detailed account of the criticisms directed against ʿUthmān,[267] his efforts to respond to them,[268] the pernicious influence of Marwān ibn al-Ḥakam,[269] the dangerous divisions within Medina,[270] the gathering clouds, the storm, and the end of ʿUthmān,[271] the reaction among the major personalities in Medina, and finally the election of ʿAlī.[272] He then presents the attitude of Ṭalḥa and al-Zubayr towards the new caliph, their consultations with ʿĀ'isha, the departure of the three for Basra, their negotiations with ʿAlī prior to the fighting, and finally the Battle of the Camel.[273] After this he takes up the conflict between ʿAlī and Muʿāwiya, the battle of Ṣiffīn, the arbitration between the two contenders, and Muʿāwiya's occupation of Egypt.[274] Finally, he reports on al-Ḥasan's relations with the Kufans and his negotiations with Muʿāwiya, and ends with the abdication of al-Ḥasan.[275]

Al-Zuhrī apparently did not deal with the Umayyad period. It is reported, however, that al-Walīd ibn ʿAbd al-Malik asked him about the lifespans of the Umayyad caliphs,[276] and similarly, that he wrote down for his grandfather the ages of these caliphs and the period each of them ruled.[277] Al-Ṭabarī also

[266] Al-Balādhurī, *Futūḥ al-buldān*, p. 462; *idem, Ansāb al-ashrāf*, V, 25 [ʿAbbās ed., IV, i, 512].

[267] Al-Balādhurī, *Ansāb al-ashrāf*, V, 26, 27, 38, 39, 88f. [ʿAbbās ed., IV, i, 512ff., 526, 527, 579ff.].

[268] *Ibid.*, V, 26, 27f., 89 [ʿAbbās ed., IV, i, 512ff., 581].

[269] *Ibid.*, V, 62, 67ff. [ʿAbbās ed., IV, i, 551, 556ff.].

[270] *Ibid.*, V, 26, 88ff. [ʿAbbās ed., IV, i, 513, 579ff.].

[271] *Ibid.*, V, 62, 67ff., 85, 91, 97 [ʿAbbās ed., IV, i, 551, 556ff., 577, 583, 590]; al-Ṭabarī, *Ta'rīkh*, I, 2871; II, 305ff.

[272] Al-Balādhurī, *Ansāb al-ashrāf*, V, 69ff., 91f. [ʿAbbās ed., IV, i, 559f., 583f.].

[273] Al-Ṭabarī, *Ta'rīkh*, I, 3069, 3102f., 3185ff.

[274] *Ibid.*, I, 3241f., 3341ff., 3390ff.

[275] *Ibid.*, II, 1, 5ff.

[276] *Ibid.*, II, 149.

[277] *Ibid.*, II, 428.

quotes al-Zuhrī—and this is his last citation from him—on the duration of the caliphate of al-Walīd ibn ʿAbd al-Malik.[278]

This part of al-Zuhrī's studies demonstrates that interest in the experiences of the *umma* was another factor of importance in the rise of historical writing. The principle of *ijmāʿ*, the emergence of political factions and the controversy among them over events of the past (especially the *fitna*), the question of whether succession to the caliphate should be elective or hereditary, problems of administrative organization (especially of taxation),[279] and the *dīwān*—all these issues called for clarification through historical study. Al-Zuhrī offers us the Medinan version of events, and these accounts generally show the *umma* to be in the right. We understand from him, for example, that the Prophet did not nominate anyone to succeed him in leadership of the Islamic community, which decided for the principle of elective, not hereditary succession. The *umma* elected Abū Bakr, and even ʿAlī, at first unhappy with the outcome, willingly pledged homage to him later on. Al-Zuhrī presents Abū Bakr and ʿUmar to us as paragons of righteousness.

The problem of the *fitna*, however, is enormously complicated, and the complaints against ʿUthmān were to some extent justified by his actions. But al-Zuhrī does not portray him in the same dark colors that other accounts do. It is clear from his reports that Medina was internally divided during the *fitna*. ʿAlī ibn Abī Ṭālib at first adopted the attitude of an advisor, then withdrew and stood aside during the storm, though he was shocked when it ended with the murder of ʿUthmān. ʿAlī was then elected as caliph because his status and qualifications made him the obvious candidate. In discussing the rebellion of Ṭalḥa and al-Zubayr, the accounts offered by al-Zuhrī side with ʿAlī and cast a slight shadow on the revolu-

[278] *Ibid.*, II, 1269.
[279] See al-Balādhurī, *Futūḥ al-buldān*, pp. 19f., 59, 68, 80, 384.

tionaries. In the confict between ʿAlī and Muʿāwiya, ʿAlī's case appears to be the just one, although Muʿāwiya is made to appear more astute. Al-Zuhrī nevertheless reports that al-Ḥasan renounced the caliphate in favor of Muʿāwiya, and with this terminates the story. These observations demonstrate that al-Zuhrī was not influenced by political partisanship, and tried to offer a portrayal of the events as they were viewed in Medina. Here a few words must be said concerning al-Zuhrī's relations with the Umayyads.[280]

Al-Yaʿqūbī states that during the conflict with Ibn al-Zubayr ʿAbd al-Malik ibn Marwān tried to prevent the Syrians from going on the pilgrimage, and in order to support his position attributed to al-Zuhrī a *ḥadīth* endorsing pilgrimage to the al-Aqṣā mosque in Jerusalem.[281] The *ḥadīth* is dubious in itself, and likewise, al-Zuhrī was only a young man at the time (ca. A.H. 72-73) and not famous as he was later. The sources report that al-Zuhrī journeyed to Damascus and by coincidence happened to meet ʿAbd al-Malik, who had a personal legal problem. The caliph did not know him, but was impressed by his learning and acumen during their encounter, and so rewarded him by paying his debts and presenting him with a gift. He then advised him to continue his studies, and with that al-Zuhrī returned to Medina.[282] This account shows that he was still a young scholar at the time, and similarly, one would hardly expect the caliph to advise him, during the conflict with Ibn al-Zubayr, to return to Medina if he was as important as al-Yaʿqūbī's account makes him out to have been.

[280] See al-Dhahabī, *Tarājim*, p. 72. Goldziher's remarks on this in *Muhammedanische Studien*, II, 35f., 37f., 40[= *Muslim Studies*, II, 44f., 46f., 48f.] are not very critical.

[281] Al-Yaʿqūbī, *Taʾrīkh*, II, 311.

[282] Ibn Qutayba, *Maʿārif*, p. 239 [ʿUkāsha ed., p. 472]; al-Dhahabī, *Tarājim*, p. 70; Ibn Kathīr, *Al-Bidāya wa-l-nihāya*, IX, 340f., adding that ʿAbd al-Malik granted al-Zuhrī a stipend (*rātib*) in accordance with the latter's request. See also Ibn Saʿd, VII, ii, 157; Ibn Qutayba, *Maʿārif*, p. 228 [ʿUkāsha ed., p. 447].

And on the other hand, there is an account reported from al-Zuhrī which indicates that he was critical of ʿAbd al-Malik during the period of the struggle with Ibn al-Zubayr.[283] We must accordingly reject the account of al-Yaʿqūbī and instead accept al-Zuhrī's own report in which he says, "I came to Damascus during the rebellion of Ibn al-Ashʿath,"[284] about A.H. 80, i.e., seven or eight years after the revolution of Ibn al-Zubayr.[k]

Though he did make occasional and intermittent visits to the Umayyad court, al-Zuhrī's studies probably kept him in Medina most of the time. Later he moved to Adāma, in southern Palestine near the border of the Hijaz, and from there made trips to the Hijaz and to Damascus (the Umayyad court) "for academic purposes" (*li-ʿilmihi*).[285] ʿUmar ibn ʿAbd al-ʿAzīz held him in high regard,[286] and it is most likely that he came to take up residence in Damascus in the days of Yazīd ibn ʿAbd al-Malik and Hishām. The former appointed him as a *qāḍī*, and he was on very good terms with Hishām, who made him his son's tutor, indicating the increasing authority of the Islamic perspective. Hishām also asked him to dictate *ḥadīth* for the benefit of his sons,[287] and likewise later told

[283] Al-Balādhurī, *Ansāb al-ashrāf*, XI, 163.

[284] Al-Bukhārī, *Al-Taʾrīkh al-kabīr*, IV, 93. [Cf. also Abū Zurʿa, *Taʾrīkh*, I, 408, 583f.]

[k] [On this famous controversy, in which Duri's position is now generally accepted, see Horovitz, "Biographies," II, 35ff.; Johann Fück, "Die Rolle des Traditionalismus im Islam," *ZDMG*, XCIII (1939), pp. 23f.; Muḥammad ʿAjjāj al-Khaṭīb, *Al-Sunna qabla l-tadwīn* (Cairo, 1963), pp. 501ff.; Werner Caskel, *Der Felsendom und die Wallfahrt nach Jerusalem* (Köln and Opladen, 1963), pp. 25f.; S.D.F. Goitein, "The Sanctity of Jerusalem and Palestine in Early Islam," in his *Studies in Islamic History and Institutions* (Leiden, 1968), pp. 135ff.; M. J. Kister, "'You Shall Only Set Out for Three Mosques': a Study of an Early Tradition," *Le Muséon*, LXXXII (1969), pp. 173ff.; Azmi, *Studies*, pp. 289ff.]

[285] Ibn al-Jawzī, *Ṣafwat al-ṣafwa*, II, 79; al-Dhahabī, *Tarājim*, p. 70; Ibn Kathīr, *Al-Bidāya wa-l-nihāya*, IX, 341f.

[286] Ibn al-Jawzī, *Ṣafwat al-ṣafwa*, II, 78. See also Ibn ʿAbd al-Ḥakam, *Futūḥ Miṣr*, p. 104.

[287] Al-Dhahabī, *Tarājim*, pp. 70f.; Ibn Kathīr, *Al-Bidāya wa-l-nihāya*, IX, 342.

two secretaries to accompany him, attend his classes, and write down his *ḥadīth* materials, which they did for the period of a year.[288] This probably explains the presence of so many of his works in the library of the Umayyad court. However, from a fierce argument which transpired between him and Hishām, we can see that al-Zuhrī had not fallen under the influence of the Umayyads. Hishām asked him who was meant in the Qur'ānic verse, "whichever of them takes upon himself the greater part of it."[1] and al-Zuhrī replied, "It was ʿAbd Allāh ibn Ubayy." "You lie!" Hishām cried, "It was ʿAlī!" Al-Zuhrī replied, "I lie?! May you have no father! By God, even if a herald were to cry out from heaven that God had permitted lying, still I would not lie."[289] Such was al-Zuhrī the scholar.

Al-Zuhrī's contribution to historical studies was not limited to his view of history and his study of early Islamic history. He also rendered a great service to historical writing by setting his *ḥadīth* materials down in writing. In his house, his books surrounded him on every side.[290] The Umayyad library contained numerous loads of "books" (*dafātir*) of his learning written for Hishām ibn ʿAbd al-Malik.[291] There is a statement attributed to him, "We disliked writing (*al-kitāb*) until the authorities (*al-umarāʾ*) compelled us to do so; then I decided not to prevent any Muslim from doing likewise,"[292] but this appears to echo the views of *ḥadīth* scholars of later times.

[288] Abū Nuʿaym, *Ḥilyat al-awliyāʾ*, III, 361.

[1] [I.e., the greater responsibility for the slandering of ʿĀʾisha, referred to in Sūrat al-Nūr (XXIV), 11.]

[289] Al-Dhahabī, *Tarājim*, p. 72.

[290] Al-Yāfiʿī, *Mirʾāt al-janān*, I, 261; [also al-Fasawī, *Kitāb al-maʿrifa wa-l-taʾrīkh*, edited by Akram Ḍiyāʾ al-ʿUmarī (Baghdad, 1974), I, 620ff.].

[291] Abū Nuʿaym, *Ḥilyat al-awliyāʾ*, III, 361, 363; al-Dhahabī, *Tarājim*, p. 72; Ibn Kathīr, *Al-Bidāya wa-l-nihāya*, IX, 344.

[292] Al-Dhahabī, *Tarājim*, p. 69; Ibn Kathīr, *Al-Bidāya wa-l-nihāya*, IX, 341. In Abū Nuʿaym (*Ḥilyat al-awliyāʾ*, III, 363) we read, "We had no desire to write down anything from al-Zuhrī, until Hishām compelled al-Zuhrī to do so. He then wrote for Hishām's sons, and then the people began to write down *ḥadīth*." Al-Zuhrī also said, "We disliked writing (*al-kutub*) until the authorities (*al-sulṭān*) compelled us to do so; then we did not want to prevent other people from doing likewise."

The truth of the matter is that al-Zuhrī had been accustomed to writing down his *ḥadīth* materials and other accounts ever since his days as a student.[293] The following report, which is contemporary, regards his habit of setting his learning down in writing as a matter of course. According to al-Layth, "I said to Ibn Shihāb, 'O Abū Bakr, if only you would make these books available to the people, record them, and thus free yourself [for other work].' He replied, 'No one has spread this learning as I have, or offered it as I have.' "[294] Al-Zuhrī granted writing a certain value when he said, "There is no difference, God willing, between reading a scholar's book and hearing him."[295] ʿUbayd Allāh ibn ʿUmar reported, "I used to see al-Zuhrī give [someone] a book which he neither recited [to the students] nor had recited to him [by the students]; someone would say, 'May we transmit this on your authority?' and he would reply, 'Yes,' "[296] Mālik ibn Anas was fully aware of al-Zuhrī's role when he said, "Ibn Shihāb was the first to set *ʿilm* down in writing."[297] Such writing cleared the path for others to follow.

It is clear from the above that al-Zuhrī established the outlines and structure for writing the biography of Muḥammad, and played an important role in stabilizing the *ḥadīth*s and accounts of Medina. If ʿUrwa ibn al-Zubayr was the forerunner of historical writing, then it was al-Zuhrī who founded

[293] See pp. 96-97 above.

[294] Al-Dhahabī, *Tarājim*, pp. 72ff.

[295] Ibn Kathīr, *Al-Bidāya wa-l-nihāya*, IX, 344 [and much earlier, Abū Zurʿa, *Taʾrīkh*, I, 415. This sentence could also be interpreted as meaning, "There is no difference, God willing, between reading a scholar's book out loud to him (*al-qirāʾa*) and hearing him recite it himself (*al-samāʿ*)." On this sense of the terms, which result in important differences for the interpretation of the passage, see *GAS*, I, 58f.]

[296] Al-Dhahabī, *Tarājim*, pp. 69, 70. [Cf. al-Khaṭīb al-Baghdādī, *Taʾrīkh Baghdād*, I, 266. On this practice, the *munāwala*, see *GAS*, I, 59; Abbott, *Studies*, II, 35; Azmi, *Studies*, p. 286, with further references.]

[297] Ibn al-Jawzī, *Ṣafwat al-ṣafwa*, II, 78; Abū Nuʿaym, *Ḥilyat al-awliyāʾ*, III, 260.

the historical school of Medina. We can say with certainty that the foundations for the ***maghāzī*** were laid by his serious studies, and were not engendered by the *qiṣaṣ* tales of storytellers like Wahb ibn Munabbih, as some have believed. His students, such as Mūsā ibn 'Uqba and Ibn Isḥāq, traveled in the path he had laid out; and although Ibn Isḥāq, at the expense of historical balance, took much of his material from popular *qiṣaṣ* lore and the *Isrā'īliyāt*, the accounts of al-Zuhrī remained the fundamental core of his *Sīra*.

It is also clear from the studies of al-Zuhrī that interest in the experiences of the *umma* was a further motive for historical study. And here we feel that the simple basic steps taken by 'Urwa were completed and brought to fruition at the hands of al-Zuhrī.

Finally, his writing down of his learning helped to establish historical studies on a firm foundation, and served to preserve the earliest historical sources.

CHAPTER THREE

The Beginnings of Historical Folklore: Wahb ibn Munabbih

The study of Wahb ibn Munabbih takes us beyond the scope of an investigation of historical writing among the Arabs.[a] But as some researchers in the past have placed him within these domains,[1] and some have stressed his importance in the *sīra*,[2] we are compelled to examine him here in order to show, in no uncertain terms, that he is not to be regarded as one of the *maghāzī* authors, and that his field and his influence lie within the domain of *qiṣaṣ* and the *Isrā'īliyāt*.

Wahb ibn Munabbih was born in Yemen in Dhimār, two days' journey from Ṣan'ā'. There is disagreement on the dates of his birth and death. The sources place his death variously between A.H. 110 and 114, but it seems that the latter date is more likely, as his nephew 'Abd al-Ṣamad ibn Ma'qil confirms that he died on 11 Muḥarram 114/732.[3] Al-Dhahabī states that he was born in the caliphate on 'Uthmān, and this causes us to view favorably the account reporting that he died at the age of eighty, which would place his birthdate in 34/654-55.[4]

[a] [Wahb ibn Munabbih has more recently been studied in a number of important contributions by Raif Georges Khoury. See his "Der Heidelberger Papyrus des Wahb b. Munabbih," *ZDMG*, Supp. I.xvii (1969), pp. 557ff.; "Un Ecrit inédit attribué à Wahb b. Munabbih: la *Risāla fī sīrat an-nabī*," *Al-Mashriq*, LXIV (1970), pp. 591ff.; and particularly his *Wahb b. Munabbih*, with extensive bibliography; also *GAS*, I, 305ff.]

[1] Horovitz, ["Biographies," I, 553ff. =] *Al-Maghāzī al-ūlā*, pp. 27ff.

[2] *EI*[1], IV, 441 (G. Levi Della Vida).

[3] See al-Bukhārī, *Al-Ta'rīkh al-kabīr*, IV, ii, 164; Ibn Qutayba, *Ma'ārif*, p. 233 ['Ukāsha ed., p. 459]; Yāqūt, *Mu'jam al-udabā'*, VII, 232; al-Yāfi'ī, *Mir'āt al-janān*, I, 250; al-Dhahabī/Fischer, p. 442.

[4] Ibn Ḥajar, *Tahdhīb al-tahdhīb*, XI, 168.

Wahb was one of the *abnā'*;[b] his father Munabbih, from Herat in Khurāsān, had been sent to Yemen during the reign of Chosroes Anushirvan and converted to Islam in the lifetime of the Prophet. Wahb grew up in Yemen and was known for his ascetic tendencies. As al-Dhahabī says, "Wahb remained forty years without cursing any living thing, and twenty years without performing any ablution between the evening prayer and the morning prayer the next day."[5] The sources very frequently extol him for his piety and asceticism. He was at first a Qadarite, but then abandoned this doctrine, so it is said, after reading the books of past prophets. There is, however, one reference to his continued adherence to anti-predestinarian doctrine up until the last days of his life.[6] He was also a firm believer in dreams.[7]

Wahb held the position of *qāḍī* under ʿUmar ibn ʿAbd al-ʿAzīz.[8] Yāqūt claims that he died while in office in Ṣanʿā',[9] but this is impossible. He was imprisoned in his last years, and eventually flogged for reasons which remain uncertain.[10] He seems to have been a fierce-tempered man fanatically devoted to his Yemenite heritage.[11]

From this it is clear that Wahb was far removed from the school of Medina, a Yemenite who differed in approach from the scholars of *ḥadīth*. From all appearances, he was a com-

[b] [The *abnā'* were Yemenites descended from Persian troops sent into the area in pre-Islamic times. For details, see Ibn Khallikān, *Wafayāt al-aʿyān*, VI, 35f.; Nöldeke, *Geschichte der Perser und Araber*, pp. 220ff.; *EI*², I, 102 (K. V. Zetterstéen); Khoury, *Wahb b. Munabbih*, pp. 189f.]

[5] Al-Dhahabī/Fischer, p. 439 [also Ibn Saʿd, V, 396. The implication here is that Wahb's continent life style rendered superfluous any further ablution for the morning prayer.]

[6] Yāqūt, *Muʿjam al-udabā'*, VII, 232; al-Dhahabī/Fischer, p. 440; Ibn Ḥajar, *Tahdhīb al-tahdhīb*, XI, 168; also Ibn Hishām, *Kitāb al-tījān*, pp. 47f. [Cf. Khoury, *Wahb b. Munabbih*, pp. 206, 270ff., 314, concerning Wahb's writings and views on this subject.]

[7] Al-Dhahabī/Fischer, p. 440; Ibn Kathīr, *Al-Bidāya wa-l-nihāya*, IX, 293.

[8] Al-Yāfiʿī, *Mir'āt al-janān*, I, 248f.

[9] *Muʿjam al-udabā'*, VII, 232.

[10] Al-Dhahabī/Fischer, p. 442; Ibn Ḥajar, *Tahdhīb al-tahdhīb*, XI, 168.

[11] Al-Dhahabī/Fischer, p. 440.

piler of *akhbār* and *qiṣaṣ*: Yāqūt calls him an "*akhbārī* and teller of tales",[12] Ibn Khallikān describes him as a "narrator of *akhbār* and *qiṣaṣ*,"[13] and al-Dhahabī confirms them when he says, "Wahb was an *akhbārī* and a highly learned storyteller."[14] For these reasons we find that he was a topic of criticism and controversy, for while some regarded him as a reliable authority, others were critical of him.[15]

Wahb took his materials from both oral accounts and books. He claimed to have read a wide collection of prophets' books, works which according to the various sources numbered 30, 32, 70-some, 92, and 93. Given the widely erratic numbering of these books and the sources to which they are attributed, we cannot lend any credence to such accounts.[16] At any rate, however, Wahb was renowned for his familiarity with books of the ancients. Ibn al-ʿImād states, "He was intensely interested in the books of the ancients and narratives and tales of the nations,"[17] works which his brother reportedly used to

[12] *Muʿjam al-udabāʾ*, VII, 232.

[13] *Wafayāt al-aʿyān*, II, 238 [ʿAbbās ed., VI, 35].

[14] Al-Dhahabī/Fischer, p. 438.

[15] See Ibn Saʿd, V, 395ff.; Ibn Ḥajar, *Tahdhīb al-tahdhīb*, XI, 167. Al-ʿIjlī said that he was a trustworthy *tābiʿ*, and Abū Zurʿa, al-Nasāʾī, and Abū Ḥayyān also considered him trustworthy (*thiqa*). Yāqūt deemed him "one of the best of the *tābiʿūn*, a trustworthy veracious man" [*Muʿjam al-udabāʾ*, VII, 232]. Al-Dhahabī (Fischer, p. 438) said, "He transmitted from Ibn ʿAbbās, Jābir . . . and others."

[16] Ibn Saʿd, V, 395; Ibn Qutayba, *Maʿārif*, p. 233 [ʿUkāsha ed., p. 459]; Ibn Ḥajar, *Tahdhīb al-tahdhīb*, XI, 167. Ismāʿīl . . . I heard Wahb saying, "I have read 92 books, all of which had been sent down from heaven: 72 in the churches and in general circulation, and 20 known only to a few." Yāqūt (*Muʿjam al-udabāʾ*, VII, 232) has him saying, "I have read 70-some books of the prophets," and in the *Tījān* (p. 2) he states, "I have read 93 of the books revealed to the prophets," and offers details: "two rolls (*ṣaḥīfa*) sent down to Adam, 50 to Seth, son of Adam, 30 to Idrīs, two to Noah, 40 to Hūd, two to Ṣāliḥ, 20 to Abraham, 50 to Moses, the Psalms revealed to David, the Gospel revealed to Jesus, and the Qurʾān (*al-Furqān*) revealed to Muḥammad." Al-Sakhāwī, *Al-Iʿlān bi-l-tawbīkh*, p. 48, "I have read 30 books revealed to 30 prophets"; al-Dhahabī (Fischer, p. 439); Abū Nuʿaym, *Ḥilyat al-awliyāʾ*, I, 24: "I have read 90-some . . . 91."

[17] Ibn al-ʿImād, *Shadharāt al-dhahab*, I, 150.

buy for him. As Ibn Kathīr says, "He was learned in the books of the ancients."[18] Likewise, Yāqūt mentions that "Wahb transmitted much material from the ancient works known as the *Isrā'īlīyāt*."[19]

From the accounts ascribed to him it is evident that Wahb fairly accurately transmitted fragments of the Old Testament which were later quoted by al-Ṭabarī in his *Tafsīr*, and also reported fragments of the Psalms; certain of his narratives also indicate knowledge of the Talmud.[20] As Horovitz points out, he gave the names and personalities of the Book of Genesis in accordance with the Hebrew text, and also noted the deviations in the Syriac translation.[21] There are a number of passages which indicate his knowledge of Hebrew, and possibly also Syriac.[22] He apparently drew information on the birth and life of Jesus from the Gospels and other Christian writings.[23] Moreover, his data on the origins of Christianity and its spread in Yemen are related to the Syriac text of the *Letter of Simeon*, with the embellishments demanded by popular folklore.[24] Much of his information seems to have been drawn from folktales circulating among the Christians and Jews. Al-Dhahabī mentions that he was "intensely interested in the

[18] *Al-Bidāya wa-l-nihāya*, IX, 276.

[19] *Mu'jam al-udabā'*, VII, 232.

[20] 'Alī, "Mawārid ta'rīkh al-Ṭabarī," I, 193.

[21] ["Biographies," I, 557 =] *Al-Maghāzī al-ūlā*, p. 33.

[22] The following examples appear in the *Tījān*, p. 21: "Qaynān, a Hebrew name which in the Arabic language means 'purchaser' (*mushtarī*)"; "Mahlīl, a Hebrew name which in the Arabic language means 'glorified' (*mamdūḥ*), and which in the Syriac version of the Bible is given as Mālālī, which in Arabic means 'anointed of God' (*masīḥ Allāh*)." [For this last example, Krenkow's edition of the *Kitāb al-tījān* must be emended to read *musabbiḥ Allāh*, "praiser of God," to accord with the sense of the Syriac. For further examples, see Khoury, *Wahb b. Munabbih*, I, 215f.; also cf. Ramzi Baalbaki, "Early Arab Lexicographers and the Use of Semitic Languages," forthcoming in *Berytus*, on the knowledge and use of other Semitic languages in early Islamic times.]

[23] Al-Ṭabarī, *Tafsīr*, I, 102; cf. Genesis 10:21ff. And on the birth and life of Jesus, see al-Ṭabarī, *Tafsīr*, III, 77, 147; XVI, 43.

[24] See Axel Moberg's introduction to his *The Book of the Himyarites* (Lund, 1924).

Isrā'īlīyāt."[25] As we shall see below, he also made use of many popular Yemenite tales.

Some of Wahb's information, however, shows points of variance from the scriptural texts. Ibn Qutayba noted the discrepancies between his information on the beginning of Creation and the Book of Genesis, and Ibn Qutayba's collation of Wahb's data indicates that the latter added material to the passages he took from the Old Testament and other texts.[c] Parts of this material derive from exegesis of Qur'ānic verses, from the *Isrā'īlīyāt*, and from Wahb's own reflections on the books of the *ahl al-kitāb*.[26] That Wahb's accounts contradict each other is obviously a factor pointing to the conclusion that they suffered either corruption or interpolation in later times.[27] Al-Sakhāwī regards his accounts as impermissible to historians.[28] And we should also note that Wahb was not above making claims to learning he did not possess, such as his ability to read a Greek inscription in the mosque of Damascus for al-Walīd ibn ʿAbd al-Malik.[29]

A number of works on the pre-Islamic period are attributed to Wahb, although there is disagreement concerning their titles.[d] Ibn Saʿd states that Wahb composed a book entitled *Aḥādīth al-anbiyā' wa-l-ʿubbād wa-aḥādīth Banī Isrā'īl*, "Accounts of the Prophets and Saints, and of the Israelites."[30] Ibn al-Nadīm refers to *Al-Mubtada'* and attributes it to Wahb's grandson ʿAbd al-Munʿim,[31] and Ibn Qutayba makes men-

[25] Al-Dhahabī/Fischer, p. 438.

[c] [Cf. further on this, Lecomte, "Citations," pp. 34ff.; *idem, Ibn Qutayba*, pp. 77, 192ff.]

[26] See Ibn Qutayba, *Maʿārif*, pp. 8f., 9ff. [ʿUkāsha ed., pp. 14f., 17ff.].

[27] Horovitz, ["Biographies," I, 557 =] *Al-Maghāzī al-ūlā*, p. 32.

[28] *Al-I'lān bi-l-tawbīkh*, p. 48.

[29] Al-Masʿūdī, *Murūj al-dhahab*, edited by Barbier de Meynard and Pavet de Courteille (Paris, 1861-77), V, 361f. [ed. Charles Pellat (Beirut 1966-79), III, 366].

[d] [Cf. Khoury, *Wahb b. Munabbih*, I, 210ff.]

[30] Ibn Sa'd, VII, ii, 97.

[31] *Fihrist*, p. 138.

tion of a *Qiṣaṣ al-anbiyā'*, "Tales of the Prophets," and a *Mubtada' al-khalq*, "Beginning of Creation," also called *Al-Mabda'*, or *Al-Mubtada'*.[32] Al-Mas'ūdī also refers to the *Mubtada'*.[33] Ḥājjī Khalīfa probably has parts of the same work in mind when he attributes to Wahb a *Qiṣaṣ al-akhyār*, "Tales of Righteous Men," and a *Qiṣaṣ al-anbiyā'*, "Tales of the Prophets," and likewise when he speaks of a *Kitāb al-isrā'īliyāt*.[34] Rosenthal considers this last work and the *Kitāb al-mubtada'* to be one and the same.[35] From this and from the selections which have come down to us, it appears that Wahb dealt with the beginning of Creation and tales of the prophets and holy men. No book has survived on any of the subjects mentioned in the titles given by later authorities, but some of his work has reached us as quotations cited in al-Ṭabarī (both the Qur'ān commentary and the history), Ibn Qutayba, Ibn Isḥāq, and others. Whereas his accounts in al-Ṭabarī for the most part come to us from Ismā'īl ibn 'Abd al-Karīm ibn 'Abd al-Ṣamad ibn Ma'qil (this Ma'qil was the brother of Wahb) and hence from Wahb, we have the *Kitāb al-tījān* in the recension of 'Abd al-Mun'im (d. A.H. 228) ibn Idrīs, a descendant of Wahb through his daughter.

There is no question that the accounts and tales of Wahb became a kind of inheritance, as it were, for his family, which tried to circulate them, and perhaps also to add to them through the work of 'Abd al-Mun'im ibn Idrīs and Ismā'īl ibn 'Abd al-Karīm ibn Ma'qil ibn Munabbih (d. A.H. 210), both of whom probably resorted to fabrication in order to glorify Wahb's name.[36] But on the other hand, Wahb did become a

[32] Ibn Qutayba, *Ma'ārif*, p. 6 ['Ukāsha ed., p. 9]; Ibn Ḥajar, *Tahdhīb al-tahdhīb*, XI, 168.

[33] *Murūj al-dhahab*, I, 127 [Pellat ed., I, 73; cf. also II, 292].

[34] *Kashf al-ẓunūn*, edited by Gustav Flügel (Leipzig and London, 1835-58), IV, 518, no. 9436; V, 40, no. 9826 [Istanbul ed., II, 1328, 1390].

[35] *History of Muslim Historiography*, p. 265, n. 2 [2nd ed., p. 335, n. 2]; Becker, *Papyri Schott-Reinhardt I*, pp. 8ff.

[36] "'Abd al-Mun'im ibn Idrīs, the famed storyteller, fabricated stories, bought

prominent authority on the *Isrā'īlīyāt*, and as we sense a certain discrepancy in the accounts ascribed to him in such primary sources as al-Ṭabarī, Ibn Qutayba, and al-Masʿūdī, it is probable that there were others who added to or altered his stories.[37]

Let us now attempt to reconstruct a provisional outline for the *Mubtada'* of Wahb by comparing the first part of the *Kitāb al-tījān* with the accounts attributed to Wahb in the history and Qur'ān commentary of al-Ṭabarī, and in Ibn Qutayba's *Kitāb al-maʿārif*:[c]

1. Age of the earth, and the creation of the heavens, earth, and seas in seven days;[38] the story of Adam and Eve in the Garden (*al-Janna*);[39] Adam's fall to earth, and his knowledge that his progeny will populate it, and that God will create in Mecca "the house of sacred refuge" (*al-bayt ḥaraman āminan*);[40] the sons of Adam.[41]

2. Noah, his sons, the propagation of his descendants upon the earth, and the peoples and languages ascribed to them.[42]

3. Wahb follows the Torah in his tales of the prophets, especially those of the Israelites, and also elucidates some Qur'ānic references. He mentions Isaac, son of Abraham, the story of Jacob, son of Isaac, the tribes descended from

books, including biographical works, transmitted the stories they contained, and attributed it all to his illustrious grandfather Wahb"; see Ibn Ḥajar, *Tahdhīb al-tahdhīb*, I, 315; *idem, Lisān al-mīzān*, II, 73. In Ibn Saʿd, V, 395, we find the *ḥadīth*, "In my community there will be two men, the first of them Wahb, to whom God will grant (*yahabu*) wisdom," a manifest forgery intended to glorify Wahb.

[37] See *EI*[1], IV, 1085 (J. Horovitz).

[c] [Cf. Khoury, *Wahb b. Munabbih*, pp. 222ff.]

[38] See al-Ṭabarī, *Tafsīr*, XII, 4; *idem, Ta'rīkh*, I, 36ff.; Ibn Qutayba, *Maʿārif* (al-Ṣāwī), pp. 8f. [ʿUkāsha ed., pp. 14f.].

[39] Al-Ṭabarī, *Tafsīr*, VII, 106; VIII, 184f.; *idem, Ta'rīkh*, I, 106. [The *Tījān* devotes a long discussion to the question of whether *al-Janna* here means paradise or a place somewhere on earth.]

[40] Al-Ṭabarī, *Ta'rīkh*, I, 130f.

[41] Ibn Qutayba, *Maʿārif*, p. 10 [ʿUkāsha ed., pp. 17f.].

[42] *Ibid.*, pp. 11ff. [ʿUkāsha ed., pp. 21ff.]; al-Ṭabarī, *Ta'rīkh*, I, 211.

him,[43] the story of Moses and Aaron, Moses in the Sacred Valley, Moses and his staff and Pharaoh's magicians, the sacred cow of the Israelites, and the death of Moses.[44]

4. Succession of the Israelite prophets; tribulations suffered by the Israelites and their deliverance by the prophet Ezekiel;[45] proliferation of sin among the Israelites, and the story of the Ark of the Covenant, the *sakīna*,[f] and their role in the victory of the Israelites; loss of the Ark, followed by a 400-year period of tribulation until the appearance of the prophet Samuel and the return of the Ark; Samuel bestows his blessing on Saul, who becomes king but fails to carry out God's will, so the blessing passes to David, who kills Goliath and becomes king; details on David;[46] Solomon and his relationship with Bilqīs;[47] the two sons of Solomon and those who came after them up until the time of Jeremiah and the destruction of Jerusalem at the hands of Nebuchadnezzar.[48]

5. Later Israelite prophets;[49] birth and miracles of Jesus, his summons to his apostles for the Last Supper, Jesus' prophecy concerning his apostles.[50]

[43] Ibn Qutayba, *Ma'ārif*, pp. 16f. ['Ukāsha ed., pp. 35ff.].

[44] See Ibn Qutayba, *Ma'ārif*, p. 20 ['Ukāsha ed., p. 43f.]; al-Ṭabarī, *Ta'rīkh*, I, 471ff., also 504; *idem, Tafsīr*, I, 281f.; II, 373f., 385f., 388; XVI, 107f., 118f., 136, 139, 140, 141.

[45] Al-Ṭabarī, *Ta'rīkh*, I, 535f., 539.

[f] [The *sakīna*, a divine presence which may take a number of perceptible forms, is associated with the Ark of the Covenant in Sūrat al-Baqara (II), 248. See Ignaz Goldziher, *Abhandlungen zur arabischen Philologie* (Leiden, 1896-99), I, 177ff.; *EI*[1], IV, 78 (B. Joel); Arthur Jeffery, *The Foreign Vocabulary of the Qur'ān* (Baroda, 1938), p. 174.]

[46] Al-Ṭabarī, *Ta'rīkh*, I, 544ff., 551ff., 560ff., 571ff.; *idem, Tafsīr*, II, 390, 392, 396, 398f.

[47] Al-Ṭabarī, *Tafsīr*, XIX, 81f., 86, 88, 90, 91, 96f. [*idem, Ta'rīkh*, I, 572, 584ff. This is the famous story of Solomon and the Queen of Sheba; see *EI*[2], I, 1219f. (E. Ullendorff).]

[48] Al-Ṭabarī, *Tafsīr*, III, 20, 22ff.; [*idem, Ta'rīkh*, I, 658ff.;] Ibn Qutayba, *Ma'ārif*, pp. 20ff. ['Ukāsha ed., pp. 46ff.].

[49] Ibn Qutayba, *Ma'ārif*, pp. 22ff. ['Ukāsha ed., pp. 49ff.].

[50] Al-Ṭabarī, *Tafsīr*, VI, 205; XVI, 49, 161, 192, 195, 203, 390.

Wahb usually presents the *qiṣaṣ al-anbiyā'* in a form which accords in its general outlines with what we find in the literature and lore of the *ahl al-kitāb*. In the *Kitāb al-tījān* we find Arabic folktales on the beginning of paganism,[51] ʿĀd, and the city of Iram.[52] Similarly, Ibn Qutayba quotes him on the story of Abraham, Nimrod, Abraham's emigration, the story of Ishmael,[53] and likewise on the Seven Sleepers and on Shuʿayb and Madyan.[54] Ibn Khallikān defined the scope of his interests when he said, "He was a man knowledgeable on *akhbār* of the ancients, the creation of the world, the affairs of the prophets—may the blessing and peace of God be upon them—and the lives of kings."[55] It seems that Ibn Khallikān had in mind his narratives on the kings of Yemen, in addition to the materials we have mentioned above.

Yāqūt said that Wahb ibn Munabbih wrote a book entitled *Kitāb al-mulūk al-mutawwaja min Ḥimyar wa-akhbārihim wa-qiṣaṣihim wa-qubūrihim wa-ashʿārihim*, "The Crowned Kings of Ḥimyar, Their Narratives and Tales, Tombs and Poems."[56] Ibn Khallikān saw this work and described it as being "a useful book."[57] In all probability this book was the foundation for the *Kitāb al-tījān fī mulūk Ḥimyar wa-l-Yaman*, "The Book of Crowns, concerning the Kings of Ḥimyar and Yemen," which Ibn Hishām transmitted as a work ascribed to Wahb and handed down through ʿAbd al-Munʿim ibn Idrīs.

The greater part of the *Kitāb al-tījān* deals with the story of the southern Arabs, their past history, the glorious deeds of their kings, and their migration. The book displays a mov-

[51] *Kitāb al-tījān*, pp. 203ff., 207ff.

[52] *Ibid.*, pp. 39ff.

[53] Ibn Qutayba, *Maʿārif*, pp. 15f. [ʿUkāsha ed., pp. 30ff.].

[54] *Ibid.*, pp. 19, 35 [ʿUkāsha ed., pp. 41f., 54].

[55] *Wafayāt al-aʿyān*, II, 238 [ʿAbbās ed., VI, 35].

[56] *Muʿjam al-udabā'*, VII, 232. [Cf., on this work, Krenkow, "The Two Oldest Books on Arabic Folklore," II, 55ff., 204ff.; Khoury, *Wahb b. Munabbih*, I, 286ff.]

[57] *Wafayāt al-aʿyān*, II, 238 [ʿAbbās ed., VI, 35].

ing folkloric style similar to the *qiṣaṣ* of pre-Islamic times, and thus is a pseudo-literary work consistent in both verse and prose with the style of the *ayyām* tales. It offers up popular and glorious Yemenite legend, the goal of which seems to have been to paint a magnificent portrait of the Arabs of the south, confronting the general predominance of the Arabs of the north, and reflecting the form taken by the boasting which transpired between the two sides. The book thus proclaims, "Ḥimyar on the earth was like the lamp shining in the dead of the night."[58] We hear that the Arabs of the south were familiar with monotheism (*tawḥīd*) before other peoples,[59] and that during the wars of al-Ṣaʿb Dhū l-Qarnayn, he used to summon his foes "to either the sword or the faith."[60] We find that the Yemenites regarded the Kaʿba as sacred, and that some of their kings performed the pilgrimage to it.[61] Their kings also made great conquests all over the world.[62] Also

[58] *Kitāb al-tījān*, p. 62.

[59] It is explained, for example, that Yaʿrub was the successor (*khalīfa*) to the prophet Hūd and "took up God's work after him"; *Tījān*, p. 16. Al-Ṣaʿb Dhū l-Qarnayn resembled Solomon in that "livestock, grazing animals, birds, vermin, and even wild beasts were all subject to his command" (p. 46), and even the wind obeyed him (pp. 86f.). Al-Ṣaʿb is described as an unsent prophet (*nabī ghayr mursal*), as also is Luqmān (pp. 35, 70). [On the distinction between a *nabī* and a *rasūl*, see Krenkow, p. 62.]

[60] *Kitāb al-tījān*, p. 101. Al-Khaḍır served as his guide during his conquests. [It should be noted here that the *Tījān* takes Dhū l-Qarnayn to be an ancient Yemenite hero and specifically excludes (p. 110) identification of this figure with Alexander the Great, who in the Qur'ān and in Islamic tradition is usually referred to as Dhū l-Qarnayn.]

[61] *Ibid.*, p. 35.

[62] For example, ʿAbd Shams ibn Yashjub, named Sabaʾ, conquered Babylonia, Armenia, and Syria, reached the Nile, and founded Miṣr, the capital of Egypt (pp. 47f.). In the east, Ḥimyar reached so far as even to extend beyond Gog and Magog to the land of the rising sun; he also conquered Syria, Abyssinia, Egypt, and the Maghrib as far as the Atlantic Ocean (pp. 52f.). In the west, al-Ṣaʿb Dhū l-Qarnayn conquered black Africa, Abyssinia, and Spain, and in the east he overran Armenia, Samarqand, Bāb al-Abwāb [Darband in the eastern Caucasus], and Gog and Magog, built the wall between them and other peoples, conquered India and China, and finally reached the Spring of Life (pp. 86ff.).

attributed to the Yemenites is precedence in the use of the Arabic script,[63] and in the composition of poetry in Arabic, an art which the Arabs of the north copied from them later on.[64] The work further stresses their knowledge of the sciences (*al-ḥikma*),[65] their skill and preeminence in craftsmanship, and that the rest of mankind learned these skills from them.[66]

It is clear from this that the book glorifies the Yemenites and accords them the preeminent position in monotheism, military conquests, language, literature, science, and craftsmanship. It is difficult to demarcate the role Wahb played in all this, but in any case he must have had a powerful influence.[67] And we must note that the book contains tales which go back to Ibn Isḥāq (through his students, such as al-Bakkā'ī and Abū ʿAbbād al-Hamdānī),[68] Abū Mikhnaf,[69] Muḥammad ibn al-Sā'ib al-Kalbī,[70] ʿUbayd ibn Sharya,[71] Kaʿb al-Aḥbār,[72] and other later authorities.[73] A great part of the book comes with no mention of any source, and probably some of this, or most of it, derives from Wahb ibn Munabbih.

Wahb did compose a book on the *maghāzī*, a work to which Ḥājjī Khalīfa refers.[74] Becker discovered a fragment of his *Maghāzī* as it appears in a papyrus copied in A.H. 228. This fragment is in the recension of ʿAbd al-Munʿim ibn Idrīs and

[63] *Ibid.*, p. 54.
[64] *Ibid.*, p. 35.
[65] *Ibid.*, pp. 70, 73, 74. They were also the first to make stoning the punishment for adultery and to cut off the hand of the thief.
[66] *Ibid.*, p. 162.
[67] See al-Thaʿālibī, *Laṭā'if al-maʿārif*, p. 26 [Cairo ed., pp. 37f.], where Wahb vehemently defends the Yemenites.
[68] *Kitāb al-tījān*, pp. 65f., 75, 115, 128, 251.
[69] *Ibid.*, pp. 125, 180, 183.
[70] *Ibid.*, pp. 132, 212, 213, 240.
[71] *Ibid.*, pp. 66, 209.
[72] *Ibid.*, pp. 110ff.
[73] *Ibid.*, pp. 111, 135, 164, 233.
[74] *Kashf al-ẓunūn*, II, 1747. [Cf. Khoury, *Wahb b. Munabbih*, I, 274ff.]

begins, "Muḥammad ibn Baḥr Abū Ṭalḥa told me: ʿAbd al-Munʿim ibn Idrīs told us, from his father, from Abū l-Yās, from Wahb ibn Munabbih."[75] The following subjects are discussed: the second pledge of al-ʿAqaba, discussion of Quraysh in the *Dār al-nadwa*, the Hijra and the Prophet's arrival in Medina, the expedition against Banū Khathʿam. The narratives go back to Wahb without *isnād*, and in them we find poems recited by the pagans who took part in the events, and patterned after the style of the *ayyām*. We cannot tell whether Wahb neglected the *isnād* entirely, since the author of the *Ḥilyat al-awliyā'* has quoted two fragments from Wahb—the first concerning the conquest of Mecca,[76] and the second on the death of the Prophet[77]—in which he gives the *isnād* with the indication that the account has come via ʿAbd al-Munʿim ibn Idrīs. The style of the two fragments is the very essence of the popular folkloric style with a clear legendary stamp.

The important fact here is that the *Maghāzī* of Wahb ibn Munabbih is neither referred to in the books on the *sīra*, nor regarded as a serious work. Its approach is entirely different from that of the school of Medina. Wahb ibn Munabbih was, as we have seen, a storyteller, or *qāṣṣ*, who in his *Mubtada'* and in his narratives on Yemen set forth folktales and legends which he cited as if they were history. In this way he introduced the folkloric element into the discipline of history, as is clear from the accounts quoted from him, for the pre-Islamic

[75] Becker, *Papyri Schott-Reinhardt I*, pp. 1ff.; Adolf Grohmann, *From the World of Arabic Papyri* (Cairo, 1952), p. 4. [On pp. 115ff. of his *ʿIlm al-ta'rīkh*, Duri gives the Arabic text of parts of this papyrus. For an English translation of these lines, see Gertrude Mélamède, "The Meetings at al-ʿAḳaba," *Le Monde Oriental*, XXVIII (1934), pp. 17ff.; for the full text, with a German translation, see Khoury, *Wahb b. Munabbih*, I, 117ff. Cf. also the remarks and emendations proposed by M. J. Kister in his "Notes on the Papyrus Account of the ʿAqaba Meeting," *Le Muséon*, LXXVI (1963), pp. 403ff.; *idem*, "On the Papyrus of Wahb b. Munabbih," *BSOAS*, XXXVII (1974), pp. 545ff.]

[76] Abū Nuʿaym, *Ḥilyat al-awliyā'*, IV, 79.

[77] *Ibid.*, IV, 73.

THE FAMILY OF WAHB[78]

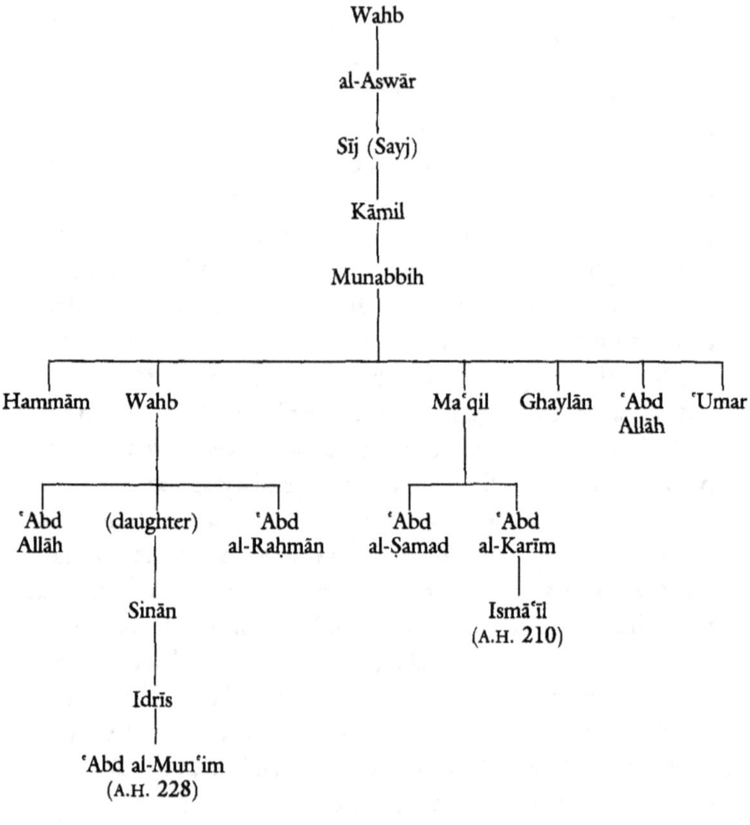

period, in Ibn Isḥāq, al-Yaʿqūbī, Ibn Qutayba, al-Ṭabarī, and al-Masʿūdī. In like manner, he had a powerful influence on the *qiṣaṣ al-anbiyāʾ*, as in the works of al-Kisāʾī and al-Thaʿālibī.[g]

[78] See Victor Chauvin, *La Récension égyptienne des Mille et une nuits* (Brussels, 1899) [also Khoury, *Wahb b. Munabbih*, p. 201].

[g] [Al-Kisāʾī, *Qiṣaṣ al-anbiyāʾ*, edited by I. Eisenberg (Leiden, 1922); al-Thaʿālibī, *Qiṣaṣ al-anbiyāʾ* (Cairo, A.H. 1286).]

It would seem that the storytellers, whether popularizers or preachers, at times influenced the tone in which the *sīra* was written in later periods by introducing a certain tendency towards exaggeration and fanciful imagination. But they are not, in any case, to be regarded as historians, nor did they produce any historical approach to the writing of the *sīra*. It is obvious that the popular folktale on the *sīra* and on the early Muslims is in its style an extension of the pre-Islamic folktale, and this is what aroused the disapproval of the *maghāzī* school of Medina. It can thus be said with certainty that the outlines and contents of the *sīra* were not products of the storyteller's craft, but rather the work of *maghāzī*-oriented *ḥadīth* scholars and others who followed their methodology in Medina.

The role of Wahb ibn Munabbih thus lies in the fact that he was the first to establish a framework, albeit a folkloric one, for the history of prophethood from the beginning of Creation until the appearance of Islam. Some later historians borrowed from, or were influenced by, this structure or the material it contained.

CHAPTER FOUR

Origins of the Historical School of Iraq: Its Rise and Development Until the Third Century A.H.

Arab historical writing is an integral part of Arab culture, and it can only be understood in terms of other cultural activities and developments.[a] To study it in isolation leads only to a confused and incomplete understanding of its origins and development.

Historical writing among the Arabs began after the rise of Islam. Activities of the Jāhilīya, such as the *ayyām* tales and genealogy, indicate one aspect of Arab interests and the beginnings of a narrative style, but they do not embody any conception of history.

In their earliest stages, historical studies followed two general perspectives in separate paths: the perspective of the *ḥadīth* scholars, and the perspective of the tribes, which was in a sense the continuation of earlier tribal activities. These two perspectives reflect two fundamental currents in early Islamic society, the Islamic and the tribal, which had an influence on various aspects of life. The activities of the two perspectives each took shape in a particular center. Medina, the cradle of Islam, was the primary center for the perspective of the *ḥadīth* scholars, while Basra and Kufa, settlements of the tribal gar-

[a] [The Arabic text of this chapter is based on a paper read by Professor Duri at a London conference on the historians of the Middle East and published as "The Iraq School of History to the Ninth Century—a Sketch," in *Historians of the Middle East*, edited by Bernard Lewis and P. M. Holt (London, 1962), pp. 46ff.]

risons and centers of tribal tradition, were the primary foci for the tribal perspective. All three cities were centers of cultural life in early Islamic times.

The Islamic perspective is not the subject of our inquiry here. It suffices for us to state that it began among the *ḥadīth* scholars who, beginning with ʿUrwa ibn al-Zubayr, devoted special attention to the life of the Prophet, rapidly advanced to the study of early Islamic history, and founded a school of *maghāzī* historians. In addition to this, tales and stories about the Prophet and the conquests were being told and circulated. These tales, or *qiṣaṣ*, did not lead to the establishment of any historical perspective, but in later times they did provide material which seeped into the works of some historians, Ibn Isḥāq in particular. Such tales remained, however, the object of suspicion and caution among serious historians. The earnest intent and critical approach of the Medinan school is apparent in its emphasis on chains of authorities and in its criticism of *ruwāt*. By the end of the first century A.H., the general lines of the *sīra* had been laid out and its basic accounts collected. Many popular tales crept in at a later time, with the shift from simple and factual narrative accounts towards those bearing elements of glorification and a certain degree of exaggeration. The idea of writing down accounts appeared at a relatively early time; the use of writing had already been established by al-Zuhrī by the end of the first century A.H., and from that time onwards accounts were taken either orally or from written sources.

The tribal perspective on the study of history began as a result of the interest in the activities and affairs of the tribes. In both style and approach it was a direct continuation of the *ayyām* tales (and also of the accounts of genealogies), but now directed at the new *ayyām*, the battles and conquests of Islam.

Arab culture was basically oral. It relied on poetry for its documentation and found verse to be the best means of preserving its heritage. There are references to registers and documents in the hands of the kings of al-Ḥīra and the Ḥimyarites in Yemen, and to some Yemenite family records and written genealogies later used by some historians, but these are exceptional cases.[1] Narratives were related primarily in tribal social gatherings (*majālis*), and in general were viewed as the collective property of the family or tribe. Certain individuals, such as narrators of poetry or tribal elders (*mashāyikh*), were its principal transmitters. At first these narratives and accounts had no *isnād*s naming specific authorities, but rather remained a part of general culture and the common concern of all. Such oral accounts as these, full of poetry, circulated in early Islamic society just as they had in pre-Islamic times.[2] Kufa and Basra, as great tribal centers in direct and continuous contact with the arid steppe lands, became active centers for circulating these accounts and narratives.[b]

On the other hand, the rise of Islam and the settlement of the tribes in the garrison towns gathered the tribes together into a single area, fostered new topics of interest among them, and introduced them to the basic skills of reading and writing. We have ample evidence of the use of writing, to aid the memory or to preserve accounts, before the end of the first century A.H. and during the first half of the second.[3] Thus accounts in written form began to appear alongside oral ones.

At the dawn of the second century A.H., we hear of the presence of elders (*ashyākh*) and narrators (*ruwāt*) learned in

[1] See Ibn Hishām (Cairo ed.), I, 321 [Wüstenfeld ed., I, i, 191]; al-Ṭabarī, *Ta'rīkh* (Cairo ed.), II, 123 [de Goeje ed., I, 770]; al-Hamdānī, *Iklīl*, I, 5; X, 30f., 111f.

[2] See al-Jāḥiẓ, *Bayān*, III, 366; al-Suyūṭī, *Muzhir*, I, 248f.; II, 355.

[b] [Pellat provides an important account of these developments in Basra in his *Le Milieu baṣrien*, pp. 123ff.]

[3] Ibn al-Nadīm, *Fihrist*, pp. 9f., 132; *Aghānī* [IV, 52], IV, 253; Ibn Ḥajar, *Tahdhīb al-tahdhīb*, II, 216. [Cf. Nabia Abbott, *The Rise of the North Arabic Script and Its Ḳur'ānic Development* (Chicago, 1939), pp. 45ff.; also her *Studies*, I, 5ff.; II, 5ff.]

the genealogies and exploits of their tribes, and also of the existence of "books" containing genealogies, poetry, and probably prose narratives, *akhbār*, of certain tribes. These works had probably been collected by some of the *ruwāt*, but still were regarded as the collective property of the tribe. The poet al-Ṭirimmāḥ (d. 105/723-24) refers to the *kitāb* of Tamīm, and Ḥammād al-Rāwiya (d. 156/773) had access to the *kutub* of Quraysh and Thaqīf.[4] From these *ruwāt* and in these books, there was abundant historical material for historians of later times.

Around the middle of the second century A.H. we encounter *ruwāt, akhbāriyūn*, genealogists, and philologists as scholars who left behind historical works or a wealth of historical accounts. This period was one of pioneering scholars in various fields who began collecting poetry, *akhbār*, and *ḥadīth*. Abū ʿAmr ibn al-ʿAlāʾ (d. 154/770) and Ḥammād al-Rāwiya collected poetry, *akhbār*, and materials on pre-Islamic Arab genealogies, primarily from tribal *ruwāt* and monographs, and made use of writing to preserve some of the work they produced.[5] From this period also derive the first collections of *ḥadīth*, compiled in various provinces, and the first works on the *sīra* which have come down to us. This is indicative of a phase of cultural development—the collecting phase—in which history had a role to play. The *akhbāriyūn* and the scholarly *ruwāt* are thus our first historians.

[4] [Al-Ṭirimmāḥ, *Dīwān*, edited by F. Krenkow (London, 1927), p. 148, no. 28]; *Aghānī* [IV, 45; V, 174], IV, 237; VI, 94; Ibn ʿAbd al-Barr, *Al-Inbāh ʿalā qabāʾil al-ruwāt* (Cairo, A.H. 1350), pp. 43ff. [Cf. also Ignaz Goldziher, "Some Notes on the Dīwāns of the Arab Tribes," *JRAS* (1897), pp. 325ff.; also in his *Gesammelte Shriften*, IV, 119ff.; F. Krenkow, "The Use of Writing for the Preservation of Ancient Arabic Poetry," in *A Volume of Oriental Studies Presented to Edward G. Browne*, edited by T. W. Arnold and Reynold A. Nicholson (Cambridge, 1922), pp. 261ff.]

[5] See Ibn Saʿd, VII, ii, 42; al-Jumaḥī, *Ṭabaqāt fuḥūl al-shuʿarāʾ*, edited by Aḥmad Muḥammad Shākir (Cairo, 1952), p. 40; *Aghānī* [III, 100f.], III, 312; *Mukhtārāt Ibn al-Shajarī* (Cairo, A.H. 1306), pp. 123, 127, 136; al-Suyūṭī, *Muzhir*, II, 304.

Just as in the historical writing on the *sīra* we find predecessors to Ibn Isḥāq—such as al-Zuhrī—on whom he to a great extent relies, so we notice that the *akhbārīyūn* very frequently quote certain *ruwāt*. For example, of the more than sixty *ruwāt* from whom Sayf ibn ʿUmar took material (as provided to us in al-Ṭabarī), we find that this scholar is particularly dependent on two, Ṭalḥa ibn al-Aʿlam and Muḥammad ibn ʿAbd Allāh, each of whom he quotes more than a hundred times. Other examples are Hishām ibn al-Kalbī's dependence on Ibn Abī Ṣāliḥ for information on ancient prophets, and al-Madā'inī's dependence on Abū l-Dhayyāl and al-Mufaḍḍal al-Ḍabbī for information on Khurāsān. One can see that these *ruwāt* were interested in general events or public affairs, not just in the narratives on a particular tribe as had earlier been the case, and in this way they took an important step forward. In the same category we can place some of the genealogists who in their writings transcended the limits of a single tribe, although along with these there continued to be *ruwāt* for the particular tribes.

The *akhbārīyūn* were thus the first historians in the tribal perspective. They differ from the *ruwāt* who related accounts of specific events, in that they sought to gather accounts relevant to a subject or event and compile them into a continuous written work. Among these *akhbārīyūn* were Abū Mikhnaf (d. 157/774), ʿAwāna ibn al-Ḥakam (d. 147/764), Sayf ibn ʿUmar (d. 180/796), and finally the doyen of the *akhbārīyūn*, al-Madā'inī (d. 225/839).

These *akhbārīyūn* displayed an interest in the affairs of the *umma* alongside their special concern for the affairs of Iraq. We thus notice among them the conception of the unity and continuity of the experiences of the Islamic community, and similarly, we perceive the idea of the intrinsic unity of Arab history. We thus find Sayf ibn ʿUmar linking the Ridda wars to the conquests. ʿAwāna ibn al-Ḥakam covers Islamic history in the first century A.H.: the Rāshidūn caliphs, the Ridda, the conquests, the *fitna*, and the history of Iraq and Syria up to the caliphate of ʿAbd al-Malik. Abū Mikhnaf deals with early Islamic history up to the battle of Ṣiffīn, then continues with events in Iraq up to the end of the Umayyad period. As for al-Madāʾinī, he ranges over all of Arab history—political, literary, and social—beginning with the Jāhilīya and continuing until the dawn of the third century A.H.

The focus of interest is thus the *umma*, not the tribe. Similarly, we can see other historical views in the works of the *akhbārīyūn*. We notice the conflict between the concept of divine foreordainment (*jabr*) in public affairs, as promoted by the Umayyads, and the concept of free will and human responsibility, as espoused by the opposition factions.[c] ʿAwāna ibn al-Ḥakam presents the Umayyad point of view in some of his accounts: Yazīd attributes Umayyad authority to the will of God,[6] and ʿUthmān predicts that political power will pass to ʿAbd al-Malik and his sons.[7] On the other hand, we find Abū Mikhnaf expressing another viewpoint, especially when we carefully examine the information he has to offer on the rebellion of al-Ḥusayn and the movement of the Tawwābūn.

Reflected in these historical works is the concept of the state, which from the Umayyad angle emphasized the rights of the *imām* and the fealty and obedience owed to him, as opposed to the tribal or factional view which placed other loyalties (regional, tribal, etc.) above those due to the state. The rebellions against the Umayyads are not regarded as illegitimate, even though they are not glorified or explained in favorable

[c] [On the concepts of *qadar* and *jabr*, see Ignaz Goldziher, *Introduction to Islamic Theology and Law*, translated by Andras and Ruth Hamori (Princeton, 1981), pp. 81ff.; Julian Obermann, "Political Theology in Early Islam: Ḥasan al-Baṣrī's Treatise on *Qadar*," *JAOS*, LV (1955), pp. 138ff.; *EI*², IV, 368ff. (Josef van Ess); Cook, *Early Muslim Dogma*, pp. 105ff.]

[6] Al-Ṭabarī, *Taʾrīkh*, II, 381. [Cf. p. 155 below.]

[7] Al-Balādhurī, *Ansāb al-ashrāf*, V, 220.

terms. And even when Muʿāwiya's revolt against ʿAlī is criticized, as is the case in the *Kitāb Ṣiffīn* of Naṣr ibn Muzāḥim, this criticism is founded on factional considerations, not on any conception of the state.[8] The surviving works of the *akhbāriyūn* accordingly show great moderation, for these historians did not sink to the level of sheer partisanship in their writing and were not representatives of only a single point of view. Some of the extreme accounts in their works may have been omitted during the selection process undertaken by the later historians (such as al-Ṭabarī and al-Balādhurī) who preserved their works for us. But it is more likely that the explanation for this goes back to the importance attached to the *riwāya* and *khabar* as opposed to personal judgment (*ra'y*), and to the spirit of historical discipline enjoined by the way in which *ḥadīth* scholars and other learned men viewed the sources at their disposal.

Factional, regional, and tribal partisanship also had their effects on historical writing. Thus we see both ʿAlid[9] and Iraqi[10] inclinations in Abū Mikhnaf, particularly where he cites the account, "I witnessed the time when people were saying, 'The first disgrace to befall Kufa was the death of al-Ḥusayn ibn ʿAlī, the killing of Ḥujr ibn ʿAdī, and the summons of Ziyād.' "[11] He also reveals a certain tendency to glorify the tribes, and in his narratives on Ṣiffīn we find a clear emphasis on noble tribal deeds. Sayf explains the role of the tribes in the conquest of Iraq and stresses the part played by Tamīm.[12] ʿAwāna's sympathies are considered to be 'Uthmānī: he clearly gives Umayyad accounts and sometimes reports from within

[8] See al-Ṭabarī, *Ta'rīkh*, II, 3f., where the *imām* of error is preferred over no *imām* at all.

[9] See al-Ṭabarī, *Ta'rīkh*, I, 2337, 3276; II, 182ff., 307f.

[10] *Ibid.*, I, 3221f.

[11] *Ibid.*, II, 145.

[12] *Ibid.*, I, 2068f., and the importance of al-Qaʿqāʿ ibn ʿAmr al-Tamīmī.

the Umayyad family.[13] Nevertheless, some of his accounts reflect a viewpoint opposed to the Umayyads.[14]

The *akhbārīyūn* made great wide-ranging efforts to collect accounts and narratives. We thus find them making use of family accounts, tribal accounts in Iraq, and a great number of individual reports. They had to complement these accounts with those of other provinces involved in the events they studied, and so we find accounts from Syria, Medina, and Arabia. This much is clear from the works of the *akhbārīyūn*. Abū Mikhnaf quoted accounts from the tribal elders of al-Azd, Numayr, Muḥārib, and Tamīm, and also cited family accounts.[15] He gives accounts from persons who participated in the events themselves, and in addition, a great number of individual reports.[16] His sources on Ṣiffīn, Muslim ibn ʿAqīl's arrival in Iraq, and the tragedy of Karbalā' were mainly Kufan ones, but he did supplement them with Syrian and Medinan accounts.[17] Sayf ibn ʿUmar also relies on Kufan accounts, especially for the conquests, and rounds them out with some Medinan and Syrian reports. On the Ridda he is dependent on accounts from Kufa, Arabia, and Medina; among his Medinan *ruwāt* are Hishām ibn ʿUrwa and Mūsā ibn ʿUqba. In many reports he goes back to those who participated in the events under discussion.[18] ʿAwāna ibn al-Ḥakam relied on family accounts, accounts from his own Kalb tribe and others, a great number of individual reports, and many Syrian and Umayyad accounts.[19] In addition, the *akhbārīyūn* used official documents—letters and treaties—probably obtained from

[13] See al-Balādhurī, *Ansāb al-ashrāf*, IVB, 31 [ʿAbbās ed., IV, i, 286, 320]; al-Ṭabarī, *Ta'rīkh*, II, 13.

[14] Al-Balādhurī, *Ansāb al-ashrāf*, V, 369; al-Ṭabarī, *Ta'rīkh*, I, 1837.

[15] Al-Ṭabarī, *Ta'rīkh*, I, 3261, 3302, 3303, 3309.

[16] See al-Ṭabarī, *Ta'rīkh*, I, 3202f.

[17] *Ibid.*, II, 279, 376, 410ff., 479.

[18] *Ibid.*, I, 1786, 1797, 1931ff., 1947f.

[19] See al-Balādhurī, *Ansāb al-ashrāf*, V, 132ff., 140; al-Ṭabarī, *Ta'rīkh*, II, 785, 791ff.

government *dīwāns* or from persons who held personal copies.[20]

The *akhbārī* could rely heavily on the accounts of his own province (as in the case of Abū Mikhnaf) or tribe (e.g., Sayf ibn ʿUmar), but he could not ignore opposing or contradictory reports.[21] By this time the *ḥadīth* scholars' method of source criticism had become fairly widespread and had influenced the *akhbārīyūn*. Thus we see that the critical method of the latter consisted of scrutinizing the *ruwāt* and assessing the value of the accounts they had transmitted. Sayf, for example, says, "This story on the affair of al-Ubulla and its conquest is contrary to what the biographical authorities (*ahl al-siyar*) know, and contrary to the traditional accounts."[22] Abū Mikhnaf says, in reference to an event pertaining to the tragedy of Karbalā', "But what al-Mujālid ibn Saʿīd, al-Ṣaqʿab ibn Zuhayr al-Azdī, and other *ḥadīth* scholars told us is in keeping with the general consensus of *ḥadīth* scholars. They said. . . ."[23]

The tales of the *majālis*, however, and the poetry pertaining to these stories, did make their way into the writings of the *akhbārīyūn*. This is particularly true of Naṣr ibn Muzāḥim, who quotes large amounts of fabricated poetry and in his *Ṣiffīn* clearly follows the style of the *majālis* tales, which in the role they play are a continuation of the *ayyām*.[24] We can also perceive a certain trace of the folkloric *qiṣaṣ* style in such other *akhbārīyūn* as Sayf ibn ʿUmar, Abū Mikhnaf,[25] and ʿAwāna. These authors wrote in a smooth direct style, and sometimes portrayed events in a graphic and vivid manner. When they

[20] See al-Ṭabarī, *Ta'rīkh*, I, 2820.

[21] See al-Ṭabarī, *Ta'rīkh*, II, 182, 202, 323, concerning Abū Mikhnaf; and al-Balādhurī, *Ansāb al-ashrāf*, IVB, 31 [ʿAbbās ed., IV, i, 286, 320]; V, 369; al-Ṭabarī, *Ta'rīkh*, I, 1833, on ʿAwāna.

[22] Al-Ṭabarī, *Ta'rīkh*, I, 2025.

[23] *Ibid.*, II, 314.

[24] See al-Khaṭīb al-Baghdādī, *Ta'rīkh Baghdād*, XIII, 482f.; al-Ṭūsī, *Fihrist kutub al-shīʿa*, edited by A. Sprenger *et al.* (Calcutta, 1855), p. 347.

[25] Al-Ṭabarī, *Ta'rīkh*, I, 2058, 2071f., 2101f.; II, 3, 8ff.

write about battles we find them quoting poetry, speeches, and dialogue throughout their narratives. The story is usually told in continuous form in their writings, and in them we sometimes sense the stylistic tone of the *ayyām* tales.

The *akhbārīyūn* furthermore represent a phase of transition from an earlier period when the *isnād* was entirely lacking to the strict method of the *ḥadīth* scholars in citing the chain of transmitters, for the *akhbārīyūn* display a great deal of freedom, and sometimes carelessness, in their use of the *isnād*. We thus find broken chains of authorities, cases where only the first name of the *rāwī* is mentioned (e.g., "from ʿUmayr ibn So-and-So (*fulān*) al-ʿAbdī"), or barren statements like "it was said," "on the authority of a man (or elder) from . . . ," or "on the authority of scholars who know." During the second century A.H. we find that a single account is usually given for each point or subject, and that reports follow each other in succession to bring the story or narrative to completion. This practice persists until we come to al-Madāʾinī, who gives more than one report on the same subject and provides us with a more balanced and impartial picture of it. *Akhbār* and *riwāyāt* were for the most part taken from oral transmission, but it is probable that some sources were written ones, as appears from such expressions as *qāla*, "he said," and *ḥaddathanī*, "he told me," in reference to the same source.

It would be appropriate here to mention that philologists also played a role in the shaping of a more strictly critical method of research through their studies on poetry and their efforts to separate genuine from fabricated poetry.[d] Likewise, they helped to collect and sift historical accounts, and in so doing introduced the method of internal criticism of source materials and established it alongside that of external criticism of the sources and the *ruwāt*. In writing, their approach was

[d] [Cf. further, Abbott, *Studies*, III, 25ff.]

similar to that of the *akhbārīyūn* in that they too collected the materials pertaining to a subject or event and compiled them into "monographs" (*kutub*).

Genealogists rendered their services to historical studies by providing the genealogies with some information on the lives of the personalities involved (especially in Muṣʿab al-Zubayrī). Here it is clear that social requirements, tribal conflicts, and political divisions among the tribes were the factors which stimulated interest. These studies provided for the notables of the tribes what the *ṭabaqāt* works provided for the scholars of *ḥadīth*, although to a much lesser extent from the standpoint of actual material produced. The controversy and cultural conflict with the Shuʿūbīya, on the one hand, and the ever-broadening ranks of the *mawālī*, on the other, led genealogists and philologists to broaden the scope of their studies and compelled them to emphasize the unity of Arab cultural history and the interrelationship of its various periods. The sources primarily used by genealogists and philologists were poetry and tribal accounts of events or subjects mentioned in poetry, or those which cited poetry in their texts to confirm their authenticity. Their studies were thus intermingled or interrelated with those in the field of historical studies.

Genealogical studies began within the limits of a single tribe. Then in the second century A.H. there appeared genealogists who collected tribal accounts and narratives from the genealogists of the various tribes and from poetry, particularly the *naqā'iḍ*, or polemic verse. Representative of these scholars were Muḥammad ibn al-Sā'ib al-Kalbī (d. 146/763) and Abū l-Yaqẓān al-Nassāba (d. 190/804). In the same period, philologists and grammarians began to gather Arabic poetry from tribal "books" and from the *ruwāt*. Some limited their interest to genealogy and grammar, but others devoted wide-ranging attention to the field of Arab history in their studies (e.g., the works of Hishām ibn Muḥammad al-Kalbī and Abū ʿUbayda

Maʿmar ibn al-Muthannā). Here again we find that the trend moved from giving an account without *isnād*, to an effort to mention some of the *ruwāt*, to full establishment of the *isnād* as a critical tool. Hishām ibn Muḥammad ibn al-Sā'ib al-Kalbī, for example, gives reports from persons of the *ahl al-kitāb*, from Ibn Abī Ṣāliḥ on the history of the prophets, from translations and registers in al-Ḥīra, and from *qiṣaṣ* on the history of the Persians and the Arab tribes, while relying on the elders (*mashāyikh*) of Kufa, Abū Mikhnaf, and ʿAwāna for Islamic history. Abū ʿUbayda cites reports from his mentors Abū ʿAmr ibn al-ʿAlā', al-Akhfash, ʿĪsā ibn ʿUmar al-Thaqafī, and Yūnus ibn Ḥabīb, as well as from Hishām ibn ʿUrwa, Wakīʿ, and a number of eloquent bedouins.[26]

There is a historical conception emerging behind these studies, the idea of the cultural continuity (in the sense of cultural unity) of Arab history and the important bearing it had on contemporary issues, particularly the claims of the Arab tribal aristocracy, the relationship between Quraysh and the other Arab tribes, the Arab attitude towards the *mawālī*, and problems pertaining to the linguistic heritage and Arabic literature. These great questions broadened the horizons of the genealogists and philologists to include the history of other peoples prior to Islam. Hishām ibn al-Kalbī studied the history of the prophets and Persian history as it related to Arab history, while Abū ʿUbayda referred back to Persian narratives (among his works are a *Kitab akhbār al-furs*, "Narratives on the Persians," and a *Kitāb al-mawālī*, "Book of the [non-Arab] Clients [of the Arab Tribes]").

Political issues are also reflected to a certain extent in their writings. We find something of an inclination towards the

[26] *Naqā'iḍ Jarīr wa-l-Farazdaq*, I, 30, 487; Abū ʿUbayda, *Majāz al-Qur'ān*, edited by Muḥammad Fu'ād Sazgīn (Cairo, 1954-62), I, 400; al-Khaṭīb al-Baghdādī, *Ta'rīkh Baghdād*, XIII, 252; Ibn Khallikān, *Wafayāt al-aʿyān*, II, 138 [ʿAbbās ed., V, 235]; al-Suyūṭī, *Muzhir*, II, 401f.

ʿAlids in Hishām ibn al-Kalbī; Abū ʿUbayda, based on what we find in the *Naqāʾiḍ*, adheres to the orientation of the Shuʿūbīya and betrays a tendency to expose Arab faults in a way which is not explained by the fact that he was a Khārijite.[27]

By the dawn of the third century A.H., historical studies had reached a stage which led to the emergence of the great historians of that century, for in the "books" which they composed, the *akhbārīyūn*, philologists, and genealogists defined the scope of historical study, and their own researches encompassed many diverse aspects of the discipline. It was in these studies that the concept of the unity of Islamic history emerged, and the idea probably took form as a historical study, with a strict chronological sequence, in al-Haytham ibn ʿAdī's work, *Kitāb al-taʾrīkh ʿalā l-sinīn*, "History According to the Years." It was also in these works that the genealogical perspective of study developed into a historical perspective set within a genealogical framework, as in the *Nasab Quraysh* of al-Zubayrī (d. ca. 233-36/844-50), and more clearly in design and scope in the *Taʾrīkh al-ashrāf al-kabīr* of al-Haytham ibn ʿAdī. The idea of universal history also emerged, and thus Hishām ibn al-Kalbī covered the history of the prophets and of the northern and southern Arabs prior to Islam, in addition to Islamic history.

From the standpoint of methodology, attention to the *isnād* increased and some scholars began to report varying accounts on the same point or subject, as was the case with al-Madāʾinī and Abū ʿUbayda. We also note the inclination towards use of written sources along with oral accounts in the works of al-Madāʾinī, Abū ʿUbayda, and Hishām ibn al-Kalbī. These authors quoted from the works of the generation of Abū Mikhnaf, ʿAwāna, Muḥammad ibn al-Sāʾib al-Kalbī, and Abū ʿAmr ibn al-ʿAlāʾ.

[27] See Ghannāwī, *Naqāʾiḍ*, p. 146.

The third century A.H. witnessed a new phase of cultural development. Enormous numbers of historical accounts transmitted or written down in various regions were accumulating, and this was the era of the *riḥla fī ṭalab al-ʿilm*, "journey in search of learning," a movement initiated by *ḥadīth* scholars to collect and classify *ḥadīth* materials. The contacts made in the course of such travels led to reciprocal influences on matters of method and historical perspective. Use of the *isnād* henceforth became widespread and more firmly established than before, and the rules pertaining to it were more strictly defined. In addition, informed opinion among scholars and historians was beginning to formulate definitive judgments on the value of previous works and the extent to which one could trust their authors. This was a development which enormously facilitated the task of collecting and criticizing accounts, and produced more accurate results.

When the historians of the third century appeared—al-Balādhurī (d. 279/892), al-Yaʿqūbī (d. 284/897), al-Dīnawarī (d. 282/898), Ibn Qutayba (d. 270/882), and al-Ṭabarī (d. 310/923)—they wrote continuous histories of the Islamic community which differed from the "monographs" which preceded them. Here it will suffice for us to make some general observations on these works.

The historical concepts underlying the writings of these scholars were the unity and continuity of the experiences of the *umma*, and the universal vision of history. Al-Balādhurī represents the first concept, the other historians the second. Their motives for writing history varied. Al-Balādhurī wrote his history, the *Ansāb al-ashrāf*, or "Genealogies of the Notables," as a work woven around the Arab tribal aristocracy, and in so doing indicated the focus of importance in his view, and likewise stressed an Arab view of society. His *Futūḥ al-buldān*, "Conquests of the Nations," expresses the fundamental mission of the Islamic community—the *jihād*—and fills certain juridical and administrative needs. Al-Yaʿqūbī wrote a universal history not devoid of Shīʿī tendencies, and accorded pre-Islamic history a spiritual and cultural significance. Ibn Qutayba had in mind the class of secretaries (***kuttāb***) and their need for a concise, comprehensive history in which numerous approaches were synthesized—those of the ***ayyām***, universal history, and juridical considerations. Al-Dīnawarī, meanwhile, sought to demonstrate the role of Iraq and Iran in his universal history, and in doing so found justification for this approach in the history of the Sāsānian and ʿAbbāsid periods. As for al-Ṭabarī, he sought to elucidate the will of God in his history, and to make the work a guide, complementary to his great Qur'ān commentary, to the activities of the ***umma***.

In this century we find the critical method of the ***ḥadīth*** scholars becoming more thoroughly applied. Al-Ṭabarī was a ***ḥadīth*** scholar who strictly adhered to the method of his peers, as is apparent from his emphasis on ***isnāds*** and his aversion to criticism of the substance of accounts. Ibn Qutayba criticizes his sources to the extent of referring back to the Torah in order to verify the material Wahb ibn Munabbih offers on the beginning of Creation and the prophets, and takes from his sources only what could be verified as accurate. Al-Yaʿqūbī maintains a critical attitude towards his sources, especially those pertaining to pre-Islamic times; he scrutinizes the sources for the Islamic period as well, but considers it sufficient to refer to them in his introduction since their chains of authorities are already well known. Al-Balādhurī follows a middle course, quoting earlier historians and naming them in each instance, but as their chains of authorities are well known, omitting the ***isnād*** except in instances where providing one seemed necessary.

Al-Balādhurī and al-Ṭabarī both provide divergent accounts on the same subject, and there is little in them and in the other historians that is partisan or prejudicial. Likewise, the way these two authors compare the materials offered by earlier historians is of great assistance in providing a balanced picture of events.

These historians undertook special wide-ranging studies on historical, geographical, and literary topics, added their work to the legacy of the *akhbārīyūn*, and used written materials (after reading them to a teacher, or *shaykh*) along with oral accounts. At times they also consulted documents and official registers. In their histories they synthesized the approaches of the genealogists, *akhbārīyūn*, and philologists, and also derived great benefit from the school of Medina. The emergence of these historians signaled the end of the phase of the *akhbārīyūn*, for it was they who laid down the lines for historical writing among the Arabs, and consolidating their views and conceptions of history.

CHAPTER FIVE

Motives for the Writing of History and the Historical Views Embodied in the Works of the First Historians

The factors which led to the writing of history among the Arabs are related to cultural developments on the one hand, and to general currents and perspectives in Arab society on the other.

Originally we find that the pre-Islamic Arab interest in *ayyām* and genealogies, as well as their prose and verse accounts pertaining to these subjects, were closely associated with the social views predominant among them on *ḥasab* and *nasab*. As one might expect, these accounts, in keeping with the prevailing cultural order, were oral ones. *Qiṣaṣ* and *akhbār*, transmitted as the collective property of the family or tribe, were in general circulation in the social milieu and were not the exclusive work of particular individuals. Such narratives were a part of general culture, and the concerns which they represented continued to endure after the rise of Islam.

Islam set forth the idea of the *umma*, or community, a concept which took root in Medina and then gradually began to establish itself in Iraq. Islam also motivated the tribes to settle in the garrison towns and encouraged the introduction of basic literary skills into cultural life.

Historical studies among the Arabs began in two independent schools, the Iraqi school in Kufa and Basra and the Hijaz school in Medina. For each there were factors contributing to its rise and growth, and both had their own views of history.

In Iraq, the following factors were responsible for the rise of historical studies. The ancient interest in the exploits and splendid military achievements of the tribes continued into Islamic times, and gradually there emerged among the tribes a partisan spirit, or *ʿaṣabīya*, for the province in which they had settled, a sentiment which manifested itself in their feelings of loyalty to these centers. This was closely linked to the question of the Islamic conquest and the insistence of the tribes on maintaining their right to benefit from the revenues of the countries they had conquered, or more simply put, the prerogatives of the Iraqi tribes in Iraq. Likewise, this partisan spirit was related to the feeling of the people of Iraq, who held the leadership of the Islamic world in the time of the fourth caliph, that they were more worthy of preeminence than others.

There was also the question of the imāmate, or the caliphate, and the emergence of political factions. Thus we find that many Iraqis felt, for historical reasons, that the Iraqi cause was related to that of the ʿAlids. Also at issue was the concept of the state, or the sense of state in the form instituted and advocated by the Umayyads, and opposed by the provinces and the tribes. And also involved was the clash between the principle of *qadar*, or freedom of the will and human responsibility in public affairs, and the principle of *jabr*, or acceptance of prevailing public circumstances as foreordained by God. The Umayyads embraced and advocated the principle of *jabr*, while the opposition factions proclaimed the principle of freedom and the responsibility of man for the prevailing state of affairs.

On the other hand, there took shape among the Arabs an awareness of their own importance and a realization that in Islam they were participants in a universal mission. This awareness was related to the establishment of the Arab Islamic empire and had an influence on the Arab attitude towards the *mawālī*. Moreover, the concept of the *umma* exerted its own influence in causing the interest in *akhbār* and *qiṣaṣ* to transcend the limits of the tribe to include society as a whole, and in this way opened the door to historical study. In like manner, the sympathies and interests of the Iraqis, opposed to the Umayyad political order, comprised another factor affecting the path historical study would follow. All of these issues manifested themselves in the study of history, and the role they played appears in the concern over such events as the Ridda, the conquests, the *shūrā*, the *fitna*, and such related events as the battles of the Camel and Ṣiffīn.

The works of the *akhbārīyūn*, the first historians in Iraq, articulated the prevailing views in Iraq on the issues mentioned above. We find Sayf ibn ʿUmar dealing with the Ridda and the conquests in this manner. His narratives on the conquests proclaim the glorious deeds of the tribes in a way which to a great extent obscures their role in the Ridda, and similarly, the image he proffers of the Ridda is, as one might expect, not a dark one. Abū Mikhnaf covered the Ridda, the conquests, the *shūrā*, the *fitna*, Ṣiffīn, and then the affairs of Iraq up to the end of the Umayyad era. Devotion to Iraq (or partisan spirit for the province) is reflected in his *akhbār*; likewise, he proclaims the justice of ʿAlī's cause and places Muʿāwiya and his followers in the wrong. He links the cause of ʿAlī to that of Iraq and considers them one, but does this without associating himself with the ʿAlid faction.[1] Similarly, he highlights the glorious deeds of the tribes in his narratives on the conquests and Ṣiffīn. Naṣr ibn Muzāḥim offers a Shīʿī approach in his *Ṣiffīn*. The factional influence is clearly evident in his narratives, and he unequivocally asserts the boastful deeds of the tribes.

ʿAwāna ibn al-Ḥakam was probably ʿUthmānī in his sym-

[1] See the example cited on p. 142, n. 11 above.

pathies, i.e., he stood closer to the Umayyads. We see him setting forth Umayyad accounts, and find him displaying a certain indulgence even with Yazīd, concerning whom he quotes the statement of Sukayna, "We never saw a disbeliever in God better than Yazīd."[2] Although he cites the judgment of Jābir ibn ʿAbd Allāh deeming the pledge of fealty sworn to Muʿāwiya to have been a "mistaken oath of allegiance," he presents the struggle during the *fitna* as a conflict between the "faction" (*shīʿa*) of ʿUthmān and the "faction" of ʿAlī. ʿAwāna gives free rein in his *akhbār* to the Umayyad point of view by emphasizing fate and divine decree. He cites an account relating how Yazīd ibn Muʿāwiya addressed ʿAlī ibn al-Ḥusayn, a survivor of the tragedy of Karbalā', and explained to him that his father had not heeded the Qur'ānic verse, "Say: 'O God, dominion is thine. Thou givest dominion to whomever thou willest, and seizest dominion from whomever thou willest. Good is in your hand, and indeed, thou art powerful over every thing.' "[3]

At any rate, the *akhbāriyūn* generally stressed human responsibility for the course of events and did not approve of the concept of *jabr* in public affairs. In the narratives on the Tawwābūn we find a powerful illustration of this perspective. Moreover, the concept of the state as the Umayyads tried to consolidate it, and the stress laid on obedience and loyalty to its ruling head, found no endorsement in the monographs of the *akhbāriyūn*. Instead, we find sympathy in their works for the revolutions and uprisings, or at the very least, an interpretation favorable to them. Also reflected in these works are suspicion of the Quraysh and jealousy of their prestigious position and the special privileges they enjoyed.[4] We note that

[2] Al-Ṭabarī, *Ta'rīkh*, II, 381.

[3] *Ibid.* [citing Sūrat Āl ʿImrān (III), 26].

[4] See al-Ṭabarī, *Ta'rīkh*, II, 1955-56: "Quraysh will not tolerate this or anything like it, for they are jealous folk . . . they are a perfidious people." [The reference is misprinted here and could not be traced in the history of

the contempt of the tribes for the *mawālī* is conspicuous in some writings, and find a clear example of this in the narratives on the revolt of al-Mukhtār.

By the end of the second century A.H., we can perceive other developments. The conflict between the Arabs and the *mawālī*, friction between the Muslims and the non-Muslim communities under their suzerainty (*ahl al-dhimma*), the claims of the Arab aristocracy, and the relationship between the Quraysh and the other tribes—all of these exerted their influence on historical writing. It was at this time too that the concept of cultural continuity in Arab history emerged. Moreover, the gradually increasing importance of the *ijmāʿ* in a general sense, in contrast to its earlier signification of the consensus of the people of one particular province, provided scope for the expression in practice of the concept of the collective experiences of the *umma* and the essential unity of these experiences.

Against this background, we find al-Madāʾinī ranging over the entire field of Arab history—political, social, and cultural—both before and after the rise of Islam. Hishām ibn Muḥammad al-Kalbī referred back to the history of the prophets and discussed Persian history, the history of the Arabs—both northern and southern—in pre-Islamic times, and then Islamic history, giving expression to the general concept of the unitary and integrative nature of history. Abū ʿUbayda consulted Persian narratives and wrote books with such titles as *Akhbār al-furs*, "Narratives on the Persians," and *Kitāb al-mawālī*, "Book of the [non-Arab] Clients [of the Arab Tribes]." Here we find him clearly influenced by the trend of the *mawālī*. Al-Haytham ibn ʿAdī wrote *Al-Taʾrīkh ʿalā l-sinīn*, "History According to the Years," and in this way stressed the idea of the unity of the *umma*'s experiences. His work *Kitāb al-ashrāf al-*

al-Ṭabarī. For a similar view of Quraysh, see al-Mubarrad, *Al-Kāmil fī l-lugha wa-l-adab*, edited by Muḥammad Abū l-Faḍl Ibrāhīm (Cairo, 1376/1956), III, 165.]

kabīr, "Great Book of the Notables," expresses the attitude of the Arab aristocracy towards its privileged position in Islamic society, as well as the idea of cultural unity in Arab history.

We also notice that *Isrā'īlīyāt* and Persian accounts are not to be found in the works of the first generation of *akhbārīyūn*. They managed to creep in later on with the help of their transmitters and advocates. Similarly, we find that practical problems and cultural developments had an effect on historical ideas and broadened their horizons.

Turning to Medina, we perceive two factors influencing historical studies: firstly, the study of the *ḥadīth* and *sunna* of the Prophet, and secondly, the principle of *ijmā'*, which at first was only regional (i.e., the *ijmā'* of Medina) and then became more widespread in later times. This led to the study of the biography of the Prophet and the lives of his followers, and to the study of the Rāshidūn caliphs, the issues of the *shūrā*, the collection of the Qur'ān, and the *fitna*, and perhaps some of the points pertaining to the early Umayyads.

Studies on the subject of the *mubtada'*, or the history of Creation and the ancient prophets, relied primarily on the books and lore of the *ahl al-kitāb*. This was a subject foreign to historical study; it insinuated itself into the field through the influence of Wahb ibn Munabbih, primarily on Ibn Isḥāq, and comprised an element of exotica which did not meet with approval in the school of Medina. If Ibn Isḥāq discussed the *mubtada'*, al-Wāqidī, a contemporary of al-Madā'inī and Hishām ibn Muḥammad al-Kalbī, disregarded it and instead placed emphasis on the idea of the unity and integration of the experiences of the *umma*.

The third century A.H. witnessed a reciprocal exchange of influence between the schools and provinces of historical ideas, approaches, and methods, particularly by means of the *riḥla fī ṭalab al-'ilm*, "journey in search of learning." In like manner, fundamental Islamic concepts which made an impression on historical writing became predominant in the various provinces after already having gained ascendancy in Medina.

It is at this point that we find the concept of the integration of all prophethood and the unity of prophetic mission finally established among historians. We sense the influence of the ʿAbbāsid movement on historical writers, noting that the movement embodied the ascendancy of the Islamic current over that of the tribes. Moreover, the Shuʿūbīya movement contributed to the emphasis placed on the cultural continuity and unity of Arab history, and the Arab aristocracy, having now to share political power with the *mawālī*, felt the need to justify its position. Similarly, the Persians became increasingly more aware of their strength after the ʿAbbāsid victory. The *ijmāʿ* became a general consensus, and the principle of free will and free choice gradually receded in both the political and the cultural spheres. Finally, the stage of historical studies shifted from the centers of the provinces to the great capital of the caliphate, Baghdad.

All of these factors and perspectives found expression in the works of the third-century historians. In this survey it will suffice to give a provisional general view of some of these writers. In his *Ansāb al-ashrāf*, al-Balādhurī expresses the idea of the continuity of Arab history, weaving the threads of his narratives around the Arab notables, and in this way indicating the focus of attention and importance in this history and vigorously asserting the social attitude of the Arab aristocracy. His *Futūḥ al-buldān* asserts the mission of the Arabs in Islam and their historical role—this in addition to the assistance it provides for resolving juridical and administrative problems.

Al-Yaʿqūbī wrote a general history, the first part of which covers universal history up through the pre-Islamic period and gives this historical era a spiritual and cultural significance. His sympathies seem to be Shīʿī, and likewise, the influence of his job as a secretary appears in the second part of his history, which he apparently composed to make the book more useful.

Ibn Qutayba synthesizes two historical concepts in his book *Al-Maʿārif*: that of universal history and that of cultural unity in Arab history. He does this to fill the need of the secretarial class for a comprehensive history, and also to confront the Shuʿūbīya movement in the cultural sphere. Al-Dīnawarī wrote *Al-Akhbār al-ṭiwāl*, a universal history stressing the role of both the Arabs and the Persians in history, and offered an explanation in historical terms for the participation of both Arabs and Persians in political power in the ʿAbbāsid era.

Lastly, it was al-Ṭabarī who established in final form the *ḥadīth* scholars' approach to the writing of history. He asserted the idea of the integration of all prophetic missions in history, and also the idea of the unity of the *umma*'s experiences (or the *ijmāʿ*). History for al-Ṭabarī was an expression of divine will and he wrote it accordingly. His history is thus the counterpart to his Qur'ān commentary: just as the latter elucidates the will of God through His words, the former elucidates the will of God through the activities of mankind.

Bibliography of Works Cited

[Abbott, Nabia. *The Rise of the North Arabic Script and Its Ḳur'ānic Development*. Chicago, 1939.]

[———. *Studies in Arabic Literary Papyri*. 3 vols. Chicago, 1957-72.]

Abū l-Faraj al-Iṣfahānī, ʿAlī ibn al-Ḥusayn. *Kitāb al-aghānī*. 20 vols. Cairo, A.H. 1285; 24 vols. Cairo, 1345-94/1927-74.

Abū Nuʿaym al-Iṣfahānī, Aḥmad ibn ʿAbd Allāh. *Ḥilyat al-awliyā' wa-ṭabaqāt al-aṣfiyā'*. 10 vols. Cairo, 1351-57/1932-38.

Abū ʿUbayd al-Qāsim ibn Sallām. *Kitāb al-amwāl*. Cairo, A.H. 1353.

Abū ʿUbayda Maʿmar ibn al-Muthannā. *Majāz al-Qur'ān*. Edited by Muḥammad Fu'ād Sazgīn. 2 vols. Cairo, 1954-62.

[Abū Zurʿa al-Dimashqī, ʿAbd al-Raḥmān ibn ʿAmr. *Ta'rīkh*. Edited by Shukr Allāh ibn Niʿmat Allāh al-Qawajānī. 2 vols. Damascus, 1400/1980.]

[al-ʿAdawī, Ibrāhīm Aḥmad. *Ibn ʿAbd al-Ḥakam: rā'id al-mu'arrikhīn al-ʿarab*. Cairo, 1963.]

Aghānī, see Abū l-Faraj al-Iṣfahānī.

AIEO = *Annales de l'Institut des Études Orientales.*

AJSL = *American Journal of Semitic Languages and Literatures.*

[Āl Yāsīn, Muḥammad Ḥusayn. *Al-Dirāsāt al-lughawīya ʿinda l-ʿarab ilā nihāyat al-qarn al-thālith*. Beirut, 1400/1980.]

ʿAlī, Jawād, "Mawārid ta'rīkh al-Ṭabarī," *Majallat al-majmaʿ al-ʿilmī al-ʿIrāqī*, I, (1950), 143ff.; II (1951), 135ff.; III (1954), 16ff.; VIII (1961), 425ff.

[al-ʿAlī, Ṣāliḥ Aḥmad, "Al-Mu'allafāt al-ʿarabīya ʿan al-Madīna wa-l-Ḥijāz," *Majallat al-majmaʿ al-ʿilmī al-ʿIrāqī*, XI (1964), 118ff.]

[Amar, Émile, "Prolégomènes à l'étude des historiens arabes par Khalīl ibn Aibak aṣ-Ṣafadī," *Journal asiatique*, 10th Series, XVII (1911), 251ff.; XVIII (1911), 5ff.; XIX (1912), 243ff.]

[Arafat, Walid N., "An Aspect of the Forger's Art in Early Islamic Poetry," *BSOAS*, XXVIII (1965), 477ff.]

[———, "Early Critics of the Authenticity of the Poetry of the *Sīra*," *BSOAS*, XXI (1958), pp. 453ff.]

[ʿArmūsh, Aḥmad Rātib. *Al-Fitna wa-waqʿat al-jamal*. Beirut, 1391/1972.]

[al-Aʿẓamī, Muḥammad Muṣṭafā. *Maghāzī Rasūl Allāh li-ʿUrwa ibn al-Zubayr*. Riyad, 1981.]

[Azmi, Mohammed Mustafa. *Studies in Early Ḥadīth Literature*. Indianapolis, 1978.]

[Baalbaki, Ramzi, "Arab Grammatical Controversies and the Extant Sources of the Second and Third Centuries A.H.," in *Studia Arabica et Islamica: Festschrift for Iḥsān ʿAbbās on His Sixtieth Birthday*, edited by Wadād al-Qāḍī (Beirut, 1981), 1ff.]

[———, "Early Arab Lexicographers and the Use of Semitic Languages," forthcoming in *Berytus*, XXIX (1981).]

[Bahshal, Aslam ibn Sahl al-Razzāz. *Ta'rīkh Wāsiṭ*. Edited by Gurgīs ʿAwwād. Baghdad, 1387/1967.]

al-Balādhurī, Aḥmad ibn Yaḥyā ibn Jābir. *Ansāb al-ashrāf* [vol. IV, i. Edited by Iḥsān ʿAbbās. Wiesbaden, 1979]; vol. IVB. Edited by Max Schloessinger. Jerusalem, 1938; vol. V. Edited by S.D.F. Goitein. Jerusalem, 1936; vol. XI. Edited by Wilhelm Ahlwardt (Anonyme arabische Chronik). Greifswald, 1883.

———. *Futūḥ al-buldān* (Liber expugnationis regionum). Edited by M. J. de Goeje. Leiden, 1866; Edited Cairo, 1932.

[al-Bayātī, ʿAbd al-Jabbār. *Kitāb ayyām al-ʿarab qabla l-Islām*. Baghdad, 1976.]

Becker, C. H. *Papyri Schott-Reinhardt I*. Heidelberg, 1906.

BEO = *Bulletin d'études orientales*.

al-Bīrūnī, Abū l-Rayḥān Muḥammad ibn Aḥmad. *Al-Āthār al-bāqiya* (Chronologie orientalischer Völker). Edited by Eduard Sachau. Leipzig, 1878.

BJRL = *Bulletin of the John Rylands Library*.

Blachère, Régis. *Histoire de la littérature arabe*. 3 vols. Paris, 1952-66.

[———, "Regards sur la littérature narrative en arabe au 1er siècle de l'Hégire (= VIIe s.J.C.)," *Semitica*, VI (1956), 75ff.]

[Braimah, Abdu. "A Reconstruction of the Lost Book *Kitāb al-maghāzī* of Mūsā b. ʿUqba." M.A. Thesis. American University in Cairo, 1968.]

[Braune, Walther, "Historical Consciousness in Islam," in *Theology and Law in Islam*, edited by Gustave E. von Grunebaum (Wiesbaden, 1971), 37ff.]

Brockelmann, Carl. *Geschichte der arabischen Literatur*. 2 vols. Weimar and Berlin, 1898-1902; Supplement. 3 vols. Leiden, 1937-42; 2nd ed. 2 vols. Leiden, 1943-49.

[———, "Naṣr ibn Muzāḥim: der älteste Geschichtsschreiber der Schia," *ZS*, IV (1926), 1ff.]

[Brunschvig, Robert, "Ibn ʿAbdalḥakam et la conquête de l'Afrique du Nord par les Arabes," *AIEO*, VI (1942-47), 110ff.]

BSOAS = *Bulletin of the School of Oriental and African Studies*.

al-Bukhārī, Abū ʿAbd Allāh Muḥammad ibn Ismāʿīl. *Ṣaḥīḥ al-Bukhārī*. 8 vols. Cairo, A.H. 1296.

———. *Al-Taʾrīkh al-kabīr*. 4 vols. Haydarabad, A.H. 1360-64.

[Caetani, Leone. *Annali dell'Islam*. 10 vols. Milan, 1905-26.]

[Cahen, Claude, "Notes sur l'historiographie dans la communauté musulmane médiévale," *REI*, XLIV (1976), 81ff.]

Caskel, Werner, "Aiyām al-ʿarab: Studien zur altarabischen Epik," *Islamica*, III (1930), 1ff.

[———. *Der Felsendom und die Wallfahrt nach Jerusalem*. Köln and Opladen, 1963.]

[———. *Ǧamharat an-Nasab: das genealogische Werk des Hišām ibn Muḥammad al-Kalbī*. 2 vols. Leiden, 1966.]

Chauvin, Victor. *La Récension égyptienne des Mille et une nuits*. Brussels, 1899.

Christensen, Arthur. *L'Iran sous les Sassanides*. Copenhagen, 1936. Translated by Yaḥyā al-Khashshāb as *Īrān fī ʿahd al-Sāsānīyīn*. Cairo, 1957.

[Conrad, Lawrence I., "Arabic Plague Chronologies and Treatises: Social and Historical Factors in the Formation of a Literary Genre," *Studia Islamica*, LIV (1981), 51ff.]

[Cook, Michael. *Early Muslim Dogma: a Source-Critical Study*. Cambridge, 1981.]

Corpus inscriptionum semiticarum. Part IV. Paris, 1889-1931.

al-Dhahabī, Abū ʿAbd Allāh Muḥammad ibn ʿUthmān. *Mīzān al-iʿtidāl fī naqd al-rijāl*. 3 vols. Cairo, A.H. 1325.

———. *Tadhkirat al-ḥuffāẓ*. 2nd ed. 4 vols. Haydarabad, A.H. 1333-34.

———. *Tarājim rijāl rawā Muḥammad ibn Isḥāq raʾīs ahl al-maghāzī ʿanhum*. Edited by August Fischer. Leiden, 1890.

al-Dhahabī/Fischer = August Fischer, "Neue Auszüge aus aḏ-Ḏahabī und Ibn an-Naǧǧār," *ZDMG*, XLIV (1890), 401ff.

al-Dīnawarī, Abū Ḥanīfa Aḥmad ibn Da'ūd. *Kitāb al-akhbār al-ṭiwāl*. Edited by Vladimir Guirgass. Leiden, 1888.

[Donner, Fred M., "The Bakr b. Wā'il Tribes and Politics in Northeastern Arabia on the Eve of Islam," *Studia Islamica*, LI (1980), 5ff.]

[———. *The Early Islamic Conquests*. Princeton, 1981.]

[Dunlop, D. M. *Arab Civilization to* A.D. 1500. London, 1971.]

[al-Dūrī, ʿAbd al-ʿAzīz. *Dirāsa fī sīrat al-Nabī wa-muʾallifihā Ibn Isḥāq*. Baghdad, 1965.]

[———, "The Iraq School of History to the Ninth Century: a Sketch," in *Historians of the Middle East*, edited by Bernard Lewis and P. M. Holt (London, 1962), 46ff.]

[———. *Al-Judhūr al-taʾrīkhīya li-l-shuʿūbīya*. Beirut, 1962.]

[———, "Kutub al-ansāb wa-ta'rīkh al-Jazīra," *Journal of the Jordan Arab Academy*, II (1979), 5ff.]

———. *Muqaddima fī ta'rīkh ṣadr al-Islām*. Baghdad, 1949.

[———, "Al-Zuhrī: a Study of the Beginnings of History Writing in Islam," *BSOAS*, XIX (1957), 1ff.]

[Eche, Youssef. *Les Bibliothèques arabes*. Damascus, 1967.]

EI[1] = *The Encyclopaedia of Islam*. Edited by M. T. Houtsma *et al*. 4 vols. Leiden, 1913-34; *Supplement*. Leiden, 1938.

[*EI*[2] = *The Encyclopaedia of Islam*. 2nd Edition. Edited by H.A.R. Gibb *et al*. Leiden, 1960—.]

[Fahad, Badrī Muḥammad. *Shaykh al-akhbārīyīn: Abū l-Ḥasan al-Madāʾinī*. Najaf, 1975.]

[Faruqi, Nisar Ahmed, "Some Methodological Aspects of the Early Muslim Historiography," *Islam and the Modern Age*, VI (1975), 88ff.]

[al-Fasawī, Abū Yūsuf Yaʿqūb ibn Sufyān. *Kitāb al-maʿrifa wa-l-ta'rīkh*. Edited by Akram Ḍiyā' al-ʿUmarī. 3 vols. Baghdad, 1974.]

[Fischer, W., "Die Prosa des Abū Miḫnaf," in *Islamwissenschaftliche Abhandlungen*, edited by Richard Gramlich (Wiesbaden, 1974), 96ff.]

[Fleisch, H., "Esquisse d'un historique de la grammaire arabe," *Arabica*, IV (1957), 1ff.]

[Friedländer, Israel, "Muhammedanische Geschichtskonstruktionen," *Beiträge zur Kenntnis des Orients*, IX (1910), 17ff.]

[Fück, Johann. *Muḥammad ibn Isḥāq: literarhistorische Untersuchungen*. Frankfurt am Main, 1925.]

[———, "Die Rolle des Traditionalismus im Islam," *ZDMG*, XCIII (1939), 1ff.]

GAS, see Sezgin, Fuat.

Ghannāwī, Maḥmūd. *Naqā'iḍ Jarīr wa-l-Farazdaq: dirāsa adabīya ta'rīkhīya*. Baghdad, 1954.

Gibb, H.A.R., "The Social Significance of the Shu'ūbīya," in *Studia orientalia Ioanni Pedersen dicata* (Copenhagen, 1953), 105ff. [Reprinted in Gibb's *Studies on the Civilization of Islam*, edited by Stanford J. Shaw and William R. Polk (Boston, 1962), 62ff.]

———, "Ta'rīkh," in *EI*[1], Supplement (Leiden, 1938), 233ff. [Reprinted in his *Studies on the Civilization of Islam*, edited by Stanford J. Shaw and William R. Polk (Boston, 1962), 108ff.]

[de Goeje, M. J. *Mémoire sur la conquête de la Syrie*. 2nd ed. Leiden, 1900.]

[Goitein, S. D., "The Sanctity of Jerusalem and Palestine in Early Islam," in his *Studies in Islamic History and Institutions* (Leiden, 1968), 135ff.]

[Goldziher, Ignaz. *Abhandlungen zur arabischen Philologie*. 2 vols. Leiden, 1896-99.]

[———. "Historiography in Arabic Literature," in his *Gesammelte Schriften*, edited by Joseph de Somogyi (Hildesheim, 1967-73), III, 359ff.]

[———. *Introduction to Islamic Theology and Law*. Translated by Andras and Ruth Hamori. Princeton, 1981.]

———. *Muhammedanische Studien*. 2 vols. Halle, 1888-90. [Edited and translated by S. M. Stern and C. R. Barber as *Muslim Studies*. 2 vols. London, 1967-71.]

[———. *Die Richtungen der islamischen Koranauslegung*. Leiden, 1920.]

[———, "Some Notes on the Dīwāns of the Arabic Tribes," *JRAS*, 1897, 325ff.; also in his *Gesammelte Schriften*, edited by Joseph de Somogyi (Hildesheim, 1967-73), IV, 119ff.]

Grohmann, Adolf. *From the World of Arabic Papyri*. Cairo, 1952.

[Guidi, Ignazio, "L'Historiographie chez les sémites," *Revue biblique*, VI (1906), 509ff.]

[Guillaume, A. *The Life of Muhammad*. London, 1955.]

[Hafsi, Ibrahim, "Recherches sur le genre *ṭabaqāt* dans la littérature arabe," *Arabica*, XXIII (1976), 227ff.; XXIV (1977), 1ff., 150ff.]

al-Ḥājirī, Ṭāhā, "Abū ʿUbayda," *Al-Kātib al-miṣrī*, II (1946), 276ff., 463ff.

Ḥājjī Khalīfa, Muṣṭafā ibn ʿAbd Allāh. *Kashf al-ẓunūn ʿan asāmī l-kutub wa-l-funūn* (Lexicon bibliographicum et encyclopaedicum). Edited by Gustav Flügel. 7 vols. Leipzig and London, 1835-58. Edited by Şerefettin Yaltkaya and Kilisli Rifat Bilge. 2 vols. Istanbul, 1941-43.

al-Hamdānī, Abū Muḥammad al-Ḥasan ibn Aḥmad. *Al-Iklīl*. vol. I. Edited by Oscar Löfgren. Uppsala, 1954; vol. X. Edited by Muḥibb al-Dīn al-Khaṭīb. Cairo, 1368/1949.

[Hamidullah, Muhammad, "Le 'Livre des Généalogies' d'al-Balādurīy," *BEO*, XIV (1952-54), 197ff.]

[Ḥassān ibn Thābit. *Dīwān*. Edited by Walid N. Arafat. 2 vols. London, 1971.]

[Hodgson, Marshall G. S. *The Venture of Islam*. 3 vols. Chicago, 1974.]

[Horovitz, Josef, "Alter und Ursprung des Isnād," *Der Islam*, VIII (1918), 39ff.]

——— ["The Earliest Biographies of the Prophet and Their Authors," *Islamic Culture*, I (1927), 535ff.; II (1928), 22ff., 164ff., 495ff. Translated by Ḥusayn Naṣṣār as], *Al-Maghāzī al-ūlā wa-mu'allifūhā*. Cairo, 1949.

[———, "Zur Muhammadlegende," *Der Islam*, V (1914), 41ff. Translated by Emma Agnes Licht as "The Growth of the Mohammed Legend," *Muslim World*, X (1920), pp. 49ff.]

Ibn ʿAbd al-Barr, Abū ʿUmar Yūsuf ibn ʿAbd Allāh. *Al-Inbāh ʿalā qabā'il al-ruwāt*. Cairo, A.H. 1350.

Ibn ʿAbd al-Ḥakam, Abū Muḥammad ʿAbd Allāh. *Futūḥ Miṣr wa-akhbāruhā* (The History of the Conquest of Egypt, North Africa and Spain). Edited by Charles C. Torrey. New Haven, 1922.

Ibn Abī l-Ḥadīd, Abū l-Ḥāmid ʿAbd al-Ḥamīd ibn Abī l-Ḥusayn. *Sharḥ nahj al-balāgha*. 4 vols. Cairo, A.H. 1329. [Edited by Muḥammad Abū l-Faḍl Ibrāhīm. 20 vols. Cairo, 1959-64.]

[Ibn Abī Ṭāhir Ṭayfūr, Abū l-Faḍl. *Kitāb Baghdād* (Sechster Band des Kitāb Baġdād). Edited by Hans Keller. Leipzig, 1908.]

Ibn al-Athīr, Abū l-Ḥasan ʿIzz al-Dīn ʿAlī. *Al-Kāmil fī l-ta'rīkh*

[(Chronicon). Edited by C. J. Tornberg. 14 vols. Leiden, 1851-76.] 11 vols. Cairo, A.H. 1290.

Ibn Ḥajar al-ʿAsqalānī, Abū l-Faḍl Aḥmad ibn ʿAli. *Lisān al-mīzān*. 7 vols. Haydarabad, A.H. 1329-31.

———. *Tahdhīb al-tahdhīb*. 12 vols. Haydarabad, A.H. 1325-27.

Ibn Hishām, Abū Muḥammad ʿAbd al-Malik. *Sīrat Rasūl Allāh* (Das Leben Muhammed's). Edited by Ferdinand Wüstenfeld. 2 vols. Göttingen, 1858-60. Edited by Muṣṭafā al-Saqqā *et al.* 4 vols. Cairo, 1355/1936.

———. *Kitāb al-tījān fī mulūk Ḥimyar wa-l-Yaman*. Edited by Fritz Krenkow. Haydarabad, A.H. 1347.

Ibn al-ʿImād, Abū l-Falāḥ ʿAbd al-Ḥayy ibn Aḥmad. *Shadharāt al-dhahab fī akhbār man dhahaba*. 8 vols. Cairo, A.H. 1350-51.

[Ibn Isḥāq, Abū Bakr Muḥammad. *Sīra*. Edited by Muḥammad Ḥamīd Allāh. Rabat, 1976. Edited as *Kitāb al-siyar wa-l-maghāzī* by Suhayl Zakkār. Beirut, 1398/1978.]

Ibn al-Jawzī, Abū l-Faraj ʿAbd al-Raḥmān ibn ʿAlī. *Ṣafwat al-ṣafwa*. 4 vols. Haydarabad, 1355-56/1936-37.

Ibn Kathīr, ʿImād al-Dīn Ismāʿīl ibn ʿUmar. *Al-Bidāya wa-l-nihāya*. 14 vols. Cairo, 1351-58/1932-39.

Ibn Khallikān, Abū l-ʿAbbās Aḥmad ibn Muḥammad. *Wafayāt al-aʿyān wa-anbāʾ abnāʾ al-zamān* (Ibn Challikani vitae illustrium virorum). Edited by Ferdinand Wüstenfeld. 2 vols. Göttingen, 1835-50. Edited in 2 vols. Cairo, A.H. 1299. Edited in 2 vols. Cairo, A.H. 1310. [Edited by Iḥsān ʿAbbās. 8 vols. Beirut, 1968-72.]

Ibn al-Nadīm, Abū l-Faraj Muḥammad ibn Isḥāq. *Kitāb al-fihrist*. Edited by Gustav Flügel. Leipzig, 1871-72.

Ibn Qutayba, Abū Muḥammad ʿAbd Allāh ibn Muslim. *Kitāb al-ʿarab*. Edited by Muḥammad Kurd ʿAlī in his *Rasāʾil al-bulaghāʾ*, 3rd ed. (Cairo, 1365/1946), 344ff.

———. *Kitāb al-maʿārif* (Handbuch der Geschichte). Edited by Ferdinand Wüstenfeld. Göttingen, 1850. Edited by Muḥammad Ismāʿīl ʿAbd Allāh al-Ṣāwī. Cairo, 1353/1934. [Edited by Tharwat ʿUkāsha. Cairo, 1960.]

Ibn Saʿd, Abū ʿAbd Allāh Muḥammad. *Kitāb al-ṭabaqāt al-kabīr* (Biographien). Edited by Eduard Sachau *et al.* 9 vols. Leiden, 1904-40.

Ibn Sayyid al-Nās, Abū l-Faraj Muḥammad ibn Muḥammad. *ʿUyūn al-athar fī funūn al-maghāzī wa-l-shamāʾil wa-l-siyar*. 2 vols. Cairo, A.H. 1356.

IJMES = *International Journal of Middle East Studies.*

Inostrantsev, K. A. *Iranian Influence on Moslem Literature.* Translated by G. K. Nariman. Bombay, 1918.

al-Iṣfahānī, Ḥamza ibn al-Ḥasan. *Ta'rīkh sinī mulūk al-arḍ wa-l-anbiyā'* (Annalium). Edited and translated by J.M.E. Gottwaldt. 2 vols. Leipzig, 1844-48.

al-Jāḥiẓ, Abū ʿUthmān ʿAmr ibn Baḥr. *Al-Bayān wa-l-tabyīn.* Edited by ʿAbd al-Salām Muḥammad Hārūn. 4 vols. Cairo, 1367-70/1948-50.

[Jahn, K., "Universalgeschichte im islamischen Raum," in *Mensch und Weltgeschichte: Zur Geschichte der Universalgeschichtsschreibung*, edited by A. Randa (Salzburg and Munich, 1969), 145ff.]

JAOS = *Journal of the American Oriental Society.*

[Jeffery, Arthur. *The Foreign Vocabulary of the Qur'ān.* Baroda, 1938.]

[Jones, J.M.B., "The Chronology of the Maghāzī: a Textual Survey," *BSOAS*, XIX (1957), 245ff.]

[———, "Ibn Isḥāq and al-Wāqidī: the Dream of ʿĀtika and the Raid to Nakhla in Relation to the Charge of Plagiarism," *BSOAS*, XXII (1959), 41ff.]

JRAS = *Journal of the Royal Asiatic Society.*

JSS = *Journal of Semitic Studies.*

al-Jumaḥī, Muḥammad ibn Sallām. *Ṭabaqāt fuḥūl al-shuʿarā'.* Edited by Maḥmūd Muḥammad Shākir. Cairo, 1952.

[Khalidi, Tarif. *Islamic Historiography: the Histories of Masʿūdī.* Albany, 1975.]

[Khan, Amanullah, "Al-Wāqidī: an Assessment of His Position as an Historian," *Journal of Research (Humanities)*, V (1970), 81ff.]

[al-Khaṭīb, Muḥammad ʿAjjāj. *Al-Sunna qabla l-tadwīn.* Cairo, 1963.]

al-Khaṭīb al-Baghdādī, Abū Bakr Aḥmad ibn ʿAlī. *Ta'rīkh Baghdād aw Madīnat al-Salām.* 14 vols. Cairo, 1349/1931.

[Khoury, Raif Georges, "Der Heidelberger Papyrus des Wahb b. Munabbih," *ZDMG*, Supp. I.xvii (1969), 557ff.]

[———. *Les Légendes prophétiques dans l'Islam depuis le Ier jusqu'au IIIe siècle de l'Hégire.* Wiesbaden, 1978.]

[———, "Un Écrit inédit attribué à Wahb b. Munabbih: la *Risāla fī sīrat an-nabī*," *Al-Mashriq*, LXIV (1970), 591ff.]

[———. *Wahb b. Munabbih.* Wiesbaden, 1972.]

[al-Kisā'ī, Muḥammad ibn 'Abd Allāh. *Qiṣaṣ al-anbiyā'*. Edited by I. Eisenberg. Leiden, 1922.]

[Kister, M. J., "Notes on the Papyrus Account of the 'Aqaba Meeting," *Le Muséon*, LXXVI (1963), 403ff.]

[———, "On the Papyrus of Wahb b. Munabbih," *BSOAS*, XXXVII (1974), 545ff.]

[———, " 'You Shall Only Set Out For Three Mosques': a Study of an Early Tradition," *Le Muséon*, LXXXI (1969), 173ff.]

[———, and M. Plessner, "Notes on Caskel's *Ǧamharat an-Nasab*," *Oriens*, XXV-XXVI (1976), 48ff.]

[Krenkow, Fritz, "The Two Oldest Books on Arabic Folklore," *Islamic Culture*, II (1928), 55ff., 204ff.]

[———, "The Use of Writing for the Preservation of Ancient Arabic Poetry," in *A Volume of Oriental Studies Presented to Edward G. Browne*, edited by T. W. Arnold and Reynold A. Nicholson (Cambridge, 1922), 261ff.]

al-Kutubī, Muḥammad ibn Shākir. *Fawāt al-wafayāt*. 2 vols. Cairo, A.H. 1283. [Edited by Iḥsān 'Abbās. 5 vols. Beirut, 1973-74.]

[Lecomte, Gérard, "Les Citations de l'Ancien et du Nouveau Testament dans l'oeuvre d'Ibn Qutayba," *Arabica*, V (1958), 134ff.]

[———. *Ibn Qutayba: l'homme, son oeuvre, ses idées*. Damascus, 1965.]

[Lévi-Provençal, É., "Le *Kitāb nasab Quraysh* de Muṣ'ab al-Zubayrī," *Arabica*, I (1954), 92ff.]

[Lichtenstädter, Ilse, "Arabic and Islamic Historiography," *Muslim World*, XXXV (1945), 126ff.]

[Loth, Otto. *Das Classenbuch des Ibn Sa'd: einleitende Untersuchungen über Authentie und Inhalt*. Leipzig, 1869.]

[———, "Ursprung und Bedeutung der Ṭabaqāt, vornehmlich der des Ibn Sa'd," *ZDMG*, XXIII (1869), 593ff.]

[Mackensen, Ruth Stellhorn, "Arabic Books and Libraries in the Umaiyad Period," *AJSL*, LII (1935-36), 245ff.; LIII (1936-37), 239ff.; LIV (1937-38), 41ff.]

al-Maqdisī, Muṭahhar ibn Ṭāhir. *Al-Bad' wa-l-ta'rīkh* (Le Livre de la création et de l'histoire). Edited and translated by Clement Huart. 6 vols. Paris, 1899-1919.

[Marçais, William, "Les Origines de la prose littéraire arabe," *Revue africaine*, LXVIII (1927), 12ff.]

Margoliouth, D. S. *Lectures on Arabic Historians*. Calcutta, 1930.

[Marquet, Yves, "Le Šīʿisme au IXe siècle à travers l'histoire de Yaʿqūbī," *Arabica*, XIX (1972), pp. 1ff., 101ff.]

al-Masʿūdī, Abū l-Ḥasan ʿAlī ibn al-Ḥusayn. *Murūj al-dhahab wa-maʿādin al-jawhar* (Les Prairies d'or). Edited and translated by Barbier de Meynard and Pavet de Courteille. 9 vols. Paris, 1861-77. [Edited by Charles Pellat. 7 vols. Beirut, 1966-79.]

———. *Al-Tanbīh wa-l-ishrāf.* Edited by M. J. de Goeje. Leiden, 1894.

[Mélamède, Gertrude, "The Meeting at al-ʿAḳaba," *Le Monde oriental*, XXVIII (1934), 17ff.]

[Meyer, E. *Der historische Gehalt der Aiyām al-ʿArab*. Wiesbaden, 1970.]

[Millward, William G., "Al-Yaʿqūbī's Sources and the Question of Shīʿa Partiality," *Abr-Nahrain*, XII (1971-72), 47ff.]

[Miquel, André. *La Géographie humaine du monde musulman jusqu'au milieu du 11e siècle*. 3 vols. Paris, 1967-80.]

Moberg, Axel. *The Book of the Himyarites*. Lund, 1924.

[Mottahedeh, Roy P., "The Shuʿūbīyah Controversy and the Social History of Early Islamic Iran," *IJMES*, VII (1976), 161ff.]

[al-Mubarrad, Abū l-ʿAbbās Muḥammad ibn Yazīd. *Al-Kāmil fī l-lugha wa-l-adab*. Edited by Muḥammad Abū l-Faḍl Ibrāhīm. 3 vols. Cairo, 1376/1956.]

Mukhtārāt Ibn al-Shajarī. Cairo, A.H. 1306.

[Mursī, Salwā Mamdūḥ. "ʿUrwa ibn al-Zubayr wa-bidāyat madrasat al-maghāzī." M.A. thesis. Jordan University, 1979.]

[Murtaza, Hamida, "The Origin of the Muslim Historiography," *Journal of the Pakistan Historical Society*, XVI (1968), 198ff.]

[Nagel, Tilman. *Die Qiṣaṣ al-anbiyāʾ: ein Beitrag zur arabischen Literaturgeschichte*. Bonn, 1967.]

[Nallino, C. A. *La Littérature arabe des origines à l'époque de la dynastie umayyade*. Translated by Charles Pellat. Paris, 1950.]

Naṣr ibn Muzāḥim al-Minqarī. *Waqʿat Ṣiffīn*. Edited by ʿAbd al-Salām Muḥammad Hārūn. Cairo, A.H. 1365.

al-Nawawī, Muḥyī al-Dīn Abū Zakariyāʾ Yaḥyā ibn Sharaf. *Tahdhīb al-asmāʾ* (Biographical Dictionary of Illustrious Men). Edited by Ferdinand Wüstenfeld. Göttingen, 1842-47.

Nöldeke, Theodor. *Geschichte der Perser und Araber zur Zeit der Sasaniden*. Leiden, 1879.

[———. *Geschichte des Qorāns*. 2nd edition revised by Friedrich Schwally *et al.* 3 vols. Leipzig, 1909-38.]

———. *Das iranische Nationalepos*. 2nd ed. Berlin and Leipzig, 1920. [Translated by Leonid T. Bogdanov as *The Iranian National Epic*. Bombay, 1930.]

[Noth, Albrecht, "Der Charakter der ersten grossen Sammlungen von Nachrichten zur frühen Kalifenzeit," *Der Islam*, XLVII (1971), 168ff.]

[———, "Iṣfahān-Nihāwand: eine quellenkritische Studie zur frühislamischen Historiographie," *ZDMG*, CXVIII (1968), 274ff.]

[———, "Die literarisch überlieferten Verträge der Eroberungszeit als historische Quellen für die Behandlung der Unterworfenen Nicht-Muslims durch ihre neuen muslimischen Oberherren," *Studien zum Minderheitproblem im Islam* (Bonn, 1973), I, 282ff.]

[———. *Quellenkritische Studien zu Themen, Formen und Tendenzen frühislamischer Geschichtsüberlieferung*. Vol. I, *Themen und Formen*. Bonn, 1973.]

[Obermann, Julian, "Early Islam," in *The Idea of History in the Ancient Near East*, edited by Julian Obermann (New Haven, 1955), 237ff.]

[———, "Political Theology in Early Islam: Ḥasan al-Baṣrī's Treatise on Qadar," *JAOS*, LV (1955), 138ff.]

[Paret, Rudi. *Die legendäre Maghāzi-Literatur: arabische Dichtungen über die muslimischen Kriegszüge zu Mohammeds Zeit*. Tübingen, 1930.]

[Pauliny, J., "Einige Bemerkungen zu den Werken *Qiṣaṣ al-anbiyā'* in der arabischen Literatur," *Graecolatina et Orientalia*, I, (1969), 111ff.]

[Pedersen, J., "The Criticism of the Islamic Preacher," *Die Welt des Islams*, New Series, II (1953), 215ff.]

[———, "The Islamic Preacher," in *Ignace Goldziher Memorial Volume*, edited by Joseph de Somogyi (Budapest, 1948), I, 226ff.]

[Pellat, Charles, "Ibn Qutayba wa-l-thaqāfa al-ʿarabīya," in *Mélanges Taha Husain*, edited by Abdurrahman Badawi (Cairo, 1962), 29ff.]

———. *Le Milieu baṣrien et la formation de Ǧāḥiẓ*. Paris, 1953.

[Petersen, Erling Ladewig. *ʿAlī and Muʿāwiya in Early Arabic Tradition*. Copenhagen, 1964.]

REI = *Revue des études islamiques*.

REJ = *Revue des études juives*.

Repertoire d'épigraphie sémitique. Vols. V-VIII. Edited by J. Ryckmans. Paris, 1929-50.

[Richter, G. *Das Geschichtsbild der arabischen Historiker des Mittelalters*. Tübingen, 1933. Translated by M. Saber Khan as "Medieval Arabic Historiography," *Islamic Culture*, XXXIII (1959), 240ff.; XXXIV (1960), 139ff.]

[Robson, J., "Ibn Isḥāq's Use of the Isnād," *BJRL*, XXXVIII (1955-56), 449ff.]

[———, "The Isnād in Muslim Tradition," *Transactions of the Glasgow University Oriental Society*, XV (1955), 15ff.]

Rosenthal, Franz. *A History of Muslim Historiography*. Leiden, 1952; [2nd ed. Leiden, 1968.]

[———. *Knowledge Triumphant*. Leiden, 1970.]

[———. *The Technique and Approach of Muslim Scholarship*. Rome, 1947.]

[Rotter, Gernot, "Abū Zurʿa ad-Dimašqī (st. 281/894) und das Problem der frühen arabischen Geschichtsschreibung in Syrien," *Die Welt des Orients*, VI (1971), 80ff.]

[———, "Formen der frühen arabischen Geschichtsschreibung," in *Deutsche Orientalistik am Beispiel Tübingens*, edited by Gernot Rotter (Tübingen and Basel, 1974), 63ff.]

[———, "Zur Überlieferung einiger historischer Werke Madāʾinīs in Ṭabarīs Annalen," *Oriens*, XXIII-XXIV (1974), 103ff.]

Ryckmans, J. "Inscriptions Sud-Arabes," *Le Muséon*, XLV (1932), 285ff.

———. *L'Institution monarchique à l'Arabie méridionale*. Louvain, 1951.

[Sachau, Eduard, "Das Berliner Fragment des Mūsā ibn ʿUḳba: ein Beitrag zur Kenntnis des ältesten arabischen Geschichtsliteratur," in *Sitzungsberichte der Preussischen Akademie der Wissenschaften* (Berlin, 1904), 445ff.]

al-Sakhāwī, Muḥammad ibn ʿAbd al-Raḥmān. *Al-Iʿlān bi-l-tawbīkh li-man dhamma l-taʾrīkh*. Damascus, A.H. 1349.

al-Samʿānī, Abū Saʿd ʿAbd al-Karīm ibn Muḥammad. *Kitāb al-ansāb*. Published in facsimile by D. S. Margoliouth. Leiden, 1912.

[al-Ṣanʿānī, Abū Bakr ʿAbd al-Razzāq ibn Hammām. *Al-Muṣannaf*. Edited by Ḥabīb al-Raḥmān al-Aʿẓamī. 11 vols. Beirut, 1390-92/1970-72.]

[Sarasin, W. *Das Bild Alis bei der Historikern der Sunna*. Basel, 1907.]

[Schacht, Joseph, "On Mūsā b. ʿUqba's *Kitāb al-maghāzī*," *Acta Orientalia*, XXI (1953), 288ff.]

———. *The Origins of Muhammedan Jurisprudence*. Oxford, 1950.

[Sellheim, Rudolf, "Prophet, Chalif, und Geschichte: die Muhammed-Biographie des Ibn Isḥāq," *Oriens*, XVIII (1967), 33ff.]

[Sezgin, Fuat. *Geschichte des arabischen Schrifttums*, I. Leiden, 1967.]

[Sezgin, Ursula. *Abū Miḫnaf*: ein Beitrag zur Historiographie der umaiyadischen Zeit. Leiden, 1971.]

al-Shā'ib, Aḥmad. *Ta'rīkh al-naqā'iḍ*. 2nd ed. Cairo, 1954.

[Shoufani, Elias S. *Al-Riddah and the Muslim Conquest of Arabia*. Toronto, 1972.]

Smith, Sidney, "Events in Arabia in the 6th Century A.D.," *BSOAS*, XVI (1954), 425ff.

[de Somogyi, Joseph, "The Development of Arabic Historiography," *JSS*, III (1958), 373ff.]

[Spuler, B., "Islamische und abendländische Geschichtschreibung: Ein Grundsatz-Betrachtung," *Saeculum*, VI (1955), 125ff.]

al-Suyūṭī, Jalāl al-Dīn Abū l-Faḍl ʿAbd al-Raḥmān ibn Abī Bakr. *Al-Muzhir fī ʿulūm al-lugha*. Edited by Aḥmad Jād al-Mawlā *et al.* 2 vols. Cairo, n.d.

———. *Al-Shamārīkh fī ʿilm al-ta'rīkh*. Edited by C. F. Seybold. Leiden, 1894.

al-Ṭabarī, Abū Jaʿfar Muḥammad ibn Jarīr. *Jāmiʿ al-bayān ʿan ta'wīl āy al-Qur'ān*. 30 vols. Cairo, A.H. 1323-29.

———. *Al-Muntakhab min kitāb dhayl al-mudhayyal*. Cairo, A.H. 1336.

———. *Ta'rīkh al-rusul wa-l-mulūk* (Annales). Edited by M. J. de Goeje *et al.* 15 vols. Leiden, 1879-1901. Ḥusaynīya edition. 13 vols. Cairo, A.H. 1336. Istiqāma edition. 8 vols. Cairo 1358/1939.

al-Thaʿālibī, Abū Manṣūr ʿAbd al-Malik ibn Muḥammad. *Laṭā'if al-maʿārif*. Edited by P. de Jong. Leiden 1867. [Edited by Ibrāhīm al-Abyārī and Ḥasan Kāmil al-Ṣayrafī. Cairo, 1960.]

[———. *Qiṣaṣ al-anbiyā'*. Cairo, A.H. 1286.]

al-Tibrīzī, Abū Zakariyā' Yaḥyā ibn ʿAlī. *Sharḥ al-ḥamāsa*. 2 vols. Cairo, 1335/1916.

[al-Ṭirimmāḥ ibn Ḥakīm al-Ṭā'ī. *Dīwān*. Edited by Fritz Krenkow. London, 1927.]

[Togan, Zeki Velidi, "Kritische Geschichtsauffassung in der islamischen Welt des Mittelalters," *Proceedings of the Twenty-Second Congress of Orientalists*, edited by Zeki Velidi Togan (Istanbul, 1953-

57), I, 76ff. Translated by M. S. Khan as "The Concept of Critical Historiography in the Islamic World of the Middle Ages," *Islamic Studies*, XIV (1975), 175ff.]

al-Ṭūsī, Abū Jaʿfar Muḥammad ibn al-Ḥasan. *Fihrist kutub al-Shīʿa* (Tusy's List of Shyʿah Books). Edited by A. Sprenger *et al.* Calcutta, 1855.

ʿUmar ibn Yūsuf (al-Malik al-Ashraf). *Ṭurfat al-aṣḥāb fī maʿrifat al-ansāb*. Edited by K. V. Zetterstéen, with an introduction by Ṣalāḥ al-Dīn al-Munajjid. Damascus, 1369/1949.

[Vajda, Georges, "Judéo-Arabica: Observations sur quelques citations bibliques chez Ibn Qutayba," *REJ*, IC (1935), 68ff.]

[Veselý, Rudolf, "La Bataille d'Uḥud chez al-Wāḳidī," in *Studia semitica philologica necnon philosophica Ioanni Bakoš dicata*, edited by Stanislaus Segert (Bratislava, 1965), 251ff.]

[Wansbrough, John. *The Sectarian Milieu: Content and Composition of Islamic Salvation History*. Oxford, 1978.]

al-Wāqidī, Abū ʿAbd Allāh Muḥammad ibn ʿUmar. *Kitāb al-maghāzī*. Edited by ʿAbbās al-Shirbīnī. Cairo, 1947. Manuscript edition by Marsden Jones. [Edited by Marsden Jones. 3 vols. London, 1966.]

[Watt, W. Montgomery, "The Materials Used by Ibn Isḥāq," in *Historians of the Middle East*, edited by Bernard Lewis and P. M. Holt (London, 1962), 23ff.]

[———. *Muhammad at Mecca*. Oxford, 1953.]

[———. *Muhammad at Medina*. Oxford, 1956.]

Wellhausen, Julius. *Prolegomena zur ältesten Geschichte des Islams*. Published in his *Skizzen und Vorarbeiten*, VI (Berlin, 1899), 3ff.

West, E. W., "Pahlavi Literature," in *Grundriss der iranischen Philologie*, edited by Wilhelm Geiger and Ernst Kuhn (Strassburg, 1895-1904), II, i, 75ff.

Wüstenfeld, Ferdinand. *Die Geschichtschreiber der Araber und ihre Werke*. Göttingen, 1882.

al-Yāfiʿī, Abū l-Saʿāda ʿAbd Allāh ibn Asʿad. *Mirʾāt al-janān wa-ʿibrat al-yaqẓān*. 4 vols. Haydarabad, A.H. 1337-39.

Yaḥyā ibn Ādam, Abū Zakariyāʾ. *Kitāb al-kharāj*. Edited by Aḥmad Muḥammad Shākir. Cairo, A.H. 1347.

al-Ya'qūbī, Aḥmad ibn Abī Ya'qūb. *Kitāb al-buldān*. Edited by M. J. de Goeje. Leiden, 1892.

———. *Ta'rīkh*. Edited by M. T. Houtsma. 2 vols. Leiden, 1883.

Yāqūt, Abū 'Abd Allāh Ya'qūb ibn 'Abd Allāh. *Mu'jam al-udabā'* (Dictionary of Learned Men). Edited by D. S. Margoliouth. 2nd ed. 7 vols. London, 1923-31.

ZDMG = *Zeitschrift der Deutschen Morgenländischen Gesellschaft*.

[Zetterstéen, K. V., "Ibn Sa'd ock hans arbete Kitāb eṭ-Ṭabaqāt el-Kebīr," *Le Monde Oriental*, I (1906), 66ff.]

ZS = *Zeitschrift für Semitistik und verwandte Gebiete*.

[al-Zubayr ibn Bakkār, Abū 'Abd Allāh. *Al-Akhbār al-muwaffaqīyāt*. Edited by Sāmī Makkī al-'Ānī. Baghdad, 1392/1972.]

al-Zubayrī, Abū 'Abd Allāh al-Muṣ'ab ibn 'Abd Allāh. *Nasab Quraysh*. Edited by É. Lévi-Provençal. Cairo, 1953.

Index

In the arrangement used below, the definite article (*al-*, *l-*) and *banū* ("tribe") are ignored for purposes of alphabetization. Numbers in italic type indicate page numbers where explanations for some of the terminology used in this book may be found. More detailed information is provided in the relevant articles in the *Encyclopaedia of Islam*.

Aaron, 129
Abān ibn 'Uthmān ibn 'Affān, 24-25, 96
al-'Abbās, 89, 110
'Abbāsids, 49, 54n, 64, 66, 67, 69, 150, 158, 159
'Abd Allāh ibn 'Abbās, 78, 98n
'Abd Allāh ibn 'Abd al-Muṭṭalib, 101
'Abd Allāh ibn Abī Bakr ibn Ḥazm, 27, 34
'Abd Allāh ibn 'Amr ibn al-'Āṣ, 78, 93, 98n
'Abd Allāh ibn Jaḥsh, 83, 84, 88, 90, 91, 103
'Abd Allāh ibn Salām, 31
'Abd Allāh ibn Ubayy, 83, 85, 103, 105, 119
'Abd Allāh ibn al-Zubayr, 52, 54n, 76, 77, 79, 117, 118
'Abd al-Malik ibn Marwān, 45, 54n, 63, 90n, 141; his relations with 'Urwa ibn al-Zubayr, 79, 80, 82, 83, 83n, 87, 88, 92; with al-Zuhrī, 117n, 117-18
'Abd al-Mun'im ibn Idrīs, 126, 127, 130, 132, 133
Banū 'Abd al-Muṭṭalib, 102
'Abd al-Raḥmān ibn Abī l-Zinād, 99
'Abd al-Ṣamad ibn Ma'qil, 122
abnā', 109, *123*
Abraham, 100, 124n, 128, 130
Abū l-'Abbād al-Hamdānī, 132
Abū 'Amr ibn al-'Alā', 55, 139, 147, 148
Abū Bakr, 28, 49, 81, 82, 89, 90, 93, 107, 110, 114, 116. *See also* Rāshidūn
Abū l-Dayyāl, 140
Abū Dharr al-Ghifārī, 93
Abū l-Faraj al-Iṣfahānī, *see* al-Iṣfahānī
Abū Hurayra, 78
Abū Jahl, 104
Abū Muslim, 67
Abū Mikhnaf, 7, 49, 52, 62, 63, 132, 140, 147, 148; attitude of *ḥadīth* scholars toward, 44n; influence of the *ayyām* on, 45; influence of the *qiṣaṣ* on, 144; sources of, 44, 143, 144; use of poetry by, 45; use of the *isnād* by, 44; viewpoint of, 44, 142, 154; works of, 43-44, 141
Abū Salama ibn 'Abd al-Raḥmān ibn 'Awf, 98n
Abū Sufyān, 48, 83, 85, 87, 108
Abū Ṭālib, 66n, 102
Abū 'Ubayda, 19, 146; as a Khā-

Abū ʿUbayda (*cont.*)
rijite, 57, 148; as a Shuʿūbī, 57, 148; critical attitude of, 57, 148; sources of, 55-56, 147; works of, 55-56, 57, 147
Abū l-Yaqẓān al-Nassāba, 51, 146
Abū l-Zinād, 94, 99
Abyssinia, 64, 81; *hijra* to, 27, 80, 82, 90, 94, 102. *See also* Negus
ʿĀd, 130
Adam, 54n, 100, 124n, 128; and Eve, 128
Adāma, 118
Adhriʿāt, 108
Adhruḥ, 108
Aḥādīth al-anbiyāʾ wa-l-ʿubbād wa-aḥādīth Banī Isrāʾīl (Wahb ibn Munabbih), 126
ahl al-kitāb ("People of the Book," esp. Christians and Jews), 31, 34, 35, 52, 113, 126, 130, 147, 157. *See also* Christians, Jews
ahl al-taswiya, 57
Āʾīn-nāmag, 59
ʿĀʾisha, 26, 76, 78, 88, 90, 93, 94n, 115, 119n
ʿajam (non-Arabs, esp. Persians), *34*, 55
Ajnadayn, Battle of, 89
akhbār, sing. *khabar* (accounts, stories), *42-75 passim*, 90, 99, 100, 112, 113, 124, 130, 139, 142, 145, 152, 154, 155
Akhbār al-furs (Abū ʿUbayda), 57, 147, 156
Akhbār al-khulafāʾ al-kabīr (al-Madāʾinī), 49
Al-Akhbār al-ṭiwāl (al-Dīnawarī), 68-69, 159
akhbāriyūn, sing. *akhbārī* (transmitters or compilers of *akhbār*), 39, 42, 42-50, 65, 66, 68, 72, 124, 151; as first historians in the tribal perspective, 43, 139, 140; "books" of the, 60, 61, 62, 74, 75, 148, 149; historical views in the works of, 141-43; sources of the, 143-44; their reliance on the *ruwāt*, 140, 144; their special interest in Iraq, 140, 154; their stress on human responsibility, 155; their style influenced by the *ayyām*, 144-45; use of documents by, 43, 143-44; use of the *isnād* by, 43, 145, 148. *See also* historical school of Iraq
al-Akhfash, 147
Alexander the Great, 59
ʿAlī ibn Abī Ṭālib, 28, 45, 47, 48, 66n, 110, 114, 115, 116, 117, 119, 142, 154, 155. *See also* Rāshidūn
ʿAlī ibn al-Ḥusayn, 155
ʿAlids, 39, 44, 46n, 47, 63, 66, 142, 148, 153, 154. *See also* Shīʿa
Āmina bint Wahb, 101
Banū ʿĀmir ibn Ṣaʿṣaʿa, 102
ʿAmra, 78
ansāb (genealogies), *see* genealogy
Ansāb al-ashrāf (al-Balādhurī), 53, 61, 62, 64, 149, 158
Anṣār (Medinan supporters of the Prophet), 35, 81, 98, 99, 106, 108
al-ʿAqaba, 82, 103, 133
al-Aqṣā mosque, 117
Arab tribes: as a topic of historical interest, 40, 41, 71, 73, 137; "books" of the, 17, 139, 146; limited notion of time among the, 20; no concept of history among the, 19, 20; northern (Muḍar), 16, 17, 18, 32, 56, 113, 131, 132, 148, 156; rivalry among the, 17, 42, 44, 50, 55, 60, 142, 147, 153; southern (Yemenite), 17, 32, 148, 156;

glorification of the, 16, 130-32. See also *'aṣabīya, ayyām*
Arabia, pre-Islamic, 14-18; as a topic for historical study, 27, 40, 52, 64, 69, 73, 101. *See also* Jāhilīya
Ark of the Covenant, 129
'aṣabīya (partisan feeling or rivalry), 17, *17n, 42,* 60, 73, 153, 154
al-Ash'ath, 89
Ashja', 85
ashrāf (tribal notables), *49*
'Āṣim ibn 'Umar ibn Qatāda, 27, 34
Asmā' bint Abī Bakr, 76
astrology, 65
astronomy, 65, 66, 75
al-Aswad al-'Ansī, 88
'Ātika bint 'Abd al-Muṭṭalib, 103
Avesta, 58
'Awāna ibn al-Ḥakam, 7, 52, 63, 140, 147, 148; citation of poetry by, 46; influence of the *qiṣaṣ* on, 144; pro-Umayyad attitude of, 46, 141, 142-43, 154-55; sources of, 45, 46, 143; use of the *isnād* by, 46; works of, 45, 140-41
al-Aws, 104
Ayla, 88, 90, 108
ayyām, ayyām al-'Arab ("Battle Days" literature), *16,* 18-20, 26, 28, 31, 32, 45, 46, 48, 52, 55, 56, 57, 68, 72, 113, 131, 133, 136, 137, 144, 145, 150, 152
al-Azd, 44, 143

Al-Bad' wa-l-ta'rīkh (al-Maqdisī), 31
Bādhān, 109
Badr, Battle of, 27, 38, 83-85, 85, 90, 91, 92, 93, 94, 103-104
Baghdad, 48, 54n, 69; shift of historical studies to, 158
Bahshal, 71
al-Bakkā'ī, 36, 132
Bakr, 84, 87, 108
al-Balādhurī, 43, 52, 53, 54n, 99; critical method of, 62-64, 142, 150; his attitude toward chronology, 62; sources of, 61-64; use of the *isnād* by, 62, 63, 150; works of, 61-64, 149, 158
Barmakids, 67
Basra, 69; activities of the *akhbārīyūn* in, 42; as center for the tribal perspective of historical writing, 10, 22, 55, 72, 73, 136-37, 138; attitude toward *jabr* in, 60; *ḥadīth* scholars in, 39; history of, 49, 53, 115. See also *miṣr*
Al-Bidāya wa-l-nihāya (Ibn Kathīr), 7
Bilāl, 93
Bi'r Ma'ūna, 85
Buḥrān, 105
Byzantium, 69

calendar: Persian, 59, 65; pre-Islamic Arabian, 15, 17, 20; Roman, 65; the *hijra*, 17, 21, 100. *See also* chronology, dating, time
Camel, Battle of the, 39, 46, 47, 77, 90, 154
Chosroes, 101, 109, 113, 123
Christians, 41, 125. See also *ahl al-kitāb*
chronology: attitude toward, among early Islamic historians, 28, 38, 46, 54, 62, 64, 65, 67, 68, 100, 148; confusion of, in the *ayyām*, 19; in Persian literary works, 59; in tribal society, 20. *See also* calendar, dating, time
Companions (*ṣaḥāba*) of the Prophet, 22, 24, 27, 29, 41, 80, 97, 98, 99, 107; as subjects of *ḥadīth*, 41
conquests, 21, 41, 45, 46, 49, 61-

conquests (*cont.*)
62, 73, 141, 143, 154; as the "new *ayyām*," 137; linked to the Ridda by Sayf ibn 'Umar, 46, 140, 154. *See also* Iraq, Syria
Creation, 20, 31, 33, 64, 68, 71, 126, 127, 128, 130, 135, 150, 157

dalā'il (proofs, esp. of prophethood of Muḥammad) literature, *40*, 101
Damascus, 63, 77, 79, 117, 118, 126
dār al-nadwa (council chamber), 133
dating, 72, 75; in pre-Islamic Arabia, 15, 17, 20; in works of early Islamic historians, 28, 32, 37, 38, 48, 65, 86, 90, 100, 105, 110-11; of births, uncertainty of, 75, 95; of deaths, 75, 110, 111. *See also* calendar, chronology, lifespans, time
David, 124n, 129
Dhāt al-Anwāṭ, 108, 112n
Dhāt al-Aṭlāḥ, 108n
Diḥya al-Kalbī, 109
al-Dīnawarī, 149, 150; works of, 68-69, 74, 159
Ditch, Battle of the, 30, 38, 85, 90, 91, 106
divine will: historical attitude toward, 41, 141, 150; history as an expression of, 74, 75, 159. See also *jabr, qadar*
dīwān (government office), *43*, 144; (register), *18*, 50, 57; (registration system), 21, 22, 28, 29, 43, 50, 114, 116. *See also* documents
Dīwān al-khātam (Office of the Seal), *43*
documents: genealogical registers, 15, 17, 50, 138; government registers, 43, 151; in pre-Islamic Arabia, 15, 138; Lakhmid "books" in churches of al-Ḥīra, 17, 147; used by Islamic historians, 26, 32, 36, 38, 40, 43, 52, 143-44, 151. See also *dīwān*, Muḥammad, *zubur*
Dūmat al-Jandal, 109

Egypt, 69, 71, 115

Faḍā'il al-furs (Abū 'Ubayda), 57
Fadak, 89, 90, 107, 114
al-Farazdaq, 51
Fāṭima, 89, 114
Fazāra, 85
al-Fijār, War of, 101
First Civil War, see *fitna*
fitna (the First Civil War), 28, 46, 114, 116, 141, 154, 155, 157
Futūḥ al-buldān (al-Balādhurī), 61-62, 64, 149, 158
Futūḥ Miṣr (Ibn 'Abd al-Ḥakam), 71

Gāh-nāmag, 59
garrison town, see *miṣr*
genealogy, 35, 66, 72, 75, 136, 139, 151; and philology, 55, 56; interest in, 41, 43, 45, 49, 50-54, 61, 62, 63, 113-14, 137, 139, 140, 147, 152; rendered important by *dīwān* system, 21; role of poetry in, 18; studies on, 19, 28, 42, 50-54, 60, 68, 72, 146-47, 148. *See also* historical school of Iraq
Genesis, 125, 126
geography, topography, 38, 53, 64, 65, 72, 75, 151
Ghaṭafān, 85, 105
Goliath, 129
Gospels, 124n, 125
grammarians, 146

ḥadīth (tradition of the Prophet), 7, 21, 23, 27, 39, 47, 56, 65, 72, 73, 78, 92, 93, 96, 97, 111, 117, 120; collection of, in the individual provinces, 43, 71, 139, 149; scholars of, 8, 10, 22, 23, 24, 25, 30, 32, 35, 36, 44n, 49, 53, 61, 71, 72, 74, 78, 95, 98, 123, 136, 142, 145, 146, 149, 150, 159. *See also* historical writing
Hajar, 88
Ḥajjāj ibn Abī Manīʿ, 99
al-Ḥajjāj ibn Yūsuf, 46n
Ḥājjī Khalīfa, 19, 91, 97, 99, 127, 132
al-Ḥakam ibn Abī l-ʿĀṣ, 76
ḥalaqāt (academic circles), *76*
Hamdān, 44
al-Hamdānī, 15, 16n, 17, 52
Ḥammād al-Rāwiya, 139
Ḥamza ibn ʿAbd al-Muṭṭalib, 105
Banū l-Ḥārith, 109
al-Ḥārith ibn ʿAbd Kulāl, 88
al-Ḥarra, Battle of, 54n, 63, 78
Ḥarūrāʾ, Battle of, 54n
ḥasab (distinction of great deeds), *18*, 152
al-Ḥasan ibn ʿAlī, 45, 66, 115, 117
Banū Hāshim, 66, 102
Ḥāṭib ibn Abī Baltaʿa, 87
Hawāzin, 87, 108
al-Haytham ibn ʿAdī, 46, 66, 148; use of the *isnād* by, 54; works of, 53-54, 54n
Heraclius, 86, 109, 113
Hijra (emigration, esp. of the Prophet to Medina), 9, 10, 25, 54n, 81-83, 90, 92, 93, 94, 103, 105, 110, 133. *See also* Abyssinia, calendar
ḥilf al-fuḍūl, *101*
Ḥilyat al-awliyāʾ (Abū Nuʿaym al-Iṣfahānī), 31, 133
Ḥimyar, Ḥimyarites, 15, 130, 131, 138
al-Ḥīra, 17, 18, 20, 52, 138
Hishām ibn ʿAbd al-Malik, 54n, 118, 119
Hishām ibn ʿUrwa, 46, 78, 143, 147
historical accounts: ʿAbbāsid, 66, 67; ʿAlid, 66; Basran, 49; collection of, *in the individual provinces*, 43; family, 43, 44, 50, 56, 143; from the *ahl al-kitāb*, 31, 34, 35, 52, 126, 130, 147, 157; Iraqi, 46, 63, 69; Kufan, 44, 143; Medinan, 43, 44, 46, 49, 62, 63, 66, 69, 143; oral transmission of, 18, 19, 23, 32, 35, 36, 53, 54n, 60, 63, 68, 72, 92, 124, 137, 138, 145, 148, 149, 151; Persian, 17, 59, 69, 156, 157; regional, 56, 62, 144, 149; Syrian/Umayyad, 63, 142, 143; tribal, 18, 19, 43, 44, 46, 50, 51, 56, 143, 144, 146, 147; written transmission of, 18, 19, 24, 25, 27, 29, 33, 35, 36, 52, 54n, 57, 60, 63, 68, 72, 96-97, 119-20, 124, 137, 138, 139, 145, 148, 149, 151; Yemenite, 16, 17, 31, 34. *See also* documents, *isnād*, poetry
historical school of Iraq, 10, 136-51; accounts of, as collective property of a family or tribe, 42, 138, 139; as center for tribal perspective of historical writing, 22, 42, 60, 73, 136-37; influenced by critical method of *ḥadīth* scholars, 60-61, 144; motives for works of the, 153-57; origins of, 41-43, 60, 136-37, 137-39, 152. See also *akhbāriyūn*, genealogy, philology
historical school of Medina, 10, 23,

historical school of Medina (*cont.*) 27, 30, 32, 34, 36, 38, 39, 95, 114, 120, 121, 123, 133, 151, 152; as center for Islamic perspective of historical writing, 22, 60, 72, 73, 136, 137, 152; collective studies of, 26, 38, 39, 76; development of, 40-41; its convergence with the *akhbārīyūn*, 39; its emphasis on the *isnād*, 137; its viewpoint on the *fitna*, 114-15; on early Islamic history, 116; motives for works of the, 157; origins of, 76, 136-37. *See also* ʿUrwa ibn al-Zubayr, al-Zuhrī

historical writing: administrative factors in, 29, 50, 60, 64, 74, 116, 149; ʿAlid tendencies in, 39, 44, 47, 63, 66, 142, 148; and the *Isrāʾīlīyāt*, 21, 30, 31, 32, 34, 69, 113, 121, 122, 128, 157; concept of continuity and unity in, 64, 73, 140, 147, 148, 149, 156, 157, 158, 159; connections with Qurʾānic exegesis, 26, 29, 34, 35, 38, 79, 82, 83, 85, 92-93, 101-102, 104-105, 110, 111-12, 119, 126, 128; cultural factors in, 12, 48, 51, 57-58, 60, 61, 65, 67, 72, 95, 136, 139, 146, 149, 152; element of exaggeration in, 30, 33, 35, 41, 94, 135, 137; influence of *qiṣaṣ* lore on, 23-24, 28, 30, 31, 33, 34, 35, 38, 39, 47, 52, 112-13, 121, 122, 131, 135, 137, 144, 147, 154; influence of the *ayyām* on, 20, 22, 31, 32, 45, 46, 48, 56, 68, 72, 131, 133, 137, 144, 145, 150, 152; Islamic perspective of, 22, 43, 60, 61, 72, 118, 136, 137, 158; links with belles-lettres, 13; origins of, 29, 40-41, 72, 76, 136-37, 152-54; political factors in, 13, 35, 36, 41, 60, 72, 74, 116, 146, 147-48, 153; pre-Islamic background of, 14-18; related to and influenced by *ḥadīth* studies, 12-13, 23, 24, 25, 28, 30, 32, 33, 34, 35, 39, 40-41, 49, 51, 60-61, 69, 72, 94, 95, 111, 112, 135, 144, 157; Shīʿī tendencies in, 36, 47, 51, 66, 150, 154, 158; social factors in, 22, 29-30, 41, 50, 60, 72, 74, 95, 146, 156; the *umma* as a concept and topic of interest in, 26, 28, 29, 41, 61, 64, 67, 70, 72, 73, 74, 75, 94, 114, 116, 121, 140, 141, 149, 150, 152, 154, 156, 157, 159; tribal perspective of, 22, 41, 43, 46, 53, 60, 61, 72, 136, 140

history: limited sense of, in Persian literary works, 60; in pre-Islamic Arabia, 15, 17, 18, 19, 136; notion of, in Islam, 20-22, 74, 94; Persian and Iranian, 52, 53n, 57, 58-60, 64, 65, 69, 150, 156; regional, 53, 71, 72, 73; universal, conception of, 21, 32, 37, 41, 61, 64, 65, 68, 73, 148, 149, 150, 158, 159

Hūd, 124n, 131n

al-Ḥudaybiya, 86, 87, 90-91, 91, 92, 106-107, 108, 112

Ḥujr ibn ʿAdī, 47, 142

Ḥunayn, 87, 88, 91, 108

al-Ḥusayn ibn ʿAlī, 47, 141, 142

Ibn ʿAbd al-Ḥakam, 71

Ibn ʿAbd Rabbih, 19

Ibn Abī l-ʿAwjāʾ al-Sulamī, 107n

Ibn Abī l-Ḥadid, 48

Ibn Abī Hunayda, 92

Ibn Abī l-Ḥuqayq, 104

Ibn Abī Ṣāliḥ, 140, 147

Ibn Abī Ṭāhir Ṭayfūr, 71

Ibn al-Ash'ath, 118
Ibn al-Athīr, 19
Ibn al-Dughunna, 81
Ibn al-Ḥaḍramī, 84
Ibn Hishām, 7, 36, 78, 130
Ibn Hubayra, 67
Ibn Isḥāq, Muḥammad, 7, 8, 25, 27, 37, 38, 39, 47, 49, 66, 68, 99, 127, 132, 134, 137, 140, 157; and the *ahl al-kitāb*, 34, 35; attitude of other historians toward, 35, 36, 39; citation of genealogies by, 35; citation of Qur'ān by, 35; critical attitude of, 35-36; exaggerating tendency of, 33, 35; his attitude toward *qadar*, 36; influence of the *qiṣaṣ* on, 32, 33, 34, 35, 121, 157; Shī'ī tendencies of, 36; sources of, 34, 36; use of poetry by, 34, 35, 36; use of the *isnād* by, 34-35, 35-36; use of the *Isrā'īliyāt* by, 34, 121; works of, 33, 36
Ibn Ka'b ibn Mālik, 97n
Ibn al-Kalbī, Hishām ibn Muḥammad, 7, 15n, 46, 52, 66, 68, 146, 148, 156, 157; sources of, 52, 140, 147; use of *qiṣaṣ* by, 52, 147; works of, 51-52
Ibn Kathīr, 7, 8, 25, 33
Ibn al-Muqaffa', 58
Ibn al-Nadīm, 56, 57, 126
Ibn Qutayba, 19, 31, 56, 77, 126, 127, 128, 130, 134, 149, 150; critical attitude of, 68, 126, 150; his consultation of the Old Testament, 68, 126; sources of, 68; works of, 67-68, 74, 159
Ibn Sa'd, Muḥammad, 7, 39, 77, 126; his contribution to the structure of the *sīra*, 40
Ibn Sayyid al-Nās, 7, 8, 25, 33, 99
Ibn al-Zubayr, *see* 'Abd Allāh ibn al-Zubayr
Ibrāhīm ibn al-Ashtar, 54n
Ibrāhīm ibn Sa'd, 98, 99
Ibrāhīm ibn al-Walīd, 54n
Idrīs, 124n
al-'Ijlī, 78
ijmā' (consensus): its relation to historical writing, *21*, 41, 61, *72*, 73, 74, 116, 156, 157; of a local area, 156, 157; of the *umma*, 21, 156, 157, 158, 159
'ilm (formal religious learning), 111, 120; contrasted with *ra'y*, *40*-41, 73
Īmā' ibn Raḥḍa, 104
inscriptions, 14-15, 126
Iram, 130
Iraq: conquest of, 39, 43, 46, 142, 153; government registers in, 43; historical writing in, 19, 44, 140; history of, 44, 45, 69, 141, 143, 150, 154; study of *sīra* in, 40. *See also* Basra, conquests, historical school of Iraq, Kufa
'Īsā ibn 'Umar al-Thaqafī, 147
Isaac, 100, 128
al-Iṣfahānī, Abū l-Faraj, 19, 56
Ishmael, 100, 130
Ismā'īl ibn 'Abd al-Karīm ibn 'Abd al-Ṣamad, 127
isnād (chain of authorities), *23*, 31; as a critical tool, 23, 29, 35, 69, 73, 75, 137, 147, 149, 150; broken, 145; collective, 29, 36, 38, 63, 102, 103, 105, 106, 107n, 108, 110, 111; criticism of, 39, 70, 73, 145; use of, by historians, 25, 29, 33, 34-35, 38, 44, 46, 48, 54, 62, 63, 65, 69, 83, 92, 111, 133, 138, 145, 148, 149
Isrā'īliyāt (tales of the Israelites), 8, 10, *16*, 21, 30, 31, 32, 34, 69, 113, 121, 122, 125, 126, 128, 157. *See also* Old Testament, prophets, Talmud, Torah

Jābir ibn ʿAbd Allāh, 155
jabr (divine foreordainment, fatalism), 75; attitude of historians toward, 30, 46, 112, 155; promoted by the Umayyads, 30, 46, 60, 141, 153; rejected in the provinces, 60, 141, 153, 155. *See also* divine will, *qadar*
Jacob, 128
Jāhilīya ("Age of Ignorance"), 14, 20, 53, 56, 136, 141. *See also* Arabia
al-Jāḥiẓ, 56
Jamharat al-nasab (Ibn al-Kalbī), 51-52
Banū Jawn, 89
Jeremiah, 129
Jerusalem, 90, 117, 129
Jesus, 124n, 125, 129
Jews, 85, 103, 104, 105, 106; traditions of, their influence on historical writing, 41, 125. See also *ahl al-kitāb*, al-Naḍīr, Qaynuqāʿ, Qurayẓa
jihād (struggle for the cause of Islam), 149
al-Jiʿrāna, 88
jizya (poll-tax on non-Muslims), 108, 109
Job, 100
Jurash, 108
Juwayriya bint al-Ḥārith, 86

Kaʿb, 86
Kaʿb al-Aḥbār, 7, 31, 100, 113, 132
Kaʿb ibn al-Ashtar, 104
Kaʿba, 80n, 81n, 86, 101, 103, 108, 131
Kalb, 45, 51, 143
al-Kalbī, Muḥammad ibn al-Sāʾib, 51, 53, 132, 146, 148
Karbalāʾ, 143, 144, 154
Khadīja bint Khuwaylid, 76, 79, 88, 101, 102
Khaḍir, 100, 131n
Khālid ibn al-Walīd, 87, 89, 109
Khālid al-Qasrī, 54n, 113
Khārijites, 44, 49, 53n, 56, 57, 148
khātam al-anbiyāʾ ("Seal of the Prophets"), *21*
Banū Khathʿam, 133
Khaybar, 89, 90, 107, 111
al-Khazraj, 104
khiṭaṭ (residential and administrative districts), *53*
Khodāy-nāmag, 58-59, 60
Khuzāʿa, 87, 88, 106, 108
Kināna, 86
Kinda, 44, 89, 102, 109, 111
al-Kisāʾī, 134
Kitāb Baghdād (Ibn Abī Ṭāhir Ṭayfūr), 71
Kitāb al-buldān (al-Yaʿqūbī), 64
Kitāb as-isrāʾīlīyāt (Wahb ibn Munabbih), 127
Kitāb al-mawālī (Abū ʿUbayda), 57, 147, 156
Kitāb al-mulūk al-mutawwaja. . . (Wahb ibn Munabbih), 130
Kitāb al-ṭabaqāt (al-Wāqidī), 39
Kitāb al-ṭabaqāt al-kabīr (Ibn Saʿd), 39, 40
Kitāb al-taʾrīkh (ʿAwāna ibn al-Ḥakam), 45
Kitāb al-taʾrīkh ʿalā l-sinīn (al-Haytham ibn ʿAdī), 53-54, 148, 156
Kitāb al-tījān fī mulūk Ḥimyar wa-l-Yaman (Wahb ibn Munabbih), 127, 128, 130
Kufa, 69; activities of the *akhbārīyūn* in, 42, 43, 44, 45, 46, 47; as a center for tribal perspective of historical writing, 10, 22, 72, 73, 136-37, 138; attitude toward *jabr* in, 60; *ḥadīth* scholars in, 39; his-

tory of, 46n, 53, 54n, 142. See also *miṣr*
kuttāb (secretaries), *58*, 64, 68, 150

Lakhmids, *see* al-Ḥīra
Last Supper, 129
Letter of Simeon, 125
Lie, Affair of the (*ḥadīth al-ifk*), 86, 106
life-spans, records of, 65, 110, 114, 115. *See also* dating
literary studies, 13, 51, 151
Banū Liḥyān, 106
Luqmān, 31, 131n

Maʿān, 86
Al-Maʿārif (Ibn Qutayba), 31, 67-68, 128, 159
Al-Mabʿath (Ibn Isḥāq), 33
Al-Mabdaʾ (Wahb ibn Munabbih), 127
al-Madāʾinī, 7, 19, 46, 63, 66, 140, 156, 157; critical method of, 145, 148; influenced by *ḥadīth* scholars, 49; sources of, 49, 140; use of the *isnād* by, 48; works of, 49, 141
Madyan, 130
mafākhir (tribal boasts) literature, 56. See also *manāqib, shamāʾil*
maghāzī (military expeditions of the Prophet), 23, *24*, 94, 97, 99, 122, 132, 137; as term for entire career of the Prophet, 24, 76n; connections with *ḥadīth* studies, 24-25, 76, 95; links with Qurʾānic exegesis, 92-93; studies on the, 24, 25, 26, 27, 30-31, 34, 121
Al-Maghāzī (Ibn Isḥāq), 33, 37; (ʿUrwa ibn al-Zubayr), 90, 91; (Wahb ibn Munabbih), 31, 132, 133; (al-Wāqidī), 7, 37, 39; (al-Zuhrī), 28, 99-110, 113
al-Mahdī, 54n, 67
majlis, pl. *majālis*, *19*, 42, 45, 48, 138, 144
Mālik ibn Anas, 98, 120
Mālik ibn Aws al-Ḥadathān, 98n
Maʿmar ibn Rāshid, 100n
manāqib (merits) literature, *47*. See also *mafākhir, shamāʾil*
al-Manṣūr, 54n
al-Maqdisī, 31
Maʿqil ibn Munabbih, 127
Marwān ibn al-Ḥakam, 54n, 115
mashāhid al-Nabī, *101*
al-Masʿūdī, 127, 128, 134
mathālib (tribal faults) literature, *53n*, 56, 57
mawālī (non-Arab Muslims, spec. clients of the Arab tribes), 56, 57, 146, 147, 154, 156, 158
Mecca, 48, 87, 128; career of the Prophet in, 27, 34, 79-82, 92, 99, 101-103, 110; conquest of, 28, 87, 91, 108, 111, 133
Medina (Yathrib), 79, 81, 98, 100, 115, 116, 117; the Prophet's career in, 27, 37, 82-89, 90-91, 92, 99, 103-11; Qurʾānic references to, 112. *See also* historical school of Medina, Hijra
al-Mirbad, 55
miṣr, pl. *amṣār* (garrison town), 22, *42*, 43, 50, 53n, 56, 138. *See also* Basra, Kufa
Moses, 100, 124n, 129
Muʿāwiya ibn Abī Sufyān, 45, 47, 48, 50, 115, 117, 142, 154, 155
al-Mubarrad, 56
mubtadaʾ (history of Creation and ancient prophets), *157*
Al-Mubtadaʾ (Ibn Isḥāq), 33, 34, 35, 36, 37; (Wahb ibn Munabbih), 31, 126, 127, 128-29, 133

Mubtada' al-khalq (Wahb ibn Munabbih), 127
al-Mufaḍḍal al-Ḍabbī, 140
Muhājirūn (Meccans who made the Hijra with Muḥammad), 103
Muḥammad, the Prophet, 21, 22, 23, 24, 25, 26-27, 30, 33, 34, 37, 40, 49, 54n, 69, 72, 79-89, 90-91, 92, 93, 94, 98, 99-111, 120, 124n, 157; letters of, 88, 92, 109. See also *sīra*
Muḥammad ibn ʿAbd Allāh, 140
Muḥammad ibn Jubayr ibn Muṭʿim, 97n
Muḥārib, 143
al-Mujālid ibn Saʿīd, 144
mukarrib (priest-king), *14*
al-Mukhtār, 47, 156
munāwala, 120n
al-Mundhir ibn Sāwā, 88
Banū Murra, 85
muruwwa (bedouin virtue), *18*
Mūsā al-Kāẓim, 67
Mūsā ibn ʿUqba, 32-33, 97, 121, 143
Muṣʿab ibn al-Zubayr, 54n, 77, 90n
Muṣʿab al-Zubayrī, 28, 114, 146, 148; his use of poetry, 53; sources of, 52-53; works of, 52-53
Muslim ibn ʿAqīl, 143
Banū l-Muṣṭaliq, 86, 91
Mu'ta, 86-87, 91, 107
Mutammam ibn Nuwayra, 89
al-Muʿtaṣim, 49, 68
Muʿtazila, 74

Banū l-Naḍīr, 105-106, 111
Najrān, 109
Nakhla, 89
naqā'iḍ (polemic verse), *50*, 51, 146. *See also* poetry
Naqā'iḍ Jarīr wa-l-Farazdaq (Abū ʿUbayda), 148
nasab (noble family origin), *18*, 152
Al-Nasab al-kabīr (Muṣʿab al-Zubayrī), 52
Nasab Quraysh (Muṣʿab al-Zubayrī), 28, 52-53, 114, 148
Nasab Quraysh wa-akhbāruhā (al-Madā'inī), 49
Naṣr ibn Muzāḥim, 7, 142, 154; as first Shīʿī *akhbārī*, 47; citation of speeches by, 48; his negligence in matters of dating, 48; influence of the *ayyām* on, 48, 144; use of poetry by, 48, 144; use of the *isnād* by, 48; works of, 47
Nebuchadnezzar, 129
Negus (of Abyssinia), 80, 93, 102
Nimrod, 130
Noah, 100, 124n, 128
northern Arabs, *see* Arab tribes
Numayr, 143
Nuʿaym ibn ʿAbd Kulāl, 88

Old Testament: consulted by Ibn Qutayba, 68, 126; its relation to the *Isrā'īlīyāt*, 31; used by Wahb ibn Munabbih, 31, 125. See also *Isrā'īlīyāt*, prophets, Psalms, Torah

Pharaoh, 129
philologists, 19, 40, 42, 51, 54-57, 139, 145-48, 151; monographs of the, 146, 148, 149. *See also* historical school of Iraq
philosophy, 75
poetry: as authenticating evidence, 18, 53, 137, 146; fabrication of, 8, 16, 31, 34, 35, 36, 48, 144, 145; role of, in Arab culture, 26, 72, 93, 113, 132, 137, 138, 152; in genealogies, 50; in philology,

55, 56, 145; in the *ayyām*, 18, 19; use of, by historians, 26, 28, 34, 35, 38, 42, 45, 46, 48, 93-94, 113, 133, 138, 144, 145. See also *ayyām, naqā'iḍ*
prophets, historical interest in ancient, 52, 68, 69, 71, 100, 124, 125, 127, 128-29, 130, 147, 148, 150, 156, 157. See also *Isrā'īlīyāt*, Muḥammad, *qiṣaṣ al-anbiyā'*
Psalms, 124n, 125

qadar (freedom of the will), 36, *41*, 74, 123, 141, 153, 155, 158. *See also* divine will, *jabr*
qāḍī (judge), 118, 123
al-Qādisīya, Battle of, 26, 90
al-Qaḍīya, 107n
Qarārat al-Kudr, 105, 110-11
Banū Qaynuqā', 85, 90, 92, 104-105, 111
qibla (direction of prayer), 103
qiṣaṣ, sing. *qiṣṣa* (stories, fables), 30, 31, 33, 34, 35, 39, 42, 47, 52, 95, 112, 112-13, 121, 122, 124, 131, 135, 137, 144, 147, 152, 154. See also *qiṣṣa al-anbiyā', quṣṣāṣ*, Wahb ibn Munabbih
Qiṣaṣ al-akhyār (Wahb ibn Munabbih), 127
qiṣaṣ al-anbiyā' ("Tales of the Prophets"), *28*, 34, 130, 134. See also *Isrā'īlīyāt*, prophets, *qiṣaṣ*
Qiṣaṣ al-anbiyā' (Wahb ibn Munabbih), 127
Qur'ān: and the Old Testament, 31, 125, 128; as a historical topic, 25, 28, 90, 114, 156; as a motive for study of the past, 21; conception of the past in, 20; its relation to the *Isrā'īlīyāt*, 31; study of, 55, 56, 124n. *See also* historical writing
Quraysh, 28, 35, 49, 53, 76-114 *passim*, 133, 139, 147, 155, 156
Banū Qurayẓa, 85-86, 90, 91, 106
Qurra ibn 'Abd al-Raḥmān, 114
quṣṣāṣ, sing. *qāṣṣ* (storytellers), *23*, 30, 41. See also *qiṣaṣ*, Wahb ibn Munabbih

al-Rajī', 85
Rāshidūn ("rightly guided") caliphs, 26, 28, 37, 43, 45, 63, 66, 73, 89-90, 114-15, 157. *See also* Abū Bakr, 'Alī ibn Abī Ṭālib, 'Umar ibn al-Khaṭṭāb, 'Uthmān ibn 'Affān
ra'y (individual judgment): contrasted with *'ilm*, 40-*41*, 73; weakness of, 70, 142
Ridda ("Apostasy") wars, 26, 39, 43, 45, 46, *89*, 90, 140, 141, 143
riḥla fī ṭalab al-'ilm (journey in search of learning), 61, 149, 157
riwāya (lecture), *76*; (transmitted account), 142
ruwāt, sing. *rāwī* (narrators, transmitters of accounts), *17*, 23, 53, 55, 56, 57, 60, 65, 70, 73, 138, 139, 143, 144, 145, 146, 147; and the *akhbārīyūn*, 42, 47, 139, 140; as storytellers, 17; reliance upon, by early historians, 33, 93, 137

al-Ṣa'b Dhū l-Qarnayn, 131
Sa'd ibn Ibrāhīm, 98, 99
Sa'd ibn Mu'ādh, 86
ṣaḥāba, see Companions of the Prophet
Sa'īd ibn al-Musayyab, 96, 97

al-Sakhāwī, 32, 36, 91, 97, 99, 101, 126
sakīna, 129
Ṣāliḥ, 124n
Samuel, 129
al-Ṣaqʿab ibn Zuhayr al-Azdī, 144
Sāsānians, 52, 65, 71, 150; paucity of information on their history, 59
Satan, 80, 84, 100, 113
Saul, 129
al-Sawīq, 104
Sayf ibn ʿUmar, 7, 140; attitude of, 46, 142, 154; influence of *qiṣaṣ* lore on, 144; influence of the *ayyām* on, 46; sources of, 46-47, 140, 143, 144; works of, 46. *See also* conquests
Seth, 124n
Seven Sleepers, 31, 130
al-Shaʿbī, 44
shamā'il (merits) literature, *40*. See also *mafākhir, manāqib*
shīʿa (faction), *155*
Shīʿa, Shīʿism, 36, 47, 51, 66, 150, 154, 158. *See also* ʿAlids
Shuʿayb, 130
shūrā (deliberative committee that elected ʿUthmān as caliph), 28, 43, 63, 114, 154, 157
Shuraḥbīl ibn Saʿd, 26-27
Shurayḥ ibn ʿAbd Kulāl, 88
Shuʿūbīya, 7, 50, 55, 57, 58-60, 146, 148, 158, 159
Ṣiffīn (Naṣr ibn Muzāḥim), 47, 142, 144, 154
Ṣiffīn, Battle of, 39, 43, 44, 47, 48, 115, 141, 142, 143, 154
sīra, pl. *siyar* (biography), 29, 59; of the Prophet, 31, 33, 75, 99, 110, 122, 133, 135, 140; chapters of, in works of al-Madā'inī, 49; character of, 41; origins of, 30; study of, in Medina, 73, 91, 94, 137, 139; study of, in the provinces, 40, 61, 139. *See also* historical school of Medina, Muḥammad
Sīra (Ibn Hishām), 8; (Ibn Isḥāq), 7, 33, 36, 37, 121
Sīrat Muʿāwiya wa-Banī Umayya (ʿAwāna ibn al-Ḥakam), 45
Siyar al-mulūk (Ibn al-Muqaffaʿ), 58, 59
Solomon, 129
southern Arabs, *see* Arab tribes
speeches, citation of: by historians, 45, 48, 66, 114, 145; in the *Khodāy-nāmag*, 59
state, concept of the, 141, 153, 155
Suhayl ibn ʿAmr, 107
Sukayna, 155
Banū Sulaym, 105, 111
Sulaymān ibn ʿAbd al-Malik, 24n
Sulaymān ibn ʿAlī al-Hāshimī, 66
sunna, pl. *sunan* (customary practice, esp. of the Prophet), 22, *97*, 99, 111n, 157
Surāqa ibn Jasham, 103, 113
Syria, 69, 83, 101; conquest of, 39, 43, 89; government registers in, 43; history of, 45, 141; study of *sīra* in, 40. *See also* conquests

Tabāla, 108
ṭabaqāt, 39n, 53, *59*, 62, 72, 75, 146
Tabaqāt al-fuqahā' wa-l-muḥaddithīn (al-Haytham ibn ʿAdī), 53
al-Ṭabarī, 7, 25, 31, 33, 43, 48, 54n, 77, 79, 99, 115, 128, 134, 140, 149; as a *ḥadīth* scholar, 69, 150, 159; critical method of, 70, 142, 150; education of, 69; use of the *isnād* by, 69, 70, 150; works of, 70, 71, 125, 127, 128, 150, 159
tābiʿūn, sing. *tābiʿ* (descendants of

the Companions), *29*, 41, 92, 111
Tabūk, 108
Tafsīr (al-Ṭabarī), 125, 127, 128, 150
al-Ṭā'if, 80, 87-88, 91
Ṭalḥa ibn al-A'lam, 140
Ṭalḥa ibn 'Ubayd Allāh, 66n, 115, 116
Talmud, 125. See also *Isrā'īliyāt*, Old Testament, Torah
Tamīm, 44, 46, 109, 139, 142, 143
Ta'rīkh (al-Ya'qūbī), 64-67
Ta'rīkh al-ashrāf al-kabīr (al-Haytham ibn 'Adī), 53, 148, 156-57
Ta'rīkh Baghdād, see *Kitāb Baghdād*
Al-Ta'rīkh al-kabīr (al-Wāqidī), 39
Ta'rīkh al-khulafā' (Ibn Isḥāq), 36-37, 37
Ta'rīkh al-rusul wa-l-mulūk (al-Ṭabarī), 69, 127, 128
Ta'rīkh Wāsiṭ (Bahshal), 71
Tawwābūn, 54n, 141, 155
Ṭayyi', 44
al-Tha'ālibī, 134
Thaqīf, 87, 88, 139
time, notion of: in Islam, 75; in tribal society, 20. *See also* calendar, chronology, dating
al-Ṭirimmāḥ, 139
topography, *see* geography
Torah, 128, 150. See also *Isrā'īliyāt*, Old Testament, Talmud
translations: from Greek, 60, 65; from Hebrew, 125; from Persian, 52, 58-60; from Syriac, 60

'Ubayd Allāh ibn 'Abd Allāh ibn 'Utba, 96, 97
'Ubayd Allāh ibn Jaḥsh, 80
'Ubayd Allāh ibn 'Umar, 120
'Ubayd Allāh ibn Ziyād, 54n
'Ubayd ibn Sharya, 16, 132
Ubayy ibn Khalaf, 105
Uḥud, Battle of, 27, 38, 91
'Umar ibn 'Abd al-'Azīz, 78, 98, 118, 123
'Umar ibn al-Khaṭṭāb, 54n, 89, 90, 101, 107, 114, 116; establishes Hijra calendar, 21; initiates *dīwān* system, 21, 114. *See also* Rāshidūn
'Umayr ibn Wahb, 104
Umayyads: as topic of historical study, 28, 37, 44, 45, 47, 49, 66, 66n, 141, 154, 157; attitude of historians toward, 36, 44, 45, 46, 47, 60, 78, 118, 119, 141, 142, 143, 153, 154, 155; promotion of *jabr* by, 30, 46, 60, 141, 153; their court library in Damascus, 119; their interest in genealogy, 50, 113; their interest in history, 24, 25, 29, 42, 79, 80, 82, 83, 87, 88, 89, 91, 92, 94-95, 115, 117-19
Umm Qirfa, 106
Umm Yaḥyā, 76
umma (the Islamic community), *13*, 26, 28, 29, 41, 61, 64, 67, 70, 72, 73, 74, 75, 94, 100, 114, 116, 121, 140, 141, 149, 150, 152, 154, 156, 157, 159
'Urwa ibn al-Zubayr, 7, 8, 10, 27, 30, 34, 96, 97, 111n, 120, 121, 137; as a *ḥadīth* scholar, 78, 91-92; as founder of *maghāzī* studies, 25, 95; citation of Qur'ān by, 92; critical attitude of, 92, 93; dating of events by, 86, 90, 91; did not support doctrine of *jabr*, 30; his *maghāzī* writings, 25, 26, 79-89, 90-91; his relations with the Umayyads, 25, 78, 80, 82, 83, 87, 88, 89, 91, 92; influence of *qiṣaṣ* on, 93; life and career of, 76-78; not politically

'Urwa ibn al-Zubayr (*cont.*)
active, 78; on the Rāshidūn, 89-90; sources of, 92-93; style of, 25, 94; use of documents by, 92; use of poetry by, 26, 93-94; use of the *isnād* by, 25, 82, 92
Usāma ibn Zayd, 78, 88, 89, 93, 109, 110
'Utba ibn Rabī'a, 104
'Uthmān ibn 'Affān, 28, 39, 62, 114, 115, 116, 122, 141, 155. *See also* Rāshidūn
'Uyūn al-athar (Ibn Sayyid al-Nās), 7, 8

Wahb ibn Munabbih, 7, 8, 10, 16, 30, 34, 150; as a storyteller, 31, 121, 122, 124, 131, 133; attitude of Medinan scholars toward, 32, 37, 124, 133, 135, 157; his interest in the *Isrā'īlīyāt*, 10, 31, 122, 125, 125-26, 128; his neglect of the *isnād*, 133; influence of the *ayyām* on, 31, 131, 133; introduced folkloric element into historical writing, 133, 157; life and career of, 122-23; not a serious historian, 32, 121, 122, 133; on the *qiṣaṣ al-anbiyā'*, 130; sources of, 124-26; works of, 31, 126-27, 128-34, later fabrication of, 127
Wakī', 147
al-Walīd ibn 'Abd al-Malik, 92, 116, 126; his relations with 'Urwa ibn al-Zubayr, 79, 89, with al-Zuhrī, 115
al-Walīd ibn Yazīd (Walīd II), 50
al-Wāqidī, 7, 25, 27, 33, 40, 49, 62, 63, 66, 68, 96, 99, 112; 'Alid tendencies of, 39; citation of Qur'ān by, 38; critical attitude of, 37, 38; dating of events by, 37, 38; his attitude toward *qiṣaṣ*, 38, 39, 157; his attitude toward the *isnād*, 38; his use of chronological sequence, 38; not reliant upon Ibn Isḥāq, 39; sources of, 37, 38; use of poetry by, 38; works of, 37, 39
Waraqa ibn Nawfal, 79, 93, 102

al-Yamāma, 89
al-Ya'qūbī, 24, 117, 118, 134, 149; 'Abbāsid tendencies of, 66-67; 'Alid sympathies of, 66, 150, 158; critical method of, 65, 150; dispensed with the *isnād*, 65, 150; sources of, 65-66; works of, 64-67, 158-59
al-Yarmūk, Battle of, 26, 90
Yazdagird I, 59
Yazīd ibn 'Abd al-Malik, 54n, 118
Yazīd ibn Mu'āwiya, 54n, 62, 141, 155
Yemen, 15, 16, 37, 52, 69, 88, 109, 122, 123, 125, 130, 138; study of *sīra* in, 40
Yūnus ibn Bukayr al-Shaybānī, 33n, 36
Yūnus ibn Ḥabīb, 55, 147
Yūnus ibn Yazīd, 101

Zanj rebellion, 67
Zayd ibn 'Alī, 66
Zayd ibn al-Ḥāritha, 106
Ziyād ibn Abī Sufyān, 142
al-Zubayr ibn al-'Awwām, 26, 66n, 76, 115, 116
al-Zubayr ibn Bakkār, 63, 95-96
Zubayrids, 46n, 66n, 93
Zufar ibn al-Ḥārith, 54n
al-Zuhrī, 7, 8, 10, 27, 32, 33, 34, 52, 63, 76, 78, 140; as a *ḥadīth* scholar, 98, 111, 118-19; dating of events by, 28, 100, 105, 110-11; did not support doctrine of *jabr*, 30, 112; first to provide *sīra* with definite structure, 27, 110;

his attitude toward poetry, 28, 113; his attitude toward *qiṣaṣ*, 28, 112-13; his format for the *sīra*, 27-28; his interest in genealogy, 28, *110*, *113-14*; his interest in past prophets, 28, 100, 113; his *Maghāzī*, 28, 97, 99-110; his relations with the Umayyads, 29, 113, 115, 117n, 117-19; importance of, 120-21; life and career of, 95-99, 117-18; not affected by the *ayyām*, 28, 113; sources of, 97; strong memory of, 96, 98; style of, 112; treatment of the Rāshidūn by, *28*, *114-15*, 116-17; use of chronological sequence by, 28, 110; use of the *isnād* by, 28-29, 102, 103, 105, 106, 107n, 108, 110, 111

Zur'a ibn Dhī Yazan, 88

Library of Congress Cataloging in Publication Data

Dūrī, ʿAbd al-ʿAzīz.
The rise of historical writing among the Arabs.

Translation of: Baḥth fī nash'at ʿilm al-tārīkh ʿinda al-ʿArab.
Bibliography: p.
Includes index.
1. Islamic Empire—Historiography. 2. Historiography—Islamic Empire. I. Conrad, Lawrence I., 1949- II. Title.

DS38.16.D8713 1983 909'.09767101 82-24028
ISBN 0-691-05388-X

GPSR Authorized Representative: Easy Access System Europe - Mustamäe tee 50, 10621 Tallinn, Estonia, gpsr.requests@easproject.com

www.ingramcontent.com/pod-product-compliance
Lightning Source LLC
Chambersburg PA
CBHW051523230426
43668CB00012B/1716

* 9 7 8 0 6 9 1 6 1 2 9 7 3 *